CRICKET ALL THE YEAR

By the Same Author

A CRICKETER'S BOOK
DAYS IN THE SUN
THE SUMMER GAME
CRICKET
GOOD DAYS
AUSTRALIAN SUMMER
ENGLISH CRICKET
TEN COMPOSERS
AUTOBIOGRAPHY
SECOND INNINGS

Cricket
ALL THE YEAR

By
NEVILLE CARDUS

COLLINS
ST JAMES'S PLACE, LONDON
1952

PRINTED IN GREAT BRITAIN
COLLINS CLEAR-TYPE PRESS : LONDON AND GLASGOW

ACKNOWLEDGMENTS

For permission to reproduce the photographs in the text the author and the publishers are most grateful to :

Central Press

Fox Photos, Ltd.

The *Herald Sun*

The *Huddersfield Examiner*

The *Manchester Guardian* and *Evening News*

Press Association and Reuters

The Picture Post Library

The Sport and General Press Agency, Ltd.

The *Sydney Morning Herald*

The Topical Press Agency, Ltd.

CONTENTS

ILLUSTRATIONS

INTRODUCTION

Of the making of books on cricket there is seemingly no end.
I tried to break myself of the habit years ago ; I wished to devote
myself to music. But the publishers wouldn't encourage such
renunciation. Last August I was pressed into a luncheon with
W. A. R. Collins, who is not only a publisher but, better still, a
cricketer. The occasion in itself and all its allurements I could,
I think, have resisted. I could remain stony-hearted while he
drew a pathetic picture of the impoverishment that might befall
him if my name—as author of *Days in the Sun*—shouldn't appear
in next summer's or next autumn's lists of his illustrious House.
For all his pleadings I would not budge ; nor would he budge
himself when I offered to write exclusively for him a short
history of Modal Polyphony. But this lunch and the gist of it
set into train a series of influences and persuasions which
suggested that the fates themselves were against me.

Collins persisted in his blandishments in a taxi all the way
to Lord's. My ears remained sealed. But as soon as we entered
Lord's, through the W. G. Grace gates, the invisible forces got
to work. It was an afternoon of ripening sunshine, and Middlesex
were playing the West Indians. As we hurried along the drive
behind the pavilion we could hear applause, for the game had
been resumed after the luncheon interval. We were passing the
gracious lawn near the Pavilion's main door when I saw sitting
on the wall an aged parson engrossed in *Wisden*, lost for a while
to the brilliance going on in front of the Pavilion at this very

moment—and Worrell was batting—lost in another day of summer beyond recall. It was a symbolical sight not to be seen anywhere else but in England and at cricket ; and it made me realise more than ever before that cricket has no past and no present. The seasons mingle in one another as with no other game. Imagine, at an encounter between Arsenal and Newcastle, somebody reading a football annual of twenty years ago. It is not to be imagined. The parson suddenly closed his *Wisden*, got up and hurried to a seat near the Mound, his eyes all the more expectant and full of light from what he had just been reading and living through again. The thought struck me that this same aged parson might like to read as many books on cricket, old and new, as he could lay his hands on.

The die was cast during the tea interval the same afternoon. I was standing near the Green Bank when a schoolboy came to me and asked please would I give him my autograph. " But I am not a cricketer," I explained, and he answered, " I know that, sir, but you're a jolly good author." No man of letters has received a tribute better worth having and preserving than this. Straightway I looked for my publisher in the Pavilion, and the matter was settled and next morning we signed the contract.

In another and equally convincing way this schoolboy sharpened my resolve to write again about cricket. He asked me what I thought of Denis Compton as a batsman. " Why," I said, " I think he's splendid." " I think he's marvellous," continued my schoolboy ; " but when I tell my father so he says ' Oh, but you should have seen Ranji and Trumper,' but how could I, sir ?—I wasn't born when they were playing " (a good point, I thought) ; " and it's the same with everything, sir. If I say I think Danny Kaye's funny, it's the same : ' Oh, you should have seen Dan Leno.' " He was silent a moment, then added, " You know, sir, it all gets very wearing."

I felt for him and, moreover, I felt a sense of guilt. I, too, have often fallen under the sway of *laudator temporis acti* ; and it is only natural for us as we grow older, to succumb to the enchantment and pathos of distance. I remember, when I was a schoolboy, reading an article by Alfred Shaw in *Wisden* and was dismayed because he said there were no great bowlers any more. Among my " favourite " cricketers then were Walter Brearley, Blythe, J. T. Hearne, J. N. Crawford—and Rhodes and Hirst would have been among my " favourites " too, but they were Yorkshiremen. As recently as 1930 I was watching Gentlemen v. Players at Lord's and a parson—no, this time it was a bishop, in gaiters—approached me and asked if I had seen a boy selling score-cards. " He'll be round soon, sir," I told him (I couldn't say ' My Lord ' as I didn't know him well enough). " One simply *has* to have a score-card nowadays," he said, " to find out who is who." As he spoke Larwood was bowling at Chapman and in the field were Woolley, Hendren, Tate, Sutcliffe. " No individuality left," persisted the bishop, so to humour him I said, " True, there're no Ranjis now, no Maclarens, no——" " Good heavens ! " he interrupted, " good heavens, sir. No Ranjis, no Maclarens ? Why, the game had gone to the dogs long before then." I have told this moral story at least once before, and I repeat it here, as a motif which, as in music, might gain a new interest or " turn " in another context.

The critic should try not to forget that his subject, whatever it is—cricket, theatre, music, pictures, books, cabbages or kings —is bound to change if it isn't to petrify ; his difficulty is to distinguish between real evolution and that kind of change which " alters when it alteration finds." Other times, other manners. It is the spirit that matters ; and the spirit bloweth as it listeth. I shall try in this book always to keep in mind both the aged parson and his *Wisden* at Lord's, and my schoolboy. And if my schoolboy sometimes thinks that I use some rather long words I hope he'll be patient, because I think he will know the meaning of all of them when he is as old as the parson.

1951

PART ONE

★

Chapter One

MYSELF WHEN YOUNG . . .

To THIS day I can't explain why one morning in June 1899 I went to Old Trafford for the first time to watch Lancashire. I wasn't a cricketer yet, wasn't much advanced beyond my ninth birthday, and my pocket money seldom ran to twopence a week. It remains, and apparently must remain, a mystery not only what was the attraction that drew me on football that way (and long before the summer holidays had begun) ; but where did the gate-money come from ?

Lancashire were playing Gloucestershire, and as I passed through the turnstiles I heard a terrific roar and didn't know, till I was told by one of the spectators, that Board had just appealed for a catch at the wicket. I am unable to remember if I then knew much about the laws and procedure of the game. I have looked up this match in *Wisden*. Jessop played and made 28 on the day I was present, but he left no indelible impression on this occasion. Why do we retain in memory some things and not others ? C. L. Townsend made 91, and I can vaguely see him now, tall when the ball was coming to him, but he bent gracefully over it as he played forward. F. H. B. Champain drove several fours that made me, with the boy's naïve delight in a play on words, see something very apt in his name.

A year afterwards I was definitely enslaved by cricket for life. On Whit-Monday 1900 I was again at Old Trafford, up at the crack of dawn to get a front seat. For some reason I cannot fathom, Lancashire didn't play Yorkshire that year on Whit-Monday ; they played Kent. At noon Kent went in first, C. J. Burnup and Alec Hearne the opening batsmen. I sat facing the pavilion, on the grass in front of the sixpenny seats, which were occupied mainly by men and youths in bowler hats or straw " cadies." Moustaches everywhere, and scarcely a girl or woman, though away on the right there was the Ladies' Pavilion, arrayed in long skirts and puffed sleeves. Only women of the middle and upper classes attended cricket matches half a century ago.

From the Stretford end Mold bowled very fast, taking a short run, just three or four strides. At the other end Briggs bowled slow. A fast and a slow bowler to begin, new ball despite. There wouldn't be another new ball during the Kent innings, even if it lasted until to-morrow, which it did. A new ball was available in those times only at the beginning of an innings, or, as John Gunn once said, " 'till t'owd un coom in two." Mold's speed made sudden havoc of Kent's innings ; three wickets went for 11, Hearne, B. D. Bannon, W. H. Patterson. The crowd gloated. I gloated. A marvellous Bank Holiday morning. . . . J. R. Mason came in third wicket down, and to my dismay he seemed to " see " Mold's bowling at once, which I thought an impossibility. Meanwhile, at the other end of the wicket was this little Burnup man. I didn't like the look of him, for he played everything in the middle of his bat, and nothing flurried him. Burn-up, I said to myself ; a silly name.

Mason, thank goodness, was out soon after lunch ; but the " bad start " had been retrieved and he made 68. The next batsman answered to the name of Perkins—T. N. Perkins—another ridiculous name, I assured myself. He missed his stroke at Mold on the off-side time after time. The crowd laughed derision at his helplessness. I joined it. Again I was cheated and cast down. Perkins began to drive classically through the covers, as I see it now, left-leg forward. Such cricket to-day against very fast bowling, in a searching situation, would be anachronistic. And the little man, Burnup, stayed there, unobtrusive but not idle, gathering runs by neat cuts. So the warm afternoon went to cool evening. There was no tea interval; drinks were brought into the field, and the crowd rose and stretched itself. T. N. Perkins was not dismissed until he had scored 88; he and Burnup increased Kent's total from 110 for four to 350 for five. If I am not mistaken, Burnup was caught at the wicket from the last over of the day—Kent 400 for six at "close," Burnup "c. Smith, b. Cuttell, 200." A report of the match in one of the newspapers next day praised Burnup's innings something like this: ". . . occupied the crease all day . . . punctuated by judicious cutting . . . periods of slow scoring excusable in view of Kent's bad start. . . ." A score of 200, after 11 for three, wouldn't seem inordinately slow nowadays, even with Compton "occupying" the crease.

I walked home from Old Trafford on the evening of this Whitsun Monday of 1900, a sad cast-down Lancashire boy. Why had Mold allowed that Perkins to survive? All the way from the county ground—planted in the country then, next to the village of Stretford—I walked to Moss Side, down Shrewsbury Street, past Brooks' Bar. Next day I was again at Old Trafford early and I received compensation for the ruined Bank Holiday. I saw Johnny Briggs score 50—flicking his bat to the off-side in a way which in contemporary circles would quickly bring him to the notice of courts-martial; also he often blocked a ball and dashed out of his ground, pretending to run, "chancing it," to use the gamester language of the period. He bounced about the wicket as though uncontrolled and uncontrollable.

It was during this summer of 1900, I think, that I saw Johnny Briggs take all ten wickets for Lancashire against Worcestershire at Old Trafford, on a quiet, dull morning. After the fall of the ninth wicket, Arthur Mold pitched his bowling wide, so that Johnny could put the finishing touch to a performance of some distinction half a century ago. For ten minutes he couldn't find any length or direction at all; he was so worked up, so excited, eager, happy, and so afraid this last wicket might elude him after all.

Poor Briggs, it was necessary to send him to an asylum ; yet need we be sorry for him ? I am assured that during his incarceration he was bowling Australia out every day, and driving four after four through the covers. One of his attendants told me that he'd go into his patient's room to find him beaming, if a little exhausted. " Eight for 52," he would report, recovering his breath, " bring me 'alf a pint, George."

Briggs wasn't born in Lancashire, he was from Nottinghamshire, and Lockwood too ; nor was Arthur Mold a Lancashire man ; he belonged to Northamptonshire. But Briggs and Mold became household words in Lancashire, part of the rubric of the day-to-day and evening-by-evening cricket scores :

b. Mold

c. and b. Briggs . . .

and so on through many many innings—" c. and b. Briggs "— he was one of the cleverest catchers from his own bowling. I suppose in his dying moments he remembered best of all his comical days in the sun the morning at Sydney in December 1894 when he and Bobby Peel caused an astonishing collapse of Australia and won the most remarkable victory in the annals of Test cricket up to that moment. Australia batted first and amassed—for those days of moderate scores " amassed " is the word—586. England responded with 325 ; the follow-on then was automatic ; the fielding side had no option but to field again. So the Australians, tired from long labours under the sun, naturally waxed and waned in attack ; England in their second innings scored 437, leaving Australia 177 to win. At the fall of the fifth afternoon, there was no suggestion that the match wouldn't after all go to its expected end, a heavy defeat of England. The wicket was still excellent and Australia had made at close 130 or so for two ; only a handful to get in the morning, with an array of superb batsmen in hand.

But there was, in the early hours of 20th December, a violent thunderstorm in Sydney, with torrents of tropical rain. It so happened that neither Johnny Briggs nor Bobby Peel heard the thunder or the bursting of the floodgates. They slept well, having drunk deep. The morning was a blaze of sunshine from a clear sky. The earth sprouted green and was dry, Briggs and Peel went to the ground together, blue serge and watch-chains. They went straight into the " middle," according to a lifetime's habit, to "look at pitch." Bobby bent down, with a curious glint in his eye at Briggs. He pressed the earth, then said, " Eh, Johnny, but soombody's bin wa-aterin' this wicket in t'neight. Coom on—we'll bowl 'em all out in a jiffy " ("bowl" pronounced to rhyme with howl).

And "bowl" them out they did : Australia collapsed for 166 and England won by ten runs against Australia's first innings total, a record in 1894, of 586.

Other shadowy pictures from the 1900's chase one another across the film of my mind, perhaps mingling together and eluding pursuit : I saw Carpenter of Essex, also at Whitsun, caught by Tyldesley at deep long-on in front of the Ladies' Pavilion at Old Trafford, the same gracious, black-and-white gabled Ladies' Pavilion where Kenneth Hutching fielded at third-man, tawny, supple, muscular and leonine, the cynosure of all eyes. Carpenter, entirely forgotten now, was a splendid batsman, equalled in stroke-play by not more than half a dozen players of 1950. In 1901 the wicket at Old Trafford was a scandal. Fast bowling on it imperilled kneecap, breastbone and Adam's-apple alike. Something had gone wrong with the ground staff's cultivation of the turf in the early spring. I have been told— but it is too good to be true—that one of the groundsmen was at work " in the middle," separating with a riddle the impure from the pure and essential marl ; he had almost finished the task, and had made two piles of the stuff—but at this critical juncture it was time for midday refreshment.

As luck would have it, he met an old friend at the adjacent inn, where every day he relished a modest sandwich and a glass of ale ; on this occasion a reunion after long separation needed to be celebrated. When the groundsman returned to the " middle " at Old Trafford he proceeded to sow the wrong pile of marl—containing many rough and foreign bodies—into the wicket, a natural enough error, all things considered. As I say, Old Trafford was indeed unfriendly to batsmen that year and a fast bowler's joy and inspiration. I saw C. J. Kortright knock Johnny Tyldesley out of action for an hour or two ; but Johnny returned after lunch, his forehead bandaged, and he counter-attacked the fastest bowler of all time. I am not sure that it wasn't in this same match against Essex, in the early 1900's, that Tyldesley didn't win a match in an over. Seven or eight Lancashire wickets were down and nearly twenty runs still wanted when a storm broke ; for an hour black clouds had rumbled up. Suddenly great spots of rain fell ; you could hear the smack of them on the grass ; then a flash of lightning was seen across the Stretford sky. Tyldesley, quicker than the storm, hit four or five fours in one over from Buckenham ; square-cuts, flicks high over the slips, death-and-glory strokes as forked as the lightning. Before the players could reach the shelter of the pavilion, Old Trafford was a lake or an archipelago. In this season of dangerous pitches C. B. Fry one day extracted some pebbles or minerals from the wicket, and they were later exhibited in the window of Tyldesley's cricket outfit shop in Deansgate. People would look at them for hours, like students going the rounds of a museum of geology.

This same season, playing half his innings on this nasty, brutish turf, Tyldesley scored more than 3,000 runs, average more than fifty, which must remain one of the wonders of bats-manship. Consider, too, the pleasure he gave while making this 3,000, to himself as much as anybody.

By the time 1904 burgeoned for Lancashire cricket, I was an addict, hanging on to every hour's news from everywhere, Taunton to Trent, Bournemouth to Bradford. In 1904 Lanca-shire won the county championship and didn't lose a match ; and the first three in Lancashire's batting order have never been equalled by any other first three, for mingled majesty, grace and swordlike power and brilliance : Maclaren, Spooner, Tyldesley. Of Maclaren I can say no more : I have written of him

elsewhere. Nobody has occupied a batting crease with his
sovereignty, his sense of born prerogative. A youthful impression of him will not fade—yet I can't believe it is a true one. On
the other hand, I am not poet enough ever to have "invented"
a picture as evocative and as true to the Maclarenesque manner
and atmosphere as this :

On a calm morning at Old Trafford in that distant and indeed
lost world of the early 1900's, Maclaren went forth with Albert
Ward to open the Lancashire innings against Warwickshire.
Hargreave, a clever slow left-hander, began the attack, and in
his first over Maclaren played forward with the sweep of grandeur
which was for him sign of the blood-royal ; but Hargreave's ball,
"coming with the arm," beat Maclaren and bowled him. Only
the leg bail fell. And when Maclaren returned to the pavilion
the members rose for him in silence, as he passed them up the
steps. At least if they didn't, they should have.

It is a mistake, of course, to assume that Maclaren was always
playing forward or swinging an imperious bat. His back-play
was strong, though it departed from the modern method in
two important ways—he lifted up his bat even to play back late ;
and when he moved back on his right foot he didn't plant it
across and "pad-up" so that the stumps were entirely covered.
He reserved to himself some liberty to make a positive hit—and
no positive hit can be performed if both pads are facing the
bowler when bat meets ball. In some sixty-one innings for
England against Australia, Maclaren was l.b.w. only twice. Leg-
before-wicket law as such, had nothing, and couldn't possibly
have had anything, to do with the fastidious use of pads in
defence by players of the breed of Maclaren, Spooner, Trumper.
The l.b.w. law was changed to operate as at present because of
an abuse of pad play. The breed of Maclaren and Spooner and
Trumper and F. S. Jackson and Hayward would never wittingly
have taken refuge in pad obstruction when confronted by an
apparently unplayable ball. These men were reared in a world
which had some respect for what I shall briefly, if a little por-
tentously, describe as æsthetic morality. I cannot imagine even

the physical or anatomical possibility of R. H. Spooner twisting his body abruptly across the line of the ball to the off-side, right leg blindly leading the way, with a protective push of precaution, knees bent and ugly. The great game of cricket is responsive to the spirit of the age. In the 1900's cricket may not have arrived at the introspection of to-day, or at the contemporary intensive refining of technical parts. It may indeed have reflected something of Victorian pompousness. But it was seldom little, seldom mean, seldom unmanly, seldom ugly. W. G. Quaife, a man of few inches and supposed in his heyday to be an inveterate stonewaller, was always pretty to see—style in miniature, style in a band-box.

In 1905 at Old Trafford, I attended to see and witness the baptism in Test cricket of my hero, R. H. Spooner. He made 52, enough runs to let us feel sure he had established his place in the England XI against Australia as a representative batsman who also happened to be one of the finest cover-points of all time. Nowadays an innings of 50 in a Test match doesn't guarantee a cricketer's security of tenure unless he also takes a few wickets. In this 1905 Old Trafford engagement A. C. Maclaren went in first with Tom Hayward to open England's first innings. He drove a straight four, to the off-side of the sight-screen at the Manchester end from the first over bowled by C. E. McLeod. McLeod then moved Clem Hill a few yards to his right at long-off, and a few moments afterwards Maclaren, again aiming at the boundary in that direction, was caught by Hill from a grand hit which was clearing the rails when held. You see, McLeod had dared Maclaren to repeat a drive—in the preliminary overs of a Test match—and Maclaren had picked up the gauntlet. I can imagine the comment upon this episode from some of the players of 1950: " Bad cricket. Yes, even selfish. A Hutton or a Washbrook would rightly get the sack for it."

Not long ago I was talking with R. H. Spooner and he told me of a Lancashire and Yorkshire match of the 1900's : he had reached 99, so the Yorkshire field was drawn closer to his bat to prevent a quickly run single. But Wilfred Rhodes sent him a ball which he thought he could safely drive for four. He got a little " under " it and, narrated Spooner, " imagine my disgust when I saw it falling apparently into Denton's hand, at deep long-off : I had thrown a century away against Yorkshire. But the ball just managed to clear David's head and drop into the crowd. . . ." Whereat I was obliged to laugh, and Spooner naturally asked me why—what had he said that was funny ? " I was laughing at you on two counts," I replied. " First that any batsman in a Lancashire and Yorkshire match with his score 99 should even faintly dream of hitting a four in front of the wicket and, second, that in a Lancashire and Yorkshire match a man should be fielding in the ' deep ' at all. . . ."

The truth is that, before 1919, the Lancashire and Yorkshire match was usually a brilliant affair, with as much gallantry as grimness—another instance of cricket's susceptibility to the spirit, even the economy, of a given period. There was opulence rife in both teams of the 1900's : Maclaren, Jackson, Hirst, Rhodes, Frank Mitchell, T. L. Taylor, Spooner, Denton, Tyldesley . . . from these men richness and challenge were bound to come. Not until the changed post-war scene of 1919 and after did the Lancashire and Yorkshire match go underground, behind trenches, ca-canny, a fight near the bone of existence, though, as we shall see, a vastly humorous one, as true to life in the 1920's as Lancashire and Yorkshire matches had been true to the more moneyed and less careworn epoch before the Deluge.

In Lancashire's wonderful year of 1904, Old Trafford and wherever the team journeyed was ablaze with superb batsmanship. Besides Maclaren, Spooner and Tyldesley, there was L. O. S. Poidevin, who would have played for Australia if he hadn't come to England and settled in Manchester to practise medicine ; also there was James Hallows, lost to Test cricket through ill-health, a glorious left-handed batsman and slow left-handed bowler, uncle of Charles Hallows, also cut down by fortune on the upper slopes of greatness ; he should have played not only once for England against Australia but many times, as our reply to Warren Bardsley. In this Lancashire side of all the talents was Jack Sharp, who lived to score a century for England, but not only that, to be chosen on a certain dire occasion to serve as the England fast bowler. W. Findlay contributed his share as a wicketkeeper, who as a batsman was, as the reports of the period habitually said, " difficult to dislodge." Worsley, too, kept wicket this year—Worsley of *Crème de Menthe* fame. In and out of the Lancashire cavalcade of 1904 passed A. H. Hornby and Harold Garnett, a left-handed batsman worth a long journey to see, with a swinging leg-hit. It is easy to make an extensive catalogue of the fine players at Maclaren's command and yet omit names that have inexplicably escaped memory. So I will protect myself by using the symbol: O. & O.E. The bowling began with Walter Brearley and Kermode, supported by Hallows, Sharp, Cuttell, and, in rainy weather, Huddleston. Brearley was a gale of a man, high dome of forehead, prematurely bald, pink of face in repose, vermilion and purple as he swung into attack ; one or two strides, then a lurch to the right, and a powerful wheel of the body over the left hip. He hoped to get a wicket every ball ; he was the living image of expostulation when he didn't. Maclaren himself thought twice before taking him off. He often bowled from noon to evening. When Brearley wasn't bowling he chafed at mid-on. " Let me 'ave another ' go,' Archie, for God's sake." Once at Lord's, Middlesex won the toss, and P. F. Warner began the innings with Tarrant. Maclaren proceeded to set the field, moving men here and there with lordly waves of the hand. Warner took guard while Brearley's arm rotated, working-up steam. He was about to open his onslaught ; he had almost started to run, when Maclaren from first-slip called out : " Wait a moment, Walter. You'll need a fine long-leg for ' Plum.' " Walter spluttered back in reply : " No, I don't, Archie ; I'm goin' to get him caught at second-slip." But Maclaren once more insisted : " Walter, you'll want a fine long-leg for ' Plum,' I tell you." And Brearley, at the end of his patience, became testy. " I don't want any fine leg for ' Plum.' Ah tell you, Archie, Ah'm goin' to get him caught at second-slip . . ." As it happened, the last ball of Brearley's first over pitched outside Warner's pads and he glanced at it for four to the Nursery end on the leg-side. Maclaren then said, throwing up his hands, addressing no particular man but the impersonal universe : " Of course, if a fast bowler thinks he knows more about placing a field than I do—very well then, let him go on, let him go on ! "

The imagination is strained to make a picture of Maclaren and Brearley both in the same team, on the field and off, between overs, or in railway trains. Did they—could they—ever stop talking ? By the standards of his day, compared, say, to N. A. Knox or Cotter or Kotze, Brearley wasn't disconcertingly fast ; but to-day he would be easily England's fastest. He was usually accurate and could " run " the ball away from the bat. Energy was his asset, and a power of will which caused his eyes to pop out of his head. And he was strong as a lion.

Harry Dean, for countless overs Brearley's colleague in attack, swung away to leg at a good bouncing pace on hard wickets ; he ran to the crease like a great dray horse ; his boots were gallant champing hooves. On " sticky " pitches he was a slow to medium left-hander enlivening first-slip with his spin. Dean, who first played in 1906, could have served as the complete model of a Lancashire lad : his jaw was square, his cheeks lined, his nose firm. It was a rugged face and a humorous one, the eyes shrewd and twinkling. His shoulders were broad and his arms so muscular that it sometimes looked, when he was standing in the field, that he couldn't get them quite down to the sides of his body. His dialect came from the mills of the county's hinterland in a period when Lancashire was prosperous. There was the old-fashioned respect of good words in his speech. The other summer I met him at Old Trafford, and immediately we talked cricket. I asked him to name the best batsman he had ever seen. His reply was prompt : " Why—Mester Spooner— Our Man." Then I said : " You've rather got me wrong, Harry. I didn't mean who had the finest style. I mean who do you count the best, the greatest you ever played with or against in your time." He took me by the lapel of the coat. "Mester Cardus," he said, "you asked me a straight question and Ah'm tryin' to answer you in as good English as Ah can—Mester Spooner. An Ah'll tell you for why. He were a born Aristocrat, he knew the fundamentials, like second natur'. No effort. No showin' off. Mester Spooner, Our Man!"

A wonderful tribute? I can "cap" it by another one, also to Spooner. It was spoken to me one day near the Green Bank at Lord's by none other than J. T. Hearne. He said: "To bowl at Mr. Spooner was a pleasure, an honour and a privilege. . . ."

Cuttell, an all-rounder, would have gone automatically into the England XI of 1950. Kermode, a fast-medium bowler from Australia, discovered by Maclaren in New South Wales, was a burly, top-heavy man, rather like a kangaroo in shape. His attack could attain a red-hot hostility. I have seen Kermode and Brearley vying one against the other to knock batsmen clean over the stumps, each reddening like boiled lobsters. Huddleston was an unplayable off-spinner after rain and sun. He pulled Lancashire out of the fire in 1904 at the Oval, when the "unbeaten" sequence seemed certain to end. At lunch Surrey needed about a hundred to win.

After lunch Huddleston, whipping back like a knife, saved the day and oh—and oh! the relief of mind he gave to a Lancashire boy, waiting in Manchester miles away, afraid to look at the latest scores in the "Stop-press"! I wonder if schoolboys still take the doings of their cricketers very much to heart and mention them in the postscript to their prayers. A summer evening was blackened for me when I opened the close-of-play edition of *The Manchester Evening Chronicle* and read "R. H. Spooner, b. Wilson, o," against Worcestershire. I joined my companions at cricket half-heartedly. But worse was to follow the day after; again the news read: "R. H. Spooner, b. Wilson, o." A "pair of spectacles" for him. I didn't play cricket on this evening but wandered alone, bereft and melancholy.

A fact of historical significance about the bowling of

Huddleston, and the bowling of all the many off-spinners who were his contemporaries, is that he seldom if ever bowled from round the wicket. The l.b.w. rule then in force permitted batsmen to frustrate any quick off-break with their legs if the ball pitched outside the off-stump, but, as we have seen, batsmen declined to trust entirely to pads in defence. The off-spinners, after beating the bat by spin and flight, were able and free to hit the stumps. Cricketers of 1950 will smile to be told that day after day the scores in the newspapers were rendered musical and poetical by the printed iteration of :

b. Haigh
b. Haigh
b. Haigh
b. Haigh

and so on. Haigh was an off-spinner. In the post-war years of 1919 we became shrewder. Before the l.b.w. law was altered so that obstruction became fatal to a ball pitching outside the off, if any part of the batsman's person was deemed by the umpire to come between wicket and wicket, batsmen with impunity frustrated glorious off-breaks by deliberately covering.

After the first war the game, like everything else, grew cannier and keener on the main chance. Batsmen unashamedly frustrated the glorious breakbacks of Cecil Parkin on a good wicket. One day at Worcester, he appealed twenty times for l.b.w. before lunch against this sort of wilful, but then legal, obstruction ; and twenty times " Sailor " Young, the umpire, turned and stared at the cathedral—probably he was ashamed to look Parkin in the face as he said " Not out." That day Parkin was breaking-back inches, but his analysis at the end was roughly thirty overs and two for 86. " And yet they send missionaries to China ! " expostulated Parkin, as he came wearily from the field. Round about 1920–1926 the Lancashire team had a saying : " If you're bowled by an off-break, you're a bloody fool. If you're l.b.w. you're a hero." " Where were your legs ? " screamed Harry Makepeace to a Lancashire novice who had just had his off-stump knocked back by Jupp of Northamptonshire, " what d'you think pads are for ? "

I can't trace in cricket's history the first off-spinner to bowl systematically from round the wicket. Wainwright of Yorkshire bowled over the wicket ; still, against Leicestershire at Dewsbury in 1898, he took twelve wickets in the match for 85, with ten clean bowled. Haigh bowled over the wicket ; also J. T. Hearne. Possibly Hugh Trumble " went round " at Old Trafford in the Æschylean Test Match of 1902, when he got rid of Ranjitsinhji, twice l.b.w., for 2 and 0 ; and it was " Ranji's " last appearance for England.

As recently as the early 1920's, as George Macaulay was coming to his own highly-tempered mastery, one of Yorkshire's oldest and most capable and honest cricket reporters hadn't grasped the tactics behind " round the wicket " off-spinners. Macaulay would go on after the seam and polish were dwindling ; he would begin over the wicket, then as soon as a ball jumped a little, he switched round at once. And dear " Old Ebor's " report invariably announced that " Macaulay, experiencing some difficulty in obtaining a foothold, was obliged to bowl round the wicket."

Huddleston was often dropped from the Lancashire team in dry weather ; so at last some of his friends petitioned the committee on his behalf, arguing that Huddleston hadn't been given a fair chance on good wickets. The chairman of the committee asked Maclaren to include Huddleston on the approaching Midland's and Western Tour. " No use for him," said Archie, " the glass is high and it's going up. I want another quick bowler." But the supporters of Huddleston's claims to a long trial on a good wicket overcame Archie's opposition. Huddleston took the field at Edgbaston next match, in hot weather. He opened the bowling, or was first change. Kinneir and Quaife stayed in for hours. Warwickshire declared at 532 for four ; Huddleston wheeled up his off-breaks—which did not turn on the perfect lawn of Edgbaston—without surcease, unchanged before lunch, on again at a quarter-past two. He was still bowling at half-past four, when, as there was no interval for tea in those days, refreshments were brought out on a tray, alcoholic and mineral. During the slight pause in the scalding action H. G. Garnett whispered in Maclaren's ear : " For God's sake, Archie, give poor Bill Huddleston a rest. He's been on since morning." Archie replied : " My committee inform me that Huddleston's not had his fair chance on a good wicket, and that he's to be given a thorough trial. This is the best wicket in England, and I'm giving him a *bloody* thorough trial." Huddleston's analysis in this interminable Warwickshire innings was :

80 overs, 22 maidens, 187 runs, 3 wickets.

At Liverpool in July 1905 Lancashire lost a match for the first time since 1903. N. A. Knox, for Surrey, wrought havoc. There was a narrow escape from disaster at Headingley, true, in the " invincible season of 1904." Yorkshire outplayed Lancashire, then favourites for the Championship, and on the third morning, with Maclaren and Spooner out, all seemed over. It was left to J. T. Tyldesley to hold back the grimly advancing Yorkshiremen by the longest and only purely defensive innings of his career ; he obstructed till six o'clock and scored 100 in five hours. Years after, whenever I was able to lure him to talk of himself for a minute or so, he would refer to this innings with some distaste.

During the period of 1902–1909 Lancashire gave to the England XI—apart from Maclaren—Tyldesley, Spooner, Brearley, Sharp, Dean, not counting S. F. Barnes, who, though he played for Lancashire throughout 1903, cannot be said to have belonged to any county ; he was a man born not to be possessed. I saw him humble the might of Surrey on the 26th June 1902, the abandoned day arranged for the Coronation of Edward VII ; the Coronation was postponed owing to Edward's appendicitis, but the nation made holiday all the same ; and in floods of sunshine at Old Trafford I saw Tyldesley score 165, cutting Tom Richardson square and so often that white powder lay for yards on the grass in front of the pavilion, dry paint knocked from

31

the rails. In the afternoon of this same day, Barnes reduced to
frailty on a perfect and reformed Old Trafford pitch, Abel,
Hayward, Hayes and the rest. Seven wickets were down for 90,
when V. F. S. Crawford came in, and with Captain H. S. Bush
playing a tall upright defensive game, Crawford subjected Barnes
to such a thrashing as he never experienced again, except once,
and that was years afterwards at Brisbane, when J. N. Crawford
—V. F. S.'s youngest brother—drove him unmercifully for 112
for " An Australian XI " against P. F. Warner's 1911–1912
England team. V. F. S. Crawford made 90 against Barnes on
the 26th June 1902 and drove him straight over the sightscreen
at the Old Trafford end and was at the wicket an hour and a half.
What with Johnny Tyldesley's 165 and the white paint knocked
from the railings and Crawford's driving, it was a day of Coronation cricket all right.

From these vintage summers Lancashire often had to leave
out, embarrassed by riches, not only Huddleston but James Heap,
a pretty and clever slow-bowler who could bat ; then there was
Arthur Hartley, a steady opening amateur batsman, who arrived
in time to relieve the failing Maclaren ; Hartley played for the
Gentlemen at Lord's ; so did H. G. Garnett. Round about the
mid-1900's, K. G. Macleod brought heavy artillery to reinforce
the county's cavalry and infantry ; he coped with a crisis at
Sheffield against the ancient enemy—five wickets down and only
a lead of 48. He scored 121 in two hours, with three sixes and
fifteen fours. This is no figment of my imagination ; it really
did happen at Sheffield on 9th August 1911. William Cook, a
professional engaged with Burnley, played a few times for
Lancashire and at Bristol in 1905 saved a lost day, when Maclaren, Spooner, Brearley and Sharp were engaged for England
at the Oval against Australia; and Cook was one of the finest
fast bowlers of many prospering then, but he preferred the more
lucrative and leisurely life in the Lancashire League. It was left
to his brother Lawrence—" Lol "—to restore the family balance
on the side of a quiet moral persistence and energy. In the
1920's " Lol " " kept one end going " for Lancashire day by

Ernest Tyldesley

Macdonald bowling at Leicester in 1921

day, usually against the wind. He was portly and resigned ; he would droop his head on one side after he had bowled in vain an over of perfect length, or had emitted an appeal on deaf ears, an appeal which in its high-pitched tone scarcely suggested hope for the best.

And now, as I come to the years immediately before the first war, my recollections of Lancashire, or any other form of first-class cricket, are dim ; for during the summers of 1912–1914 I was serving as professional at Shrewsbury School, my heart lost to school cricket altogether. But in 1919 circumstances working behind my back conspired that I returned to county company ; and all my old love flamed forth again for the great ones—and the not so great—of the game. What is more, I was paid by the *Manchester Guardian* to revisit the glimpses of the sun at Old Trafford ; in other words, I was able to make my livelihood by doing something for which since a boy I had worn myself to a shadow—watching and praying for Lancashire cricket.

The prisoner in Reading Gaol getting a sight of the sky did not suffer emotions more poignant than mine when, in May 1919, I saw again the green circle of Old Trafford's grass after years in the confinement of Manchester, with apparently cricket dead for ever in my heart, usurped by music and other " things of the mind." I saw J. T. Tyldesley bring his bat down on an off-side ball from Bestwick and cut it square for four, exactly as I had seen him cut Richardson square in 1902. So it was true, I said ; I hadn't exaggerated impressions of long ago ; in this dazzling manner did indeed my boyhood's hero play. But J. T. Tyldesley's course was nearly run by now ; he went to Chesterfield and in five hours he put to the sword the fast bowlers and the spinners alike : 272 in five hours. Next day his legs seemed to have lost their uses ; he was never more the same man. Lancashire cricket will never see his like again. Or any other county.

Ernest, his brother, stepped into Johnny's place as first-wicket-down batsman, and he established himself amongst the great stroke players and prolific scorers of the renaissance of the 1920's and 1930's. But Makepeace was the Lancashire five-year planner when in 1919 first-class cricket enjoyed revival. As time went on, and with the advent of Macdonald from Australia, the dourly cultivated soil, not a seed wasted, came to fruit: Lancashire won the championship three years consecutively, in 1927, 1928, 1929. Myles Kenyon inspired the team through the post-war reconstruction; then his successors, Leonard Green and Peter Eckersley, took charge of a diversity of characters, and coped with them by understanding the humorous source and basis of character in the North of England during the spiritually-clouded 1920's. Lancashire cricket, as I have said, now told of county life lived near the bone. Give nothing away. Make sure. If the toss is won, stay there, "wear wicket dusty," ready for Macdonald; or hope for a "sticky-dog" and Parkin's sharp-shooting off-spin.

It was never dull to watch Lancashire, for all the ca' canny of the Makepeace doctrine. That is if you were "in the joke." Lancashire didn't score slowly because they couldn't have scored quicker; they were slow *on principle*—until the bowling wearied; and it was not spared them. To travel round England with these Lancashire "professors" was an education in more than cricket; it was as enriching to the imagination as dialect litera-ture. A match at Bristol began on a dry wicket, which would certainly crumble. Gloucestershire won the toss and batted without risk for hours. Hammond himself declined to attempt a swinging hit. The innings wasn't "declared." It went on until it died of sheer longitude, staggering to the heart, by which time the wicket resembled a sandy plain. Just before Lancashire went in I chanced to pass the dressing-room. Frank Watson, deputy stonewaller to Makepeace, who was for some reason not playing in this match, thrust his head through the window and said: "Coom in 'ere a minnit, Mr. Cardus. We want to tell thi somethin'." I entered the Lancashire dressing-room, where Watson and Hallows were padded up, ready to go forth to tackle the spin of Charles Parker. I asked the two warriors what

34

they wished of me. " Tha's seen what's bin goin' on out there since yesterday mornin' ? " asked Watson, and Hallows took up the complaint : " Aye, they've batted wicket till it's like a country road." " And so," said Watson, " we wants thi to understand we've got to play 'em at same game ; an' so no foony stoof in *Manchester Guardian* about slow scorin', if tha doesn't mind."

I told them I understood, and thoroughly sympathised with their sentiments and scheme of retaliation. I wished them good luck, and out they walked, down the pavilion steps, into the sunset. In the first over Watson was caught off a prodigious hit which dropped from a great height into the hands of straight very deep long-off on the boundary's edge. A few balls afterwards Hallows was stumped yards out of his crease, attempting the mightiest pull of his career, or anybody else's. Naturally I was at a loss to account for this strange behaviour of two men who a moment ago had determined to go slower and more obdurately even than was their habit. I went into the dressing-room and demanded an explanation. " Well, it's like this, Mr. Cardus," said Watson, " when we got out there in t'middle agen, we 'ad another look at wicket——"

" And so," continued Hallows, " we decided we'd better get a few quick before it ' went ' altogether——"

" Aye," continued Watson, " before it cracked up proper."

About this time a mayor of Hastings suggested that Lancashire were not exactly an ideal team to invite to the annual and delectable festival there. Maybe they weren't, and not only because of the lack of romantic rhetoric in the batting but also possibly because there was always a chance that Macdonald and his fast bowling might put an end to a match in two days. It was against Sussex at Brighton that a crisis occurred in Lancashire's course ; they were going neck-and-neck for the championship and dared not risk loss of a single point. At tea, on the second afternoon, Sussex had finished their first innings only four runs behind. Before Lancashire batted again a council of war was held in the Lancashire professionals' dressing-room, to which the Lancashire captain was invited, with or without portfolio. There was some speedy but abortive argument; various proposals were tabled and unanimously rejected. Watson closed the proceedings this way: " Well, la-ads, we've bin talkin' for ten minutes, and tea interval is oop and we've got nowhere. So my suggestion is this, la-ads—situation of ga-ame bein' how it is—next innings we'd better pla-ay steady."

By acts of self-discipline, which for the cause he assumed like so many hair-shirts, Ernest Tyldesley conformed perhaps too often to the Makepeace doctrine. Never dully though. He was a courteous batsman whose cricket expressed the man himself, modest yet determined in a quiet way. J. T. Tyldesley more than once assured me that Ernest was his superior in technique, and he meant it. Ernest came later and inherited the sophistication of the " dead bat " for " sticky wickets," the very late push from the pads for the in-swinger. But the difference between Johnny and Ernest was one of inner fire and a congenital distaste of maiden overs. Johnny chafed if for six balls he was forced back on the defensive. You had to bowl longer at Ernest day by day to get him out than at Johnny; but Johnny took the pride and the stuffing out of bowlers. Ernest, politeness itself as a rule, paid some compliment of respect to the bowler until the bowler himself had lost self-respect. But on those occasions which challenged him to unchain his superb range of hits, when runs were wanted quickly, or when he alone survived of the team's key batsmen, Ernest could demolish and burn up the fiercest attack. Remember his bombardment of Warwick Armstrong's conquering Australians—with Macdonald and Gregory amongst them—at Old Trafford in 1921. At the Oval in 1923 he played one of the greatest and most incisively powerful and all the time most beautifully poised innings in my experience. At close of play on the second afternoon Lancashire to all appearances had lost the match; four wickets were down, 117 needed to avoid defeat by an innings, and there was nobody likely to stay with Tyldesley to-morrow against the barrage of Hitch and Reay and the rest.

An unknown amateur, Albert Rhodes, stood his ground while Tyldesley took charge next morning. Hitch, from the pavilion end, bowled his fastest. He began with four slips and a backward point. In less than half an hour three of these four slips had been moved over to the other side, a fairly draughty leg-trap, in danger of broken skulls and fingers from Tyldesley's terrific and perfectly timed, even leisurely, hooking. The contrast of havoc, cracking fury of blade, here, there, everywhere, a headlong kaleidoscope of all the strokes of the game in techni-colour—the contrast of these with the calm, almost fastidious way in which Tyldesley disposed of this ball and that ball, was remarkable ; etiquette and assault and battery in proportion, and indistinguishable. In five hours he scored a faultless 236. His more prolific seasons held their own with Hobbs', and recalled the processional sequence of C. B. Fry's six centuries in consecutive innings. In 1926 he scored 1,128 runs between 26th June and 22nd July with an average of 141. He scored seven centuries in seven consecutive matches, four in successive innings. On a bowler's pitch he had few superiors. His place in *Wisden* and in the estimation of the statisticians is secure. Those who saw much of him understood that he was an artist, one of the glories of the brief but splendid renaissance of the Golden Age—1926–1939.

It is arguable that Lancashire has never fielded teams better for all-round technique than those between, say, 1924 and 1930. There were international "colours" enough. Makepeace, Hallows, Ernest Tyldesley, Duckworth, Watson, Paynter, Parkin, Richard Tyldesley, Hopwood, Iddon, as well as Australia's Macdonald. The fielding, maybe, fell short of that close intersticed antagonism and character which was Yorkshire's secret. Though ruthless acquisitiveness governed policy there was no inflexibility of method. At Trent Bridge in 1920 Barratt with a new ball broke the spine of Lancashire's first innings in a few overs ; the recognised stroke-players were back in the pavilion and hardly a run in the books. So Makepeace changed himself for the occasion into a stroke-player while still remaining watchfully scientific. He was out just after tea for 150 in three hours fifty minutes, and he hit fourteen fours. Watson, who preferred to "pla-ay steady," scored 300 against Surrey in 1928, with thirty-seven fours, an innings that was violent and vivid of drives and cuts. On another afternoon, and against Yorkshire, on a wicket so hard and bony that Bowes was whistling the ball about the batsman's head, Watson hooked and slashed a century in two hours or so; but so frequently and far did he retire to square-leg to perform his strokes that I was disposed to doubt whether the innings could be said to have been legal and valid, seeing that the larger portion of it was scored on the wicket which was being prepared for the next match.

A crude hit, an injudicious one, most times brought upon the culprit's head a terrible scorn from Makepeace. "Why, you played forward and left ' gate ' open—farmer's glory." A new-comer to Lancashire—and against Yorkshire at Sheffield—went in just on lunch and actually hit Macaulay for two fours in front of the wicket from the last over but one before the interval. Makepeace, not out, 37, walked down the pitch and talked to the "novitiate." I asked this young player afterwards—I think he was Malcolm Taylor—what Makepeace had said to him. "He carried on awful," confessed Taylor.

Strangers from the South of England, who now and then ventured North to watch the Lancashire and Yorkshire matches of the 1920's and 1930's, thought the cricket was unspeakably dull. They didn't understand: they were in the dark. At one match a spectator was applauding strokes and bowling with such a strange impartiality that the man next to him, from Huddersfield, asked him a civil question. "Aren't you Lancasheer?" "No, I'm not." "Where's t'a from?" "London." "Well, Ah'd advise thi keep thi clapper shut—this ga-ame's got nowt to do with thee."

I found myself hard-pressed many days to cope as a writer with Lancashire's well-connived batting policy. First of all, the

On his day Parkin was one of the quickest match-winners of all the quick-medium off-spinners I have seen. In these moods he was the embodiment of snapdragon energy and gusto for life. He walked to his bowling place as upright as a guardsman, after taking a thrown-in ball with an outward thrust at the air, as though snatching an apple from a tree. Or he would trap the ball from the ground straight up to his hand. Then, arriving at his bowling place, he suddenly swung round, ducked his head (Keith Miller reminds me of him), the sun shining on his black glossy hair; and he would run in, gathering impetus, then before he released the ball the left arm went upwards and the right arm swung with the body, a cart-wheel of rare and thrilling grace. On hard wickets he improvised gaily and recklessly a slow high "googly," followed by a really fast one that came in defying eyesight. When he was taking wickets and the turf transformed his spin into rip-rapping fireworks, he would sing to himself as he walked back to bowl and while he ran into action; he was audible at mid-off, and he sang the period's melancholy tunes: "The sky is blew, I love yew," with relish and nasal burlesque. On a June morning at Lord's—Lancashire v. Middlesex—he found himself stranded while batting, after a difference between himself and Richard Tyldesley in mid-wicket. Tyldesley kept roaring "Noa," his face now an under-cut of tough beef. They, of course, both ran into Tyldesley's crease. At the other end the bowler, having taken the throw-in, needed only to walk a yard forward to remove Parkin's bails at leisure. Possibly unhinged by Parkin's catcalls and Tyldesley's Bashan roarings, he took aim at the stumps and missed them. The ball sped towards the distant Nursery. Quick to the cue, Parkin grasped the situation, and, shouldering his bat like a rifle, he thrust his head back, threw out his chest, and, knees up, marched down the pitch safely home, declaiming rather than singing, "The British Grenadiers." A fellow of jest sadly finite! Witty, humorous, a stormy petrel, herald of the approaching times of irreverence and disrule, and all the more lovable for his delinquencies. A source of happiness to countless Lancashire men and women, and Lancashire lads and lasses. May the soil rest lightly on him.

Of Macdonald I have written elsewhere, but cannot find language yet to describe the awe-ful and mingled speed, power and effortlessness of his attack. He was a tall man who would relax at mid-off after an over of bowling, all drooping curves, chewing a blade of grass. Tawny, aquiline. If a drive went beyond his reach he might not feel the effort to grasp it worth while, and then he would motion to any adjacent fieldsman, with a toss of his head over the shoulder, to run after it for him. He disdained on many days to bowl after he had swept the great and the good batsmen out of the way; he asked for his sweater at the fall of the sixth wicket and slouched to mid-off. Anybody else could finish off the " rabbits," or rather the " rabble." His moods were strange and fitful. He indulged a private conceit; he was prouder of his medium-paced off-breaks from round the wicket than of his pace. At Dover in 1926 Leonard Green declared, leaving Kent the whole of the last day to score 400 to win : a " sporting " declaration on a small fast ground, against batsmen such as Woolley, Chapman, Hardinge, the Bryans.

Macdonald, with the new ball, began at his most menacing and soon took a wicket. He was here given some rest, for Leonard Green wished to keep him untired until the hot day's issue had been decided. When Macdonald bowled his second spell he exploited his medium off-breaks. Kent were somewhere in the region of 150 for two at lunch, Woolley 60 or 70 not out. After lunch Macdonald, instead of at once sending a barrage of speed at Hardinge and Woolley before they settled again, persisted with off-spin. The Kent total soared. Macdonald was rested again. Woolley and Hardinge had scored 253 together in two hours fifty minutes when, mercifully for Lancashire, a one-in-a-hundred throw from the off-side by Leonard Green ran Hardinge out. Still, the position for Lancashire was hazardous. Kent, nearly 300 for three, Woolley still in. Green brought " Mac " to the attack for the new man in. And again

" Mac " bowled medium off-spin, round the wicket. At tea
Kent apparently had the match in the pocket. Desperately I
sought out Green. " What in God's name is the matter with
Mac ? Has he a strain or something ? " " No, he just won't
bowl fast." " But you should order him to——" " I've tried,
and he just won't—says the wicket's too slow. Go and talk to
him yourself. I'm damned if I can do any more about it." I found
" Mac " finishing a glass of whisky. I expostulated. And he
replied : " I'm surprised at you, Mr. Cardus. I should have
thought you of all people would have appreciated some art on
this lousy turf and against Frank Woolley. . . ." I appealed to
him again and emphasised that Leonard Green in his first year
as Lancashire's captain had taken a risk with the " declaration " ;
that if Kent got the runs, Tommy Higson at Old Trafford would
play hell. " Oh, very well," snarled—yes, it was a snarl—" Mac."
Back on the field, after tea, Macdonald shattered the Kent
innings in a few overs. He did the " hat-trick." He smashed
the tops from stumps. It was bowling of terrific velocity ; it was
bowling of havoc but of rare beauty. The Kent innings collapsed
with a rattle of wickets to be heard in the remotest corner of the
lovely ground. It was bowling which seemed suddenly to have
become ignited from the burning sun above. We caught the
boat-train to London comfortably, and had an evening to spare
before travelling North to Manchester at midnight. I shall think
of that summer afternoon—or I shall try—on my death-bed. The
terrace on high, the sense of space in the blue heaven, the white
tents and the shining grass, every blade alight. And the silent
curving run of Macdonald. The sudden storm after the inexplicable calm. Stumps flying at Duckworth like spears. A band
playing on the boundary and an August day running out.
Memory will cling to these impressions to the end.

At another season's close—Lancashire's last match at
Brighton—I went one evening, after the second day's play, a
walk along the " Front " as far as Hove. When I returned to
the Grand Hotel, the senior Lancashire professors were seated
together in the lounge and they had ordered drinks to be put

this was to prove a long transition stage for them. Macdonald, Parkin, Tyldesley, Makepeace left the scene in quick succession, and though the sterling little man, Eddie Paynter, was there with Washbrook, it is surprising to remember that matches could be won by an attack consisting of Pollard, Booth, Sibbles, Iddon, Hopwood and Parkinson, the last a leg-spinner who soon gave way to Wilkinson, destined never to master his unmistakable gifts for spin. Pollard was an excellent fast-medium bowler, honest, hard working and Lancashire to the marrow. Sibbles with a new ball for a while raised not only Lancastrian hopes but the hopes of at least one England Selection Committee. Whenever he took a wicket he blew his nose hard into a handkerchief. One or two grand young players brought good, not to say pedigree, blood to the team—Oldfield and Washbrook.

I shall die in the belief that the second war stole from cricket a batsman who, had he been allowed to go his ways without interruption, would have taken his place with cricket's recognised stylists and great ones. Even as it turned out, in spite of checks and the atmosphere in a less than great county, Oldfield has established himself in the good books of the connoisseur. In his salad seasons for Lancashire the blossoming of his talents lent a refreshing flavour to an XI which for the moment was enveloped in an air that had known better days. I have in mind an innings by Oldfield against Surrey at the Oval in July 1935. Against a total of 321, sparkling from dashing play by E. R. T. Holmes, Lancashire lost two wickets for 29. At this grave juncture Oldfield came in and played so beautifully, with so many rapid and fluent strokes, that old Lancastrians babbled of Spooner and Johnny Tyldesley. His stance reminded us of " J.T.T." ; his cutting, if it lacked that incomparable cutter's power, scintillated with the rightful brilliance. He hit Gover for three fours from six balls ; a glorious off-drive, a commanding pull, and a rasping backshot through the slips. The innings was in a pretty flame by now. The bowlers didn't know where to pitch the ball— and this is my acid test of a great player. Has he the power to put an attack to confusion ? If he hasn't, he may be a very good batsman, with an average to whose giddy heights a Johnny Tyldesley never thought day by day to aspire ; but for all that I shall deny his greatness. With all his radiating swiftness of stroke-play, Oldfield was this day clean and deliberate in method ; only now and then did he traffic with fortune outside the off-stump —and we loved him for it. He hit fourteen boundaries in eighty minutes while making 73, all of them fit to be photographed and printed in a new edition of G. W. Beldam's book (and why isn't a new edition published ?).

As dapper as a dancing master. Perhaps the most admirable fact about Oldfield's cricket was—and still is—its unself-consciousness. His concern has been only with the job of serving his county and the game. When I knew and watched him week after week, his art was a visitation to him ; he attended first of all to the duty of feathering the Lancashire nest by some blessed instinct of which the builder himself was unaware. To all the great stylists, in cricket and other and loftier callings, the bloom which is style has come not because it has been deliberately cultivated and " shown off "—only the second-rate artificers do that ; but because of some act of grace, like that which gives blossom to the fruit, whose chief function is just to be fruit, and edible.

Oldfield is to this day a cricketer much respected in his maturity. Still, the thought of what he might have been !—the loss to English cricket and to the æsthetic of the game. . . . Washbrook was an earlier discovery than Oldfield ; he scored 155 in his second county match for Lancashire against Surrey in 1933. Subsequently he suffered fluctuation ; he seemed to go wrong in the use of his legs. He was dropped from the team in 1934, but I never doubted that the heart of the matter was there, and many times I attacked the Lancashire county club's committee for their stupid want of confidence in him. Indeed, my refusal to desert Washbrook daily in the *Manchester Guardian* was so touching that possibly only Mrs. Micawber could have appreciated it. We all know his quality now, or rather most of us know it ; he has critics who look at him seeing only his limitations. Maybe the soul destroying ethic and economy of cricket these recent years has hindered development in the free direction Washbrook was born to go. But we have only to look at his cap and the pouter thrust of his chest, and the champing of the front foot before the bowler runs to attack. His square-cut and his hook would have adorned cricket of the 1900's. He looks right, even when he is, against nature, pushing out an unproductive bat and a by no means handsome one. If he could have gone in first with the example before him of A. C. Maclaren—but these regrets are superfluous and vain.

Lancashire have, as I write, shared the cricket championship of 1950, and as there is plenty of young blood in the team it seems another historical chapter is about to be written in the county's annals. Tattersall with off-breaks has surpassed Mold for the largest haul of wickets in a season. Berry and Hilton are chips from the Briggs block, especially Berry because of his liveliness of spirit and limb. I do not know if the Lancashire players of 1951 contain in their souls and bodies the old soil and salt, or if they sit in their public houses at night after a match, talking " tactics." When I travelled England with the team, Peter Eckersley would say to me after dinner at the hotel where the amateurs stayed : " Come—let's go and see what the ' professors ' are doing." With his rolled umbrella he would take me to the private bar of the Star or the Bell, and there they were always to be found—Makepeace, Parkin, Watson, Macdonald and " Dick " Tyldesley—arguing, demonstrating, setting imaginary fields on the table.

Nowadays it is seldom I repair to the matches of the northern folk ; I am to-day a Londoner, always at Lord's, an apostate. But when Lancashire come South how proud I am to see the cap with the lovely red rose on it. My affection for Old Trafford and my lifelong memories of Lancashire cricket fill my heart, and as I look at Washbrook or Tattersall, Hilton and Howard, I find myself murmuring :

O my Makepeace and my Watson long ago !

the political or racing columns. Impatiently I would squeeze myself in front of them and turn over just an inch of a page to see the cricket scores in the " Stop-press " column. On this particular afternoon I read " Lancashire so and so many for six. Tyldesley, c. and b. Dixon, 221." Later, when the old fogies had finished with the Boer War, I had the full report of the game to myself. " Tyldesley's brilliant display was characterised by powerful square-cuts. Having punished Wass for the four fours in an over, he turned his attention to Anthony." The language of the old cricket reporters was good—" having punished " : we can see him at it, wreaking justice on iniquity.

Any cricket ground in the world is the better if a Spooner or a Tyldesley has trodden its grass. But I honoured the famous Nottinghamshire field for its own sake ; I knew what had happened there before I was born. Every schoolboy of the early nineteen-hundreds had heard of Arthur Shrewsbury and William Gunn. I saw both of them before I was ten years old, and I remember Gunn's unfair tallness and reach ; and the way Shrewsbury played back, left leg a little off the ground, the bat coming down straight and very strong for a little man. I was told years afterwards that Arthur Shrewsbury was never seen in public without a hat ; in the dressing-room he would go into some hole and corner to change into a cap. When W. G. Grace was asked to choose the best possible or procurable England XI he said : " Give me Arthur." Simply that and nothing more.

Another reason why Nottinghamshire cricket made its claim on me at the most impressionable time of one's life is that Tom Wass on a " sticky " pitch at Aigburth would occasionally break my heart by bowling Lancashire out for less than fifty. After sun and rain Aigburth was the worst wicket in England ; and Wass bowled fast and right-handed the unplayable ball of a slow left-hander—a ball that whipped across from the leg to off-stumps. Imagine a very fast Charles Parker or Verity. On one of these Aigburth " sticky " wickets, A. C. Maclaren once said to Reggie Spooner, before the beginning of a fourth innings against Wass : " Come on, Reggie, let's get our pads on and

George Gunn

Larwood bowling against Surrey in 1931

go out, so that the scorers can have all the particulars." (Wass, eight for 19, or thereabouts.) Tom Wass was a curiosity of cricket, a fast bowler who was not at his best on dry turf but one who chortled, as Bobby Peel used to chortle, when he heard rain falling in the night. Wass, a grand rugged lean lump of nature, out of the coalfields, was not loquacious, and his vocabulary often found relief in onomatopœia ; but he never failed to express himself. "Well bowled, 'Topsy,'" said C. B. Fry to him one morning when he got to Wass's end after a leg-spinner had just missed his off-bail. "Not so much of 'Topsy,' Mr. Fry—Mr. Buddy Wass to thee." Thus the noble diamonds of the coalfields of Nottinghamshire, right down to Larwood and Voce, and I hope nowhere near an end even in these times, when to make one's living at cricket is really a profession, with a social status. I saw Tom Wass at Trent Bridge as recently as 1950 ; there was no change in his appearance since I had last seen him decades ago—no change, that is, not wrought by the passing of years. He wore the same homespun clothes and stout boots, the same flat cap, the same thick stick. His accent and choice of words had not been influenced by the modern spread of education or by the B.B.C. I spoke to him of Johnny Tyldesley. "The little begger," he said, eyes twinkling, "he gev me soom stick mony a day—an' I gev' 'im soom ba-ack."

I admired A. O. Jones, one of Nottinghamshire's finest captains, as much as it is possible for any boy to think highly of a cricketer born of any county not his own. John Gunn I didn't like : he was obstinate with his left-handed bat and wouldn't get out. In later years I came to know him ; he had turned seventy and was mellow. Of A. O. Jones he said : "Aye, some of chaps to-day go off field with strain to ba-ack, or pooled mussel and all soarts. When we old uns went complainin' to Mr. Jones before match 'e'd just say, ' You'll be all reight, Jack, when yo' gets out in " middle." ' "

John Gunn played for England at Trent Bridge in 1905 when Cotter, in England's first innings, bowled alarmingly fast. "Nun on us liked 'im," said John, " 'e got Tom 'Ayward out quick, an' 'e broke top o' Mr. Jackson's off stoomp, and 'e made a muck o' mine first ball—an' 'e were welcome. Before we began second innings, I 'appened to pass bottom o' yon stairs leading to passage outside amateurs' dressin'-room. And there were Mr. Maclaren, all padded-oop, ready to go in. And 'e were talkin' t' 'imself as he walked oop and down—aye, talkin' t' 'imself. And Ah couldn't 'elp over'earin' what he were saying, walking oop and down, talkin' t' 'imself, mind you, wi' his pads on. 'E were sayin', ' I'll bloody well Cotter 'im, I'll bloody well Cotter 'im.' "

"And," added John, an obvious afterthought, "and 'e *did*."

Hallam, who bowled at Old Trafford for Lancashire in my early days, went to Trent Bridge and won the championship for Nottinghamshire with Tom Wass. Another link. Then at Shrewsbury, where I was junior professional, my senior was Attewell. I have since been told he couldn't possibly have been *the* Attewell, but more likely his brother Walter. He never spoke to me as though he were not the one and only Attewell, born at Keyworth. He was authentic enough in my growing, looming imagination.

In 1910 Nottinghamshire at Old Trafford left Lancashire with 400 and more to score for victory in five hours or so. It was done—by Tyldesley and Jack Sharp. If I remember well, A. H. Hornby came in late and limping, eight wickets down, time nearly up. Magnificent bowling by a medium-paced left-hander, named Riley, nearly cheated Lancashire in the end. After the winning hit had been made, the crowd rushed the ground for the first time in Old Trafford's history. Strange and rude boots touched the turf Hornby and Barlow had hallowed. A few policemen were useless to turn back the jubilant multitude. I myself ran over the field with them, but not to the front of the pavilion to help the cheering. I remained on the " wicket," afraid to put all my weight on it. I was astounded at the depth of the bowler's footholds ; one or two of them were nearly ankle deep.

A cricketer's career is as brief as his summers and his fame. Half a century ago, and less, A. O. Jones and Iremonger were names almost as closely associated with first-wicket stands, " opening partnerships," as Brown and Tunnicliffe, A. C. Maclaren and Ward, Hayward and Abel. A quick scorer and a steady one—that was the combination or ritual whereby a side began an innings in those days ; a staunch bat to wear down at one end, a busy one at the other. A. O. Jones at his best was dazzling ; his late-cut would surprise the most vigilant slips and would render third-man more or less static and decorative. Iremonger played with a most stately and correct deportment. Through many a long hour in the sun did bowlers toil away at Trent Bridge when Jones and Iremonger were together, as indeed bowlers from time immemorial had sweated long hours at Trent Bridge, often with Shrewsbury and William Gunn in possession —" Sta-ay back, Billy "—and as for ever bowlers yet unborn are apparently destined to sweat at Trent Bridge. Trent Bridge, the lotus land of batsmen, where it is always afternoon and 304 for two.

Just before the first world war descended upon the Golden Age of cricket, a Nottinghamshire batsman called Alletson scored 189 out of 227 in ninety minutes at Brighton. One drive was so powerful that the ball penetrated a wooden post supporting the pavilion and was extracted only after much effort. But Alletson never again played such an innings, or anything like one ; he didn't even try. Crowds flocked to see the new Hercules. He stonewalled. Day after day. A. O. Jones told him that if he would only make an attempt to hit his place in the team would be safe ; if the attempt was not made he, Alletson, would be dropped. Alletson never more, after riding the whirlwind at Brighton, lifted up his bat. This strange story, dramatic and of Freudian significances, is told once and for all in C. P. Foley's autobiographical *Autumn Leaves*.

In 1919 I first actually saw Trent Bridge ; for the first time of many I walked over the bridge where the landscape seems to grow spacious, and I entered for the first time the gate near the

Trent Bridge Hotel. To this same gate, in the disappearing early 'nineties, would come rather late in the afternoon " Billy " Barnes. Sometimes in mid-week the Nottinghamshire professionals were expected to help the Club and Ground XI. Every year Liverpool visited Trent Bridge and A. G. Steel would be with them. Invariably he scored a century very forcibly. One July day " Billy " Barnes appeared late, as I say, at the entrance near the Bridgford Road. The gatekeeper said : " Tha'rt la-ate, Billy, they've begun wi'out thi." " Who's battin' ? " " Liverpool." " Is Maister Steel pla-ayin' ? " " Aye, 'e is that—'e's in now." " How many is 'e ? " " Abaht fifty, Billy." " Oh, is 'e ? —well, to 'ell wi' 'im. I'm off. Good afternoon." And off he went.

Between 1919 and to-day Trent Bridge has been my favourite cricket ground after Lord's—I mean as a place to go to, not only to watch cricket at but a place to wander about in and muse and laze the afternoon away. There is grass to walk on while watching the game ; at the back of the pavilion there are apple trees and an open-air café with coloured umbrellas at the tables. In the pavilion's main room there is a most historical gallery of photographs and memorials, collected by A. W. Shelton, a great friend of Nottinghamshire's cricket and a gentleman of the type fast vanishing from the committees of our county teams. Amongst the portraits is one of Richard Daft, handsome and Oscar Wilde-ish in some way that *isn't* Oscarish or flabby or feminine. There is an old score-card recording a match between Notts Club and Ground v. Veterans of the Crimean War. At least nine of the Crimean veterans were run out—a case of hardness of hearing, maybe, or rheumatic or wooden legs. . . .

To this day there is an old-world Midland ease about Trent Bridge in mid-week ; there remains in the atmosphere some flavours of the soil (and seam) that produced the homespun stuff of the past, when there was good swearing and hard drinking, and history at Trent Bridge marched along in hob-nailed boots, and Arthur Shrewsbury took a Sunday School class, and Nottinghamshire cricketers answered to such names as Mordecai.

These old " Notts " professionals after a day's play would sit in a tavern or, like Attewell, would go home to the village they were born in and have boiled onions for supper. Their vocabularies were not wide, but now and then they spoke with an echo of biblical cadence : " If God's willin'," Attewell would say, " Ah s'll be down at ground next Saturday mornin'. . . ." He once bowled " Ranji " and George Brann on a " plumb " wicket at Brighton, each for next to nothing, each with a ball, he added, " straight as a whistle." He was proud that he had bowled them with *straight* balls, proud of simple craftsmanship. I have known players of the past who disapproved of the " new-fangled " " googlies " and swerves, not because as batsmen they couldn't cope with them, but because such devices seemed to them so much jiggery-pokery, an evasion of first principles.

" Did Kortright swing the ball ? " I asked J. T. Tyldesley one day.

" No," was the laconic answer.

" What did he bowl ? "

" Fast."

" Yes ; I know. But what did he ' do ' with ball ? "

" Nothing."

" What, no swerve ? "

" No."

" No break off the pitch ? "

" No, he just bowled fast—there was no time for anything else."

Another memorial in the pavilion at Trent Bridge is a silken card showing the scores in a Nottinghamshire v. Yorkshire match of round about 1912–1914. George Gunn made just a few more than a hundred in the first innings, and in the second just a few more than another hundred, not out this time—his share of a total of 129 for three, then the match was washed out by rain. In their first innings Yorkshire passed 400 ; Nottinghamshire could play only for a draw and George Gunn's first-innings century lasted some six hours. In the dressing-room the Yorkshire professionals scoffed at him. " 'Ast lost all thi stroaks, George?" So next innings George got his century in an hour and a half, following-on uphill.

So now I have come to a cricketer who has delighted my life, one whom I would choose next to nobody else if I wanted pure entertainment from a batsman, and suggestions of original genius. In his maturity he seemed often to play in a dimension of his own, in a region governed by science and geometry created by himself for his own private amusement. He would move out of his crease to the fastest attack as though going for a walk; he would turn right and left, to off or on, changing the axis of all manner of spin. One day he goaded George Macaulay of Yorkshire to squinting distraction. Macaulay pulled himself up in the middle of his run when he saw Gunn coming towards him down the pitch. "For God's sake keep still, George," cried Macaulay. "Stop thi' antics. Ah'm booggered if Ah knows which is off-side or which is leg-side."

During the 1920's a match between Nottinghamshire and Kent was ruined by rain on the first day. But A. W. Carr told me not to give it up and go elsewhere for my " copy " for the *Manchester Guardian*. "We are going to finish in two days." G. B. Legge was the Kent captain and he had agreed with Carr to play hard for a decision. A glorious game was the issue of this compact. But on the closing morning Kent collapsed and, after all, Nottinghamshire were left ample time to score about 180. George Gunn came in with Whysall, on a lovely afternoon, and straightaway he cut and drove all over the field, all over the place, all manner of strokes, classic cover-drives, then sudden changes of gear and position, sending first-slip scampering away to long-leg. He shaped to force a well-tossed ball from C. S. Marriott past mid-off but cut it late, on second thoughts with no time to spare, out of reach of second-slip. In an hour and a half he reached a hundred and the match ended early, the best hours of a July evening still to go.

Years afterwards, I asked Gunn about this match and why he had batted in such a fashion and at such a speed. Yes, he remembered: " I was goin' out with ' Dodge ' Whysall, all ready to play nice and quiet to get the runs and give crowd something else to watch and I particularly wanted match to last a bit, because my wife had come and were in car on grass on far side of ground. But just as I were goin' downstairs with 'Dodge' on way to the 'middle,' one of Committee come up to me and was rude to me—I forget what it was about but he got my goat. . . ."

"And ? " I said, still waiting for the explanation.

"Well," replied George, "well—I took it out of Kent bowlin'."

He was born under the classical star of his uncle William, so it was an imposing period when at the turn of the century he was given a place in the county team. The sovran rays of the sun of the Golden Age ennobled all cricket fields. Naturally he had for a while to be careful and behave himself. I have occasionally suspected that George Gunn's whimsicality came, as his technique grew instinctively masterful, from some revolt against tradition, a tradition of decorum long respected in the family. "Dost thou think, because thou art Victorian and virtuous, Uncle William, there shall be no more cakes and ale ? " Uncle William himself never made strokes as handsomely formal as Gunn's copy-book ones ; but it is pretty certain that uncle William would have thought that a characteristic innings by George went near to blasphemy.

In the 1920's during a Test match in London, a certain renowned English batsman spent an hour proceeding from ninety to a hundred. At the end of the day I met George, who had come from Nottingham, on holiday, to watch this game. He delivered censure upon the batsman in question : "—— ought not to have taken that long goin' from 90 to 100. It wasn't only selfish—a cricketer after all is a public entertainer and it's his job to consider the crowd and keep 'em amused." I congratulated George on these sentiments and wished him further good luck with them. Not long afterwards Nottinghamshire played Yorkshire at Bradford and won the toss on a wicket full of runs. On a summer Saturday morning of blue sky and sun, George and Whysall came forth, George wearing a white panama hat for the occasion. At half-past six Nottinghamshire's score was 282 for four, Whysall's share nearly 200. In four hours Gunn made exactly 48. I sought him. " What was all that fine talk of yours in London about public entertainment at cricket ? " I asked.

" Now look here, Mr. Cardus," he replied, " when Ah went out with ' Dodge ' this morning I were as willin' as anybody to get moving. But we had to watch new ball a bit against Emmott and Abe. And I hadn't played two maiden overs—if you'll cast your mind back—before a spectator at far end of ground roared out to me, ' 'It em, 'it em,' sarcastic like. So I said to myself, ' That feller's come here to-day to enjoy himself,' so, I thought, ' I'll give him somethin' to shout about.' "

One evening at Old Trafford, between half-past five and half-past six, in the early 1930's, Larwood rehearsed a little " body-line " against Lancashire. A wet day had put devil into a hard earth. Larwood was terrible to see. One or two of the more inexperienced Lancashire batsmen were soon bludgeoned out, but Ernest Tyldesley took the situation in hand until the drawing of stumps. Next morning Macdonald, the fastest bowler in the world then, or since, entered the Nottinghamshire dressing-room and advised everybody to ring up the adjacent hospital and make arrangements for beds and stretchers. That afternoon Nottinghamshire needed under 200 to win, and the wicket was so much decaying bone. Macdonald's attack affrighted eye and senses ; it imperilled breast-bone, thorax and cranium. Whysall, Walker and Carr were speedily overwhelmed. But George Gunn walked up and down the wicket, yards beyond his crease, then back to the base of the stumps, and he flicked Macdonald here and there at will. He stood high on tip-toe to a terrific " kicker," put his bat under it and sent it soaring at an unprecedented velocity over third-man's head, crash into the seats of the Ladies' Pavilion.

For the only time in his life Macdonald, usually a man of satanic unconcern, lost his temper. He paused in his onslaught and, pointing down the pitch, commanded : " Get back in your crease, George ; I'm going to knock your head off now." And to the most dangerous, the fastest and most majestic of fast bowlers—" in the kill " at that—George replied : " Why, Mac, you couldn't knock skin off a rice puddin'." He made sixty or so, and Nottinghamshire won by six wickets. I have never seen more genius put into batsmanship than by Gunn that day. He seemed to take " yards " of pace from Macdonald's bowling ; it was as though Macdonald were being reduced by some kind of cinematographic magic to " slow motion." More remarkable still, it was as though the same invisible magic were reducing George Gunn's every astounding action and stroke against bowling of fearsomely tempered velocity also to " slow motion."

Rare George Gunn. We shall not look on his like again, any more than we shall look on the like of Jessop or " Ranji " or Constantine. They were biological " sports," deviations from type and the mould.

Again—at Trent Bridge : Middlesex v. Nottinghamshire. At six o'clock on Saturday George was 90 not out and he had been enjoying an indolent but ornamental innings. The position of his county was now reasonably secure. R. W. V. Robins observed that George was wearing a thoughtful expression as the field changed over. " What's the matter, George ? " he asked. " You seem to have something on your mind." " As a matter of fact, Mr. Robins," replied George, " I have. I can't decide whether to get out to-night and come on Monday mornin' and sit and watch match with missis till we declare. I'm not sure yet if we've enough runs on board."

" Well, George," said Robins, " when you *have* made up your mind, will you let me know ? " " Yes, Mr. Robins, I'll let you know," said George, and a quarter of an hour later, when the field was crossing over again, he motioned to Robins, saying : " I've made my mind up. It's all right now, so I'm gettin' out soon." So Robins, who had so far bowled many overs for no wickets, went straight to his captain, F. T. Mann, and asked to be put on at the pavilion end. The wish was granted and Robins knew, of course, that nothing more than a straight one was necessary.

Before the ball had left Robins's hand George was moving down the pitch, pavilion-wards. He sent a return catch, never stopped walking, and as he passed the bowler's and the umpire's wicket, while removing his gloves, he gave a glance backwards over his shoulder, taking in the whole field, and said: " Good day, gentlemen."

He was called on in an emergency at Sydney for the first match in the rubber of 1907–1908. He had not been chosen as one of A. O. Jones's team but happened to be present in Australia because of his health. He scored a thoroughly impertinent century, as everybody knows.

The other season he asked me about Australia: " What's it like now ? I don't think I would enjoy Test matches there to-day—they've got too serious. When I first played at Sydney they had a band——" " A band for a Test match at Sydney ? " I queried, quite incredulous. " Yes," said George, " it began to play after lunch when I were gettin' past fifty, and they played Gilbert and Sullivan and I always likes Gilbert and Sullivan, and they played selections from all my favourites. And do you know " —he was very serious as he said this—" when they come to ' Reg'lar Royal Queen ' I were listening and hummin' tune as I were making my strokes absent-minded, you know ; tum tum tum—woof !—tum tum tum—I couldn't keep my mind on game, really ; and Sammy Carter behind stumps said : ' You seem to be takin' more notice of music than of bowlin', George.' "

Cricket was his game and way of life. He played according to his fancies, with the responsibility and occasional freedom from responsibility of a man most richly endowed. There remains in the Nottinghamshire team, as I write, a fine example and perhaps the last of the great eccentrics at cricket, Harris his name. He arrived at the wicket one day, took guard and then, after a survey of the field, said: " Good morning, fellow-workers."

Harris also contributed to the game his own whimsies—an hour of wilful strokelessness, batting of no substance or shadow, batting in a sort of void ; then a burst of spontaneous combustion, a superb drive, a blinding cut—and back again into an obscure so removed from us and the tangible sunny world, so anonymous, that it certainly seemed that there weren't no such a person.

Macdonald was in his heyday when I first saw Larwood run along the grass of Trent Bridge like a young colt. For seasons afterwards, even when Larwood was at his fastest, we of Lancashire thought there was only one really fast bowler on Trent Bridge when Lancashire played Notts in those days. But in the time of those now middle-aged no English bowler has surpassed Larwood for the speed that flashes quicker than eyesight can measure. A batsman too, and one of the most avid and certain fieldsmen close to the wicket on the on-side. Best of all, a true son of Nottinghamshire cricket, born of the original stuff, speaking the original accent enlivened, at times, by the original temper. A handsome fellow, square of shoulder, strong of jaw, aquiline of nose and cheekbone; every inch a cricketer, and not too tall. From out of the Nottinghamshire mould, too, emerged " Bill " Voce. In the beginning, when they discovered him as a lean undernourished boy, he bowled slow left-handed; but he never had the spinner's physical shape or elasticity; he suggested power and assault, and before long batsmen couldn't decide whether after all it mightn't be better to " take " and tackle Larwood at the other end, rather than cope with the swinging, bouncing pace of Voce, " coming right at you." It was " Ben " Lilley's cruel duty day by day to keep wicket to this combined and persistent blitzkrieg. Under A. W. Carr—called by J. L. Garvin in a private letter to me, " The Cid "—Nottinghamshire cricket vied in achievement and personal genius with the county's most illustrious period. In this year of 1951 Nottinghamshire cricket is in a dubious way. But it doesn't matter. Trent Bridge is too old to trouble about merely contemporary and temporal ups and downs. Every day's play there becomes part of Trent Bridge, goes into the annals of Trent Bridge, is fused with Trent Bridge's past and, what is more, its future, ripening in time to history.

Chapter Three

HUTTON AND HOBBS AND THE CLASSICAL STYLE

THE CHARACTERISTICS of the classical style in cricket, or in anything else, are precision of technique, conservation of energy, and power liberated proportionately so that the outlines of execution are clear and balanced. Hutton is the best example to be seen at the present time of the classical style of batsmanship. He is a model for the emulation of the young. We cannot say as much of, for instance, Worrell, who is the greatest stroke-player of the moment; it would be perilous if a novice tried to educate himself by faithfully observing the play of Worrell. A sudden snick through the slips by Worrell might cause us to lift an eyebrow, but we wouldn't think that something had gone wrong with the element in which Worrell naturally revels; for it is understood that Worrell and all cricketers of his kind, live on the rim of their technical scope. A snick by a Jack Hobbs is a sort of disturbance of a cosmic orderliness. It is more than a disturbance; it is a solecism in fact, as though a great writer of prose were to fall into an untidy period, or actually commit bad grammar. The classical style admits of no venturings into the unknown, of no strayings from first principles. A dissonance is part and parcel of romantic excess and effort; all right in Strauss, impossible in Mozart, where not a star of a semi-quaver may fall. The exponent of the classical style observes, and is content to observe, the limitations imposed by law, restraint, taste. He finds his liberty within the confines of equipoise.

I suppose that the three or four exemplars of the truly classic style of batsmanship have been W. G. Grace, Arthur Shrewsbury, Hayward and Hobbs: I can't include Maclaren; for something of a disturbing rhetoric now and then entered into his generally noble and correct diction. Trumper was, of course, all styles, as C. B. Fry has said, from the lyrical to the dramatic. Maclaren once paid, in a conversation with me, the most generous tribute ever uttered by one great player to another. " I was supposed to be something of a picture gallery myself," said he. " People talked of the ' Grand Manner ' of Maclaren. But compared with Victor I was as a cab-horse to a Derby winner. . . ."

In our own day, Hutton comes as near as anybody to the classical style, though there are moments when the definition of it, as expounded above, needs to be loosened to accommodate him. Dignity, and a certain lordliness, are the robes and very presence of classicism. Frankly, Hutton many times is obliged to wear the dress or " overhauls " of utility; moreover, his resort to the passive " dead bat," though shrewd and tactical, scarcely suggests grandeur or the sovereign attitude. The truth is that the classical style of batsmanship was the consequence of a classical style of bowling—bowling which also observed precision, clarity of outline, length, length, length! It is as difficult to adapt classical calm and dignity of poise to modern in-swingers and " googlies " as it would be to translate Milton into Gertrude Stein, or Haydn into Tin-pan Alley.

But Hutton, in the present far from classical epoch, follows the line of Hobbs, and if all that we know to-day of batsmanship as a science were somehow taken from our consciousness, the grammar and alphabet could be deduced from the cricket of Hutton, and codified again; he is all the text-books in an omnibus edition. Compared with him Bradman, who has been accused of bloodless mechanical efficiency, was as a volcanic eruption threatening to destroy Pompeii.

We need to be careful of what we mean if we call Hutton a stylist, which, we have agreed, he is. Style is commonly but mistakenly supposed to be indicated by a flourish added to masterful skill, a spreading of peacock's feathers. (The peacock is efficiently enough created and marvellously beautiful without that.) Style with Hutton is not a vanity, not something deliberately cultivated. It is a bloom and finish, which have come unself-consciously from organised technique rendered by experience instinctive in its rhythmical and attuned movements. His drives to the off-side have a strength that is generated effortlessly from the physical dynamo, through nerve and muscle, so that we might almost persuade ourselves that the current of his energy, his life-force, is running electrically down the bat's handle into the blade, without a single short-circuit or fusing, thence into the ball, endowing it, as it speeds over the grass, with the momentum of no dead material object compact of leather, but of animate life.

His " follow through " in his drives is full and unfettered. But the style is the man : there is no squandering in a Hutton innings. Bradman, to refer again to the cricketer known as an " adding-machine," was a spendthrift compared to Hutton, who is economical always, counting every penny, every single, of his opulent income of runs. We shall understand, when we come to consider the way of life that produced him, his *habitat*, why with Hutton, the style is indeed the man himself.

Some of us are obliged to work hard for our places in the sun ; others have greatness thrust upon them. A fortunate few walk along divinely appointed ways, the gift of prophecy marking their courses. Hutton was scarcely out of the cradle of the Yorkshire nursery nets when Sutcliffe foretold the master to come, not rolling the eye of fanaticism but simply in the manner of a shrewd surveyor of " futures." But Sutcliffe knew all the time that the apprenticeship of Hutton had been served in that world of vicissitude and distrust which are the most important factors forming the North of England character under the pressure of an outlook which thinks it's as well to " take nowt on trust " —not even a fine morning. In his first trial for the Yorkshire Second XI, May 1933, he was dismissed for nothing against Cheshire. Four years after, when he was first invited to play for England, he also made nothing, bowled Cowie. Next innings he was "slightly more successful"—"c. Vivian, b. Cowie 1" Though he was only eighteen years old when he scored a hundred for Yorkshire in July 1934—the youngest Yorkshire cricketer to achieve such distinction—illness as well as the run of the luck of the game hindered his progress, dogged him with apparent malice. When he reappeared on the first-class scene again it was just in time to take part in that dreadful holocaust at Huddersfield, when Essex bowled Yorkshire out for 31 and 99. Hutton's portion was two noughts. In his very first match for Yorkshire at Fenners in 1934, J. G. W. Davies ran him out brilliantly—for nought. Until yesteryear, in fact, the Fates tried him. The accident to his left forearm, incurred while training in a Commando course, nearly put an end to his career as a cricketer altogether.

He has emerged from a hard school. It has never been with Hutton a case of roses all the way ; he had to dig his cricket out of his bones : a bat and the Yorkshire and England colours didn't fall into his mouth like silver cutlery. According to the different threads or warp of our nature and being, a different texture is an inevitable consequence. There is no softness in Hutton's psychological or, therefore, in his technical make-up. And there are broadly two ways of getting things done in our limited world. We walk either by faith or by reason. There are, in other words, the born inexplicable geniuses and those we can account for in terms of the skill they have inherited. They are in a way the by-products of skill and experience accumulated and still pregnant in their formative years ; their contribution is to develop the inheritance to a further, though rationally definable stage of excellence. But we know where they come from and how. Hutton is one of the greatest of these. But a Compton, or, better for our illustration, a Trumper, seems to spring into being with all his gifts innate and in full bloom from the beginning. He improves in certainty of touch with experience, but as soon as he emerges from the chrysalis there is magic in his power, something that "defies augury" ; he is a law unto himself, therefore dangerous as a guide or example to others who are encased in mortal fallibility. But I am wandering from a contemplation of classicism and Hutton.

more

The unique or ineluctable genius isn't, of course, necessarily the greatest master. No cricketer has possessed, or rather been more possessed by genius, than " Ranji "; for his mastery was the most comprehensive known yet in all the evolution of the game. Hobbs summed-up in himself all that had gone before him in established doctrine of batsmanship. He was encyclopædic; we could deduce from his cricket not only grammar but history. We could infer from any Hobbs innings the various forces that had produced and perfected his compendious technique over years which witnessed changes which were revolutionary as never before, ranging from the fast bowlers of the post-Grace period, in which Hobbs was nurtured, to the advent of the most modern refinements and licences—swerve and " googly," and all the rest. When Hobbs began his career the attack he faced day by day was much the same in essentials as the one familiar enough to " W.G." But very soon Hobbs was confronted by bowling of the new order of disrule, which " W.G." couldn't understand; and Hobbs was not only the first to show how the " googly " should be detected and exposed and how swerve should be played in the middle of the blade; he taught others and led the way. Hobbs was the bridge over which classical cricket marched to the more complex epoch of the present. Hutton is the only cricketer living at the moment who remotely resembles Hobbs by possession of what I shall call here a thoroughly schooled or canonical method. He doesn't commit crudities. The " wrong " stroke at times—yes, because of an error of judgment. But never an *uninstructed* stroke.

He is a quiet thoughtful Yorkshireman, with widely-spaced blue eyes that miss nothing. And his batting is quiet and thoughtful; even in his occasional punishing moods, when his strokes are animating as well as ennobling the field, he doesn't get noisy or rampagious. His stance at the wicket is a blend of easeful muscular organisation and keen watchfulness. The left

64

Hobbs making an off-drive
in 1926

Hutton making an off-drive in 1948

Compton plays to leg

Compton is not out

shoulder points rather more to the direction of mid-on than would satisfy Tom Hayward; but here again is evidence that Hutton is a creature or rather a creation of his environment; that is to say, he is obliged to solve problems of spin and swerve not persistently put to Hayward day by day. With Hayward and his school, the left leg was the reconnoitring force, the cat's whisker, the pioneer that moved in advance to "sight" the enemy. With Hutton it is the right leg that is the pivot, the springboard. But often he allows it to change into an anchor which holds him back when he should be moving out on the full and changing tide of the game. He is perfect at using the "dead" bat—rendering it passive, a blanket of a buffer, against which spin or sudden rise from the pitch come into contact as though with an anæsthetic. He plays so close to the ball, so much over it that he has acquired a sort of student's slope of the shoulders; at the sight of a fizzing off-break he is arched like a cat. Even when he drives through the covers, his head and eyes incline downwards, and the swing of the bat doesn't go past the front leg until the ball is struck. He can check the action of any stroke extremely late, and so much does he seem to see a delivery all the way that we are perplexed that so frequently he is clean-bowled by a length well up to him. From the back foot he can hit straight for four; and all his hits leave an impressive suggestion of power not entirely expended.

We shall remember, after we have relegated his 364 against Australia at Kennington Oval in 1938 to the museum of records in sport rather than to the things that belong to cricket, his innings at Sydney in the second Test match during the 1946–1947 rubber; only 37 but so dazzling in clean diamond-cut strokes that old men present babbled of Victor Trumper. He has even while playing for Yorkshire more than once caused some raising of the eyebrows. At Nottingham in 1948 he not only played, but played well, Miller, Johnston and Johnson as though for his own private and personal enjoyment. But usually he subdues his hand to what it works in—Yorkshire cricket. I have heard people say that he is not above "playing for himself." Well, seeing that he is Yorkshire to the bone's marrow, we should find ourselves metaphysically involved if we tried to argue that he is ever not playing for Yorkshire.

There is romance even in Yorkshire cricket, though they keep quiet about it. Romance has in fact visited the life and career of Hutton. In July 1930, the vast field of Headingley was a scene of moist, hot congestion with, apparently, only one cool, clean, well-brushed individual present, name of Bradman, who during the five hours' traffic of the crease, made at will 300 runs, and a few more, before half-past six. He returned to the pavilion as though fresh from a band-box; the rest of us, players, umpires, crowd and scorers, especially the scorers, were exhausted; dirty, dusty and afflicted by a sense of the vanity of life. In all the heat and burden of this day at Leeds, more than twenty years ago, a boy of fourteen years was concealed amongst the boiling multitude; and so many of these thousands seethed and jostled that one of them, especially an infant in the eyes of the law, couldn't possibly (you might have sworn) have made the slightest difference to what we were all looking at, or to the irony of subsequent history. The solemn fact is that as Bradman compiled the 334 which was then the record individual score in a Test match, the boy hidden in the multitude was none other than the cricketer chosen already by the gods to break this record, if not Bradman's heart, eight years afterwards.

Chapter Four
DENIS COMPTON

FROM TIME to time, in most walks of life, a man appears who rises above his particular job and attracts the attention of people who are not intensely interested in his vocation. He has the appeal of what we conveniently call " personality," though few of us are able to define the term. " Handsome is as handsome does " is an old and very sensible saying, so true indeed that even a Denis Compton is obliged to prove his skill day after day, as he and the rest of us have found cause ruefully to realise only yesterday. It is, apparently, not enough that he should " look well " and embody charm and appeal in all his actions in the field. Some cricketers, on the other hand, may show abnormal technique perpetually, breaking records by rote ; yet they fail to achieve " glamour " in an age that insists on it. Also, there's something in a name.

Would our Denis seem to smell as sweet if it were Septimus Tomkinson ? He has had all the help from the fairies in the cradle (though, of course, the fairies can take away capriciously, as well as give). He was baptised Denis Charles Scott Compton, a Barrie title, and he was born only a mile or two from Lord's in the month of May, the month when the cricket season blooms and blossoms ; and his father not only loved the game but was good at it himself. He was endowed with sturdy loose limbs, square shoulders and strong wrists enlivened with suppleness. He was born with an inexhaustible flow of spirits and an eye that sees swiftly and can usually seek out the bright lining of a cloud ; and not only that, it is an eye that wins friends at a glance. He is not tall but not short ; just the right build, mingling the physical attributes of cricketer *and* footballer. Nature came to him with her cornucopia pretty full, and she let him help himself to it—for a while. Best of all, she brought to him a modest mind, without which the straight bat is only a symbol of vanity—not that Compton's bat is always straight. As we shall see, he has his own way of rendering first principles up to date.

Only the other year, it seems—time flies quickly in the cricketer's life, with wars ripping out whole chunks of summers —people going to Lord's and entering the ground at the W. G. Grace gates were buying score-cards from a bright-eyed boy, and he was Compton. Yes, his career has contained all the romantic ingredients ; upward flight from the bottom rung. But no writer of a boy's story would risk a sudden eclipse of his hero at the height of his fame, in Australia too ! Let us keep to the main pattern—" Card of the match, sir " ; then, at the age of eighteen, our hero is playing for Middlesex at Lord's, the historic place shaded by great ghosts ; and all London around him on a June day, all granted him without a hard fight, gift added unto gift, the plant in the proper soil from the start. For in his first season he scores 1,004 runs, average 34.62. He gets a century in his sixth match. At the age of twenty he is chosen to play for England, and, facing Australian bowling in a Test match for the first time, he gets a century. War merely gives him the schoolboy's second wind ; there seems no summit beyond his reach. He lowers the record of the one and only Jack Hobbs, eighteen hundreds in one memorable summer. After beating at home the record aggregate in a season of Tom Hayward, 3816 runs to the Old Master's 3,518, he goes on to score two centuries in a Test match against Australia, when he first plays there. To-day he is thirty-three years old and should have been rather in need of crutches. He throws off vicissitude without a shrug ; he even throws off a sudden dreadful blow from his deceitful fairies, and throws it off without spite. He sometimes seems to trust his stars dangerously, grateful if they are ascendant but apparently scarcely aware if they are not. But genius—even genius—needs to choose the right moment. Compton came to the high summer of his renown in a period when we all badly wanted the like of him on our fields, for the purpose of rejuvenation. His cricket, in 1947, gave a nation-wide pleasure which was somehow symbolical. In a world tired, disillusioned and thread-bare, heavy with age and deprivation, this happy cricketer spread his favours everywhere, and thousands of us, young and old, ran his runs with him. Here at any rate was something unrationed. There were no coupons in an innings by Denis Compton. He was contagious ; he liberated impulses checked for long amongst all sorts and conditions of English folk— women as well as men, girls as well as boys. He embraced a new public in search of entertainment and release, a public which knows nothing of the old divisions that restricted sport to " men's games." Denis hath his fans not less dewy-eyed than those of Hollywood.

Is he a great batsman ? I would prefer to describe him as a richly gifted one who is a stroke-player of distinction and some originality. He certainly isn't Hutton's equal in technique, and nature didn't intend that he should be. Hutton is obviously the more organised batsman of the two ; he possessed what I shall here call (and I hope I won't scare away my schoolboy) power of conception, ability to see a long way ahead in an innings. A big score by Hutton is thought out, or is the consequence of delibera-tion, either before or during the execution of it. Compton seems frequently to play according to mood, or what once on a time was called the inspiration of the moment. Hutton's cricket is old in the head, rational and responsible. Compton's cricket is never old in the head ; for all its schooling and skill it simply will not grow up. If Hutton had run into half of Compton's appalling misfortunes in Australia during the Test matches of 1950–1951 he would have extricated himself by a severe bracing of the mind and will. Compton was soon at a loss—an Aladdin who had forgotten how to rub the lamp and pronounce the necessary Abracadabra.

It is the failing of all sorts of criticism to consider an artist's or performer's technique apart from the individual who is using it, and to regard skill as a thing in itself which moves of its own volition and always in the same way. The truth is that if the technical equipment of Hutton could somehow be given to Compton, inoculated into his bones and being one night while he slept, and his own taken away from him, we should see little essential difference in his cricket next day. With Hutton we have the order and fulfilment of science ; with Compton we have the short-cuts and spontaneous illuminations of temperament. Compton one day is so quick on his feet, in and out of the crease, that the bowler seems now and then to have to change his mind while running ball in hand to the wicket. Sometimes Compton prances down the pitch, only to find a length altogether too short for forward stroke ; he will run back to cut it, and sometimes it is a scurry to save himself. He is a superb driver between the left hand of mid-off and point. He is not always too particular about placing his left foot near the line of the ball ; he is trustful of the enormous power and steering-wheel suppleness of his wrists. But on his ill-starred days he may very soon be caught because his bat has gone out to seek the ball on the off-side with no guidance apparently from Compton himself ; it is as an artificial limb. On these inexplicable days he falls under that evil spell which reduces others not fit to tie his laces to immobility of the right foot, so that, he, Compton, yesterday as impertinent and ubiquitous of movement as a young terrier tackling a mastiff, is bird-limed. Or his bat has become leaden. Not often, though, is he so reduced and chap-fallen. Yet, you see, the margin of error is there. He needs always to be " seeing " the ball with the clearest and most rapid and comprehensive eye. A Hobbs or a Hutton, because of sound grasp on the fundamentals, is able to go on and on until the age of spectacles and ear trumpets. Compton's cricket at his best belongs to youth.

He has, in fact, been called the Peter Pan of the game.[1] But the point about Peter Pan is not that he would not, but could not grow up.

The operation on Compton's knee has been a serious hindrance; still, I fancy that even if he hadn't incurred this physical damage he would to-day just the same be under the compulsion to face a transition period in his development as a batsman. As youth leaves us—and no man lives for ever—we must overhaul our catechism, as that great thinker, Captain Cuttle, advises. He has already proved his harder metal. In Australia five years ago, on his first visit there, he was put under the obligation of adopting a method and outlook foreign to his nature as then supposedly known and revealed. He found himself bowed down somewhat in heavy armour, his job grimly to " hold the fort." Nobly, if not grimly, he obeyed the orders of the day, and at Adelaide on a perfect wicket he was professionally clever enough to score 43 in two hours and a quarter, and compile two centuries in one Test match. At Trent Bridge in 1948 he defended a broken bridge for England for six and a half hours against Australians " on the kill," while darkness fell on the earth from the sky. This innings was one of the greatest ever played in all the annals of Test cricket, both for extensive skill judiciously applied and for disciplined mind and temperament. Maybe we shall not again look on the gay Lothario Compton of 1947; but let us console ourselves that " ripeness is all." He has the humour to adapt himself. When he first played Iverson at Melbourne in 1950 he was for a while completely at a loss; he tried all ways and means to deal with Iverson's peculiarly spun off-break, hopping about the pitch forward and back, quite bereft, hitting and missing. At the other end of the wicket was young Sheppard playing Iverson in the middle of the bat. But as runs were not coming England's way and nothing was being done to push the game forward, Sheppard between overs asked Denis for some advice or " lead " in procedure.

[1] In *From the Boundary* [Collins, 1951] by Ray Robinson, the best of Australian cricket writers.

"It's all right, David," said Compton. "Don't worry. You go on as you are, and I'll attend to the antics." When in 1950 a gloomy view was taken of his future, and on an afternoon that really did see him hobbling around Lord's on crutches, he told me he would be playing again in a fortnight. "You can't keep a good man down, can you?" he said without the slightest affectation.

His wonderful year, as we all know, was 1947, in a season of glorious summer. When he came down the pavilion steps at Lord's on his way out to bat, the schoolboys crowed like cocks. An innings by Compton played this year of 1947 against Kent takes its place on the sunlit frieze of all that memory holds of gallant, accomplished and beautiful batsmanship. Kent declared on this enchanted afternoon and Wright bowled at his very best. Compton consumed him, leg-spinners, "googlies" and all. His strokes were as shooting stars, gliding and skimming according to an astronomy of their own. The same sort of ball was treated in different ways and sent to different parts of Lord's. No effort, all grace; no flamboyance, but brilliance in the dress of courtesy. E. W. Swanton has written of this innings for the posterity of cricket. "He scored his last 71 . . . in forty minutes. The Kent captain and his bowlers did not make the mistake of splitting the field. If they attacked the leg-stump they had six or seven men on the leg-side, or vice versa. But Denis countered every manœuvre. Perhaps he would move sufficiently quickly to get outside the ball and chop it past slip, or, if the field were on the off-side, he drew the ball across his body to fine-leg. He was always on the move, either up the wicket or laterally and, as often as not, changed his direction as the ball left the bowler's hand."

When he got out, Kent quickly won the match, and so this great innings assumed the lustre which shines on bravely lost causes.

For my part I don't wish to think of Compton as one of the persistently masterful players. In spite of what recent trials and ordeals may have taught him, and in spite of the technical adjust-

72

ments demanded by increase of years and some inevitable check on physical elasticity, he will never, I am sure, surrender to middle-age. He will continue, at least this is the hope in the hearts of thousands of us, to convey the impression that he is capable, while batting, of (1) making a superb stroke with his feet in the " wrong " place ; (2) of making a mighty pull while falling flat on his stomach ; (3) of suddenly achieving a flawless execution so that the text-book black-and-white examples of Hutton seem to be given the illumination of colours ; (4) of getting out to the easiest ball because after having gone half-way down the pitch he has forgotten exactly what he has ventured so far to do ; (5) of running himself out or somebody else by yards, or (sixth and last) of performing all these remarkable actions at one and the same time.

Denis Compton contributes to England life and holiday at the crown of the year ; he is part of an English summer. In spite of his conquests, his record and scores, his cricket has always contained that hint of brevity which is the loveliest thing in the summer's lease.

Chapter Five

KEITH MILLER

KEITH MILLER is one of the few contemporary cricketers who if transported in time to the company of A. C. Maclaren, G. L. Jessop, Hirst and K. L. Hutchings, would not puzzle them. Test matches of our day have not clipped his wings altogether. He is still impulsive despite some increase of science in his technical equipment. But on the whole his natural gifts are liberated rather than fettered by theory and principle. He won't, I fancy, ever be refined more finer than he is. He is casual at moments, even under the humorously austere eye of Lindsay Hassett. He actually wasn't looking in the fifth Test match, played at Melbourne in March 1951, when he missed an easy chance in the slips and let the ball go by over his shoulder. He walks out to bat as though not quite sure which end of the wicket is expecting him. As he makes his way there his legs are deliberate and purposeful, toes straight ; but above the hips there is complete freedom of will. He gazes round and finds interest in the crowd. He is ready to stay his progress to give his autograph to a schoolboy who has run after him through the pavilion gate, defying red-faced authority. He will ask the boy to hold his bat while he is writing it.

He is tall and masculine, square-shouldered and loose. His dark-brown hair is always falling over his eyes and often, as he stands at the crease and the bowler is running to attack him, he shakes the mane back over his head. He is handsome in a sun

and windswept way, and at first sight he suggests the typical
Australian who " couldn't care less." But at the " smell " of a
half-volley or of a snick through the slips, or at the touch of a
new shining red ball, the life of him darts into action. The right
foot prances on the crease, and the wrists and superb forearms
whip the ball to the boundary causing a crack from the fence that
is like a rapid echo of the crack of the bat. At second-slip, while
the bowler is walking back to his starting-place, he is relaxed and
conversational, dismissing with a wave of the hand somebody's
" tip " for the 3.30, or whistling a phrase from a Beethoven
piano concerto. Not until the ball is on the way does he bend.
And I have seen him pounce at a catch a split-second before the
chance has skimmed from the bat's edge, hold it and roll over,
maybe unnecessarily, because he likes a flourish that thrills the
girls as well as the schoolboys.

Frequently he is an improviser, making-up his batting and
bowling as he goes along. He will turn round abruptly—sometimes he doesn't take the trouble to measure his " run "—and
by a convulsion of the shoulders release a " bumper " of alarming
velocity and trajectory; and it is all done, I am sure, without
premeditation or malice most times. Now and then, possibly,
some excess of devilment goes into a Miller " bouncer "; he is
then like a man having " shies " at a cokernut stall when, after
he has several times nearly knocked the Aunt Sally over, she has
come swinging back again apparently at the point of no return.
Naturally the thrower is driven to exasperation. In one and the
same over Miller is equal to all sorts, not excluding a round-arm
" skimmer " as obsolete as a cannon-ball at Sebastopol. In this
over a batsman may be asked to cope with pace and length and
awkward rise from the pitch. With slower balls of tantalising
curve he has twice overthrown Hutton, bringing the Master
down when in full command, at Nottingham in 1948 and at
Sydney in 1951. He is unpredictable and occasionally barely
credible, never to be labelled under a categorical glass-case. Call
him an improviser—next day he will put us temporarily in the
wrong by scorning delights and living laboriously while observ-

ing the canons of batsmanship and wearing a hair shirt of self-control ; this happened at Sydney in 1951 when he stayed in from noon to evening resisting the quite wicked temptation of England's crippled attack, Brown, Warr and Bedser and nobody else, on a day of merciless heat. He played a scrupulous game, nearly five hours for 99. For the cause, my soul !

Call him one of the most imperious executants of the forward stroke, the left shoulder and elbow a commanding thrust not only in unison with the front foot, but all the movements of him a swift physical manifestation of a single idea. Say that whether he knows it or not he is an exponent of the doctrine of C. B. Fry : " Play back or drive." And in his very next innings he is capable of fooling us, capable of lunging out, right foot bogged, the body stretched to immobility, the bat stiff and sightless in front of a left foot which for the time being has obviously lost organic connection with his anatomy as a whole. I have seen him, after some such elongation, stumped from a ball he should either have driven on the run or have played back off the right foot ; and as the wicketkeeper removed the bails at leisure Miller lay flat on the earth, belly down, the head and shoulders of him held up only by his right hand. Slow leg-spin is likely to double him up. Wright is always knotting the whip of his stroke-play. Miller's right-hand technique is firmer and stronger than his left hand's ; he is not masterful at playing the late going away ball (if it is doing its work quickly) with the " dead bat " of Hutton directed by a left hand and left fingers as sensitive and as much in control as those of Heifetz.

But as soon as I have written that latter sentence I am obliged to pause and remember the innings of Miller at Bradford in 1948, worth only 34 in the score-book but match-winning against Yorkshire on a bowlers' wicket. There is at least another innings to be quoted in support of Miller's batting on a nasty wicket : 99 for New South Wales against Victoria at Sydney in 1949. But whenever Miller conquers the spinning ball on a pitch of different paces, it is a case of eyesight and instinct coming to his rescue. Genius can get away with murder. From a comprehensive

critical view there is no continuous line or design in a characteristic Miller innings, yet it can be ennobled by intermittent
suggestions of the classical manner, moments when the man's
volatility is caught in a brief, arrested attitude almost sculptural :
a drive crashing to the top of a grand stand, going upward all
the time, the swing of the bat easy and free, in an arc finishing
over the shoulder, the back of the right wrist not far from the
left cheek, the poise of him aquiline and seigniorial. Or a late-
cut made by a quick bending down over the ball as it flashes past
the off-stump. He seems quite still a moment after the bat has
sent the ball speeding away and he looks as though into and
above the stroke, a Narcissus of the cricket field, seeking in
brilliance a reflection of his own art and pleased, flushed face.
Or maybe it is a leg-hit which carries all his power and body
round in a spiral, a magnificent expense of passion !

The classical poise of Miller's batsmanship is, as I have said,
here and there endangered by some imp of energy in him that
is not ready to conform and observe etiquette. This cricketer,
who can stand at the batting crease with bored impatience as the
field is set for him, stand there showing the condescension of one
of the game's aristocracy, is not entirely blue of blood in his style ;
he was born under a bar-sinister. There is the rebel in him. Born
in Victoria he has become a son of Sydney. I have written of his
late-cut in twopenny-coloured language. At other times he will
cut late and resemble in his attitude a truant urchin out fishing
when he should be in school. A bowler's fate for the day is
more or less settled when Miller wakes up in the morning and
finds out how he is feeling in mood. At Leeds in 1948 on a
crucial morning, Pollard accounted for Hassett and Bradman in
one over : Australia, 68 for three, Morris also out, in reply to
England's 496. Miller came in and ran forward yards to his first
ball, driving for three with a gesture of hell for leather and be
damned. His assault turned the day. He and young Harvey,
who in his first Test match took flame from Miller's fires and was
baptised in them, added 121 in an hour and a half. But it was
Miller who gripped the dire situation by the scruff of the neck.

It was an innings batted in a tantrum. He bowls in a tantrum on occasions—even on a special occasion. When Bradman returned to his native heath of Sydney in February 1949, the first of all men regally honoured for services to Australian cricket, a mighty crowd assembled to hail the new knight as he walked to the wicket in the Kippax-Oldfield testimonial match. The stage and the scene were perfect for him. A resplendent day, a jubilant multitude. Everything had been arranged to the minute. Bradman arrived at the crease on Saturday at the right moment. The crowd roared acclamation again as he took guard. In expectant silence everybody looked for the great man's first accoladed stroke. Frenzies of joy broke out as he cut and drove. But Miller couldn't for long resist the wish, shared by all of us in certain moments, to " cock a snook," upset a pedestal, and render courtly procedure difficult if not impossible. Whizz, whoosh ! The ball bounced with a speed and aim which in the circumstances were, I confess, side-splitting. Sir Donald was obliged to resort to genuflexion.

In England in 1945 Miller was the embodiment and emblem of the game's resurrection from the ruin and graveyard of the war. The sight of him, young and gay and reckless but with the Australian's lines of experience and realism in the face, his vital care-free air and the sense he spread about him of resurgent life, no matter how damaged the world—he expressed the feelings and wishes of thousands ; and one day at Lord's, while London's wounds had scarcely yet ceased smoking and bleeding, he caused the people to see visions. For the Dominions against England, and still in the Australian Air Force, he played an innings which will never be forgotten. He hit seven sixes and added 124 to a night before's score of 61 in ninety minutes. A colossal on-drive from Hollies landed on the roof of the broadcasters' box above the England players' dressing-room, a hit which was said to have excelled in height the mighty blow of Albert Trott. In " Victory " year at Lord's, Miller scored 568 in eight innings with three centuries and an average of 94.68.

Sir Donald has written that Miller resembles J. M. Gregory,

" whose limitations were caused mainly by his own failure to concentrate." Very true, no doubt. But there is room, surely, in cricket to-day for at least one player who comes to the game most days willing to let himself go in it, without inhibitions, without even responsibility to those austere ethical canons which teach that the game is more than the player of the game. If there is the slightest likelihood that Test matches may tend to check the impulse of Miller and curb his flights into a risky void now and again, let Test matches be anathema, and done away with.

Chapter Six

BRADMAN

BRADMAN, WHO played his last innings in England in 1948, is already becoming legendary in a way, after the manner of legends, that deprives him of human appeal as a cricketer. The notion is getting about which suggests he was a mechanical batsman, slave to his own heartless technique, an adding-machine crushing out of the game all hazard and glorious uncertainty. It is a notion true only in so far as it does honour to a mastery of skill not excelled by anybody in the conditions in which he played. It is indirectly untrue because it doesn't stress Bradman's consistent brilliance and range of strokes. It is entirely false in so far as it conveys that Bradman at the wicket was ever dull, without imagination and the personal touch. He was, if we may abuse language, a *deus ex machina*.

A hundred years after the birth of W. G. Grace the curtain fell on Bradman's career in Test matches when Hollies of Warwickshire bowled him for nothing at Kennington Oval. Twenty years earlier he had gone to the wicket for the first time in a Test match in Australia at Brisbane, a terrible match for Australia too; for J. M. Gregory broke down in it physically and, so melodrama delightfully assures us, gulped to the dressing-room: " Boys, I'm finished. I'll never bowl again." Nor did he. In this match England, leading by 399, went in again and in five hours and a half compiled 342 for eight wickets, then, mercifully if not gallantly, declared—to trap Australia on a vicious pitch

Miller bowling against Yorkshire

Miller batting in his innings of 185 for the Dominions against England at Lords 1945

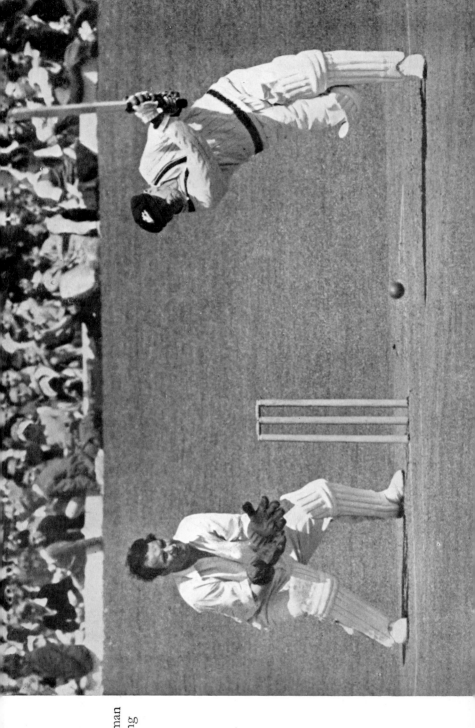

Bradman
driving

and finish them off for 66 all out. An appropriately austere baptism for the boy from Bowral. He scored 18, l.b.w. to Tate and, c. Chapman, b. White. 1. Then he was discarded from the Australian XI for the second match of the rubber, or rather he had to be content to act as twelfth man and carry the drinks to the field. When the third Test match was played at Melbourne, Ponsford could not be chosen on account of an injury, so Bradman received a recall. He jumped at the opportunity, and scored 79 and 112.

He never looked back after that, proceeding to stagger every cricketer's credulity. He changed batsmanship into an exact science, but a science with a difference ; he dwarfed precedent and known values. He came fresh to England in 1930, his age twenty-one, and began at Worcester with 236. Day after day he cut and drove and hooked bowlers right and left, never raising the ball from the ground. I followed him up and down the land for two or three weeks in May, then another engagement called me to London. One afternoon as I was walking along Whitehall I saw a newspaper placard : " Bradman Fails," and in the stop-press I read, " Bradman, b. Ryan, 58." At Nottingham, in the first Test of the summer, he scored 131, and while he was making it I asked the one and only Sidney Barnes what he thought of him. " Well," he said, " I won't say I couldn't have got him out at my best, but I would have needed to be at my very best."

It was Ranjitsinhji who gave to batsmanship a new and revolutionary direction. " Play back or drive "—it is a delusion that Ranji couldn't drive. The old lunge at the pitch of the ball became, or should have become, more or less obsolete. The Aristotle to Ranji's Alexander as he conquered new worlds was, of course, C. B. Fry. " The fallacy of reach," wrote Fry, " is fatal in true cricket. None but a giant, by advancing the left foot and pushing down the wicket, can reach within feet of the pitch of a good-length fast ball. Why, the very thing the bowler wants one to do, what he works to make one do, is to feel forward at the pitch of his bowling." At his high noon Bradman was seldom to be seen drawn out of his crease or elongated an inch. His footwork took his body closer to and more above the ball than any batsman before him.

But it was not by advancing technique that he began a new chapter. Jack Hobbs had already organised every discovered principle and device of batsmanship into a synthesis beyond which to this day no further advance seems possible. There has never been a more complete batsman than Hobbs. Bradman's contribution was eternal vigilance and a new economy. Every ball was for him a problem in itself, to be solved with no concern about its place in a context and no reference to what had happened to preceding balls. I asked him once what was his secret. " Concentration. Every ball is for me the first ball, whether my score is 0 or 200." And then he took my breath away by adding : " And I never visualise the possibility of *anybody* getting me out." (The italics were his.) In 1947 at Melbourne, Yardley clean-bowled him on a good wicket when he was thoroughly established, his score 79 ; it was a straight ball too. As he turned round and saw the disturbed stump he said to Evans, the wicket-keeper: " I must be losing my concentration." He altered the currency. In 1930 his first sequence of scores was 236, 185, 78, 9, 48 not out, 66, 4, 44, 252, 32, 191. J. S. Ryder, himself an Australian, was asked by a friend round about this period : " What sort of a batsman is this Bradman ? " Ryder, not given to abstract thinking or definition, answered : " Well, he just belts the hell out of every ball he can reach."

Not since W. G. Grace has a cricketer appealed to a public as large and world-spread as Bradman's. He filled grounds everywhere and held in thrall people with whom cricket is not a passion. He beggared description and achievement. He made the world's record individual score—452 not out ; he scored a century before lunch for Australia against England and 300 in the same day. He equalled the miracle of C. B. Fry—six centuries in six consecutive innings. He scored on an average a century in every third of his innings. But, as I say, he combined mass-production with the performance of swift and often thrilling strokes, murderous of intent and execution. He was never the conventional stylist; he was dynamic rather than polished. There was always the Bowral boy peeping out from under the armoured machine. The critics who have said he didn't enjoy himself at cricket have missed the pathos and irony of his case. Like the poor lad who in a night finds himself rich beyond all dreams, Bradman could never accept his good fortune as a natural thing to squander or take for granted. It is astonishing, in fact, that he seldom, if ever, seemed to bat with the care and tempo of thriftiness. No bowler was able to keep him quiet at his best; all were put to the sword, massacred without the turning of a hair. After he had pulverised Larwood, Geary, Tate and Richard Tyldesley at Leeds in 1930 for his 304 in a day, he came from the field at half-past six as cool and neat as though fresh from the bathroom; forty boundaries and not a spot of perspiration.

Perhaps his most remarkable innings in a Test match occurred at Lord's during the same summer of 1930, which was his " wonderful year." I doubt if he subsequently equalled, for verve and complete mastery, his batsmanship of 1930. In the Lord's Test, Ponsford and Woodfull scored 162 for the first wicket, then Bradman in two hours and forty minutes before half-past six scourged the England attack for 155 not out. The power and the ease, the fluent, rapid, vehement, cold-blooded slaughter were beyond sober discussion. I recollect that J. C. White was brought into action at once—to keep Bradman quiet— J. C. White the untouchable, or at least the scarcely drive-able. To his first ball Bradman leaped yards out of his crease and drove it to the long-on rails, near the clock at the nursery end; the stroke was just one flash of prancing white and yellow, with a crack that echoed round the ground and sent the pigeons flying. He cut and hooked G. O. Allen that evening until it seemed that soon his bat must be red hot and catch fire.

He always knew what was within his power and would, without boastfulness, face a heavy responsibility as though it had presented itself merely to be set aside. At Leeds in 1934 Bowes ran amok at the first day's end and dismissed Brown, Woodfull and Oldfield for 39, after England had collapsed on an easy wicket against a truly great attack by Grimmett and O'Reilly. That night I saw Bradman in his hotel at Harrogate ; he withdrew from a dinner engagement, went to bed early with the explanation : "Thanks, but I must make 200 to-morrow, *at least*."

He caused a revolution in bowling ; for of course the methods of Jardine with Larwood the spearhead—fast bowling on the leg-side rising head high, and a packed leg-side cordon of fieldsmen—were designed to reduce if possible Bradman's batting average by half. The plan was successful, no doubt ; but no other batsman of our or any other period could have coped as Bradman did with this formidable expedient—against Larwood faster than at any other time in his life. In spite of Larwood and the Jardinian theory, Bradman's innings were 0, 103, not out, 8, 66, 76, 24, 48 and 71.

In 1905 when Armstrong bowled slow "leg theory" at Nottingham, also to a crowded field on the leg-side, J. T. Tyldesley drew away to the on-side and, having made the pitch of the ball fall on the off-side, cracked through the covers. Against the fastest bowling seen in Australia for decades—or nearly seen—Bradman employed the same plan. Astounding and audacious ! Desperate maybe ; but what else could have been done in the circumstances ? Bradman's measures against the fast leg-side attack were severely censured by several of his playing contemporaries. Their main argument was that his improvisations suggested no long tenure at the crease and were therefore likely to disturb the confidence of less gifted colleagues sitting in the pavilion, pads on, if not securely buckled, waiting and watching, while the moth darted in and out of the flame. But there was no rational means of "digging-in," or of planning a long, deliberately executed innings against Larwood and the leg-field. The situation called for nerve and originality. In all his career Bradman did little that was more wonderful and so highly charged with his own force of character than his dazzling improvisations, his neck-or-nothing brilliance, in the face of the ruthless challenge of Jardine thrown down in 1932–1933.

We needn't call him the greatest batsman of all time, though he was the most prolific. But when W. G. Grace scored 2,739 runs in 1871, with an average of 78, the next batsman on the list was Richard Daft, whose average was not half as high. Bradman might lead the list with thousands of runs, average 90; but somebody would be on his heels, averaging 70, and somebody else averaging 60, and so on, down the rungs of the ladder. Grace in 1871 was twice as good, to say the least, as the next best; he played in another dimension, so to say. And we must remember the pitches he had to tackle, dangerous as the bowling.

It is argued, too, that Bradman seldom mastered a " sticky " wicket. Certain it is that at Lord's in 1934 he shaped against Verity as a tyro, striking horribly at the spin until he sent the ball straight up like a water-spout, and Ames came forward from behind the stumps and waited for the catch while Bradman stood aside and stroked his forehead with a sweep of the back of his right hand, a picture of humiliation. He held obtuse ideas about " sticky " wickets, arguing that they reduced science to nonsense, the best batsman to the levels of the crudest. " You might as well," he said to me, " expect an Inman to play on a torn table." But nobody expects to find a torn table in the highest circle of billiards; a " sticky " pitch is part of the natural order of things in cricket, and a great batsman should set himself to answer the challenge when it comes along.

Still, when we contemplate the cavalcade of Bradman's Test match innings from 1927 to 1948, we are forced to confess that if a cricketer with less than a masterful " sticky-wicket " technique was able to go on and on, from one prodigious performance to another, why then, "sticky" wickets would seem of no consequence whatever and seldom to occur. Besides, Bradman by the very quickness of his eye and feet, was born to conquer any turning ball; if he often appeared not to " try " on a " sticky " pitch it was surely because of his curious mental approach to such conditions. And if he *did* fail on " sticky " pitches—well, then, this was a proof that there really is a natural law of compensation. His Test match record is 80 innings, 6,996 runs, average 99.94.

Never, as I say, did he play an innings of dull negation. Always was he ready to pick up the gauntlet if it was boldly thrown before him. Whenever Bradman fell back on defence it was because the opposition had set a protective field and bowled for safety, without intent to attack. In his heyday no known species of bowler could keep him quiet or stay his course, and despite the pace of his scoring he hardly ever lifted the ball unbeautifully. Sometimes before he had scored at all, he would get a single in a rather undignified way, a mishit from the bottom of the blade ; and he would run like a hungry hen—the Bowral boy again, not born for riches but a self-made millionaire !

He kindled ravaging fires of batsmanship, but scarcely ever burned his own fingers lighting them. It has been said of him that he couldn't bear admitting he was ever out : that is, technically beaten. But to use such an assumption as evidence in him of conceit is humourless and very English, as though Heifetz were accused of conceit if he expressed bewilderment if for a split second he played his violin other than impeccably.

Bradman " murdered " all sorts of bowling, not only loose or mediocre stuff but the best. In a match between South Australia and South Africa at Adelaide, S. J. Pegler bowled his leg-spin and " googlies " over after over, and Bradman belaboured him mercilessly. At the tea interval one of the South African players came to Pegler and said : " What's the matter to-day, Sid ; can't you turn 'em to the little devil ? " And Pegler replied : " I have never bowled better in my life." Every bowler did his utmost to bring down Bradman, if only momentarily, from his eminence. Nobody ever " gave " him an easy one to get off the mark or to complete a double—or triple century. That is why Bradman was himself reluctant to make a batsman an object for his charity. I firmly believe that throughout his career most bowlers would have supported any legal means whereby, before a match, Bradman could have been bought off, or compounded with, by the gift of 100 runs on condition that he did not bat. But day by day he was himself under an obligation to bat ; crowds came from far and near to see him, and departed in disappointed droves when he got out. If he announced his inability to play through sheer physical and mental staleness, some English county club was likely to drift nearer than usual to bankruptcy. When Bradman is accused of not knowing the English secret of cricket, the jolly approach in the school cap, the fact is conveniently forgotten that the master was made slave to circumstances not of his choosing. It is doubtful if any cricketer of our time has responded with more than Bradman's conscientiousness to all demanded and expected of him. If he didn't throw his wicket away after reaching a century, might he not have been thinking of those of us, myself included, who were content to watch him all day ? In any case, how many batsmen have we known, since Jack Hobbs, who *do* throw their wickets away : unfortunately they do not. If Bradman stayed in all day he was not only placing his team in a position which in a few hours would be pretty safe from defeat ; he was winning the match all the time, holding the crowd in thrall all the time, old and young, connoisseur and layman. Of how many English batsmen can as much as this be said, how often even of Compton or Hutton ? There is probably, as I write these lines, only one English cricketer of whom it can be said that he never bores or disappoints his admirers—he either plays true to his spirit or gets out. I refer, of course, to Gimblett. I can recollect only two or three occasions on which Bradman batted with the mute on and sternly held his strokes in check. He was then past his meridian. At Trent Bridge in 1938 he was not out on the closing morning, Australia faced with more than the possibility of defeat. The wicket was dusty too. That morning, before we went to the ground, I saw him in the hotel writing a letter to his wife in Adelaide. He called me over to him and very frankly and simply told me the gist of his message. He was very serious as he read : " A pretty gruelling day's work is before us but

I'm going to see it through, and I don't think we'll lose." He scored 144 and was not out after five or six hours' martyrdom. At Melbourne in 1937, after the terrible " sticky " pitch which broke the heart of G. O. Allen and all of us, the wicket rolled out comfortably on the Monday, but Australia had lost five wickets for 90 or so runs when Bradman joined Fingleton. For an hour he hardly lifted his bat. I happened at the time to be reporting for an evening paper, so I was obliged to send messages away piecemeal in a sort of running commentary. I had just written a paragraph to the effect that Bradman after all could be kept quiet in a Test match, when applause in the crowd announced that he had reached fifty—in seventy-five minutes. He had got them in ones and twos by thoroughly safe placing, with an entirely protective bat.

He played hard but not meanly. He was all for the rigour of the game. He respected an opponent and declined to patronise him. There is a point of view from which something " soft," if not hypocritical, can be seen in the English show of condescension in games. The style should be romantic ; execution should not run away from challenge. But the temper, the will to play without flabbiness of smile, should in great cricket never be relaxed. Bradman seldom patronised and insulted keen antagonism or ran away from it. And he rightly was ruthless in the presence of the Laodicean. Occasionally his ruthlessness had a grim humour. During G. O. Allen's tour of Australia in 1936–1937, Worthington of Derbyshire couldn't find his form until the fifth Test match at Melbourne ; then, having gone in first and after scoring a brilliant 44, he trod on his wicket while making a superb pull to the fence. That evening I said to Bradman I thought poor Worthington had been shabbily treated by fortune. " There he was, thoroughly happy, looking like a hundred ; and he gets out that way." Bradman was sympathetic ; but after consideration he said : " Still, you know, a batsman ought not to tread on his wicket, ought he ? "

It is forgotten as we wonder for ever at the runs he amassed that when he was young he had no superior as an outfielder, none more thrilling in chase and pick-up and deadly return. He could run a man out from strokes which it seemed might be " walked " with time to spare. He threw Hobbs's wicket down at Leeds in 1930 with a rapidity and dash which snatched the breath away. His catching was equally agile ; I have seen him run after a ghost of a chance on the off-side and hold a spinning mishit while his body was swivelling round like a top released from the whip. And he was a shrewd far-seeing captain who commanded from everybody an emotion less common in ordinary human nature than affection : he commanded respect. He didn't easily make friends, and appeared not to go out of his way to retain those who were proud to call him a friend. He was, they say, a bad mixer ; but many of us come under this designation if we decline to go half-way to meet all sorts of birds of passage and prefer our own company. His unpopularity was partly the price he had to pay for his mastery and power : his achievement transcended normal humanity's scope and normal humanity's magnanimity. He easily aroused the most common failing of our kind—jealousy. I found him difficult as a man but not—as Doctor Johnson might say—impossible. His integrity to his conception of the game was not to be questioned. Much of his austerity sprang from that almost moral economy which is the self-made man's guiding principle. When he first came to England in 1930, a socially uninstructed youth, he asked me to make him a list of books which I thought might help him to develop his mind and enlarge his conversation. I wrote out for him a number of titles, none of them easy reading and covering a wide field of politics and letters. A year or two later he had got through them all—and he had assimilated much.

The greatest batsmen of them all ? We are bound to answer the question, because generations yet young insist on asking. We elders can see with the mind's eye a man with a great beard, stroking it contemplatively, looking down from Olympus on the years from 1928 to 1948. " He was a good 'un, not the least of my progeny. Eh yes—he put the bat to the ball all right. And he knew how to deal with umpires. What ?—one of my first choices for a World XI ? . . . eh, yes . . . but all the same, give me Arthur."

So the game goes on, its genius fruitful and multiplying. Bradman is already a legend, and the imagination boggles at the thought of the like of him again.

Chapter Seven

LORD'S AND MIDDLESEX

THOUGH TO-DAY I watch Middlesex nearly every hour of their every match at Lord's, my interest in Middlesex cricket and my affection for it began when a schoolboy aged eighteen played his first innings for Lancashire against Middlesex at Lord's, and scored 44, making his runs with an ease of style that announced that a peer of L. C. H. Palairet had come to adorn the game, now and for ever, on the field of play and by the inspiration he would surely kindle in writers of cricket's history and literature.

In August 1899 R. H. Spooner, fresh from Marlborough, drove his elegant way through the covers not only to the boundary and not only into the fadeless annals of *Wisden*, but into the cricketer's Debrett. The pavilion at Lord's that afternoon cast upon Spooner the approving, if rather glazed eye of the connoisseur. The bowlers serving young Spooner's pleasure were J. T. Hearne, Trott, Rawlin, C. M. Wells. J. T. Tyldesley was always happy to remember this début of Spooner. Johnny was a gentleman and a Christian, as well as one of the three or four greatest professional batsmen of all time. So before the match began he took the boy aside to give him words of advice, especially with reference to Albert Trott's slow ball. "He brings his left foot down bang just the same when he's bowling his fast one. Watch him, Mr. Spooner—all the time and all the way."

The shy and grateful Spooner thanked Tyldesley. He had

scored about twenty when Johnny came in to bat, first wicket down, as ever. Johnny scored a single, then Master Spooner from the other end of the wicket saw Johnny clean-bowled, playing yards " too soon " at Albert Trott's slow floating ball. Johnny gave Spooner a humorous look as he passed him returning to the pavilion. Still, in spite of the fact that Spooner made 44, Tyldesley again took him aside at the outset of Lancashire's second innings. " You saw what the old fox did with me after I had warned you, Mr. Spooner ? Well, don't take him on trust and get over-confident simply because he couldn't trick you yesterday. Watch him every inch." When Tyldesley came in to bat his second innings Spooner was thoroughly set ; what is more he again looked on while Tyldesley was clean-bowled yet again by Albert Trott's slow ball. After his warning words to Spooner, Tyldesley was " b. Trott, 1, b. Trott, 0." Spooner went on to score 89 in his second innings.

Albert Trott's name was famous in his day. He played for Australia against A. E. Stoddart's first tour of 1894–1895 in three matches at Adelaide, Sydney and Melbourne. His first appearance was tremendous : he scored 38 not out and 72 not out, and took eight for 43 in England's second innings. At Sydney he scored 85 not out, but didn't bowl in a match in which Australia needed to bat only once. At Melbourne he failed : 10 and 0, and one for 84 and nothing for 56. He left Australia for London and Middlesex, and became as familiar to Lord's as the Tavern and as naturally to be looked for there by the crowds ; for he assimilated Cockney nature, racy and rich and uninhibited. He was as strong as a lion ; huge hands and a moustache that needed copious wiping after he had swallowed a pint of ale at one pull. The cricketer's life is of brief duration, and his seasons come and go, soon forgotten except in the museum of *Wisden* ; even there his petrified statistical greatness is sadly subject to the law of diminishing returns, for year by year " record " after " record " goes by the board and nothing is left remarkable under the visiting sun. But at least one " record " or two of Albert Trott's seem likely never to be broken. He drove a ball over the pavilion at Lord's, clearing the topmost roof. To this day, in spite of proof and living testimony that Trott really did perform this mighty stroke, wonder and belief are yet strained as we measure, by eye and imagination, the height and distance of it, while a contemporary match is being played at Lord's. Such a drive could not have happened by accident. The solemn fact is that Trott in an important match (against the Australians at that!) thought an attempt at something of the kind was worth serious consideration. Trott's big hit won't be equalled until another cricketer is seized by as grandiose a conception. But Trott himself apparently spent the rest of his career trying to repeat the stroke. " Ted " Wainwright, of Yorkshire and England, once told me of an experience he went through while fielding in the " deep " at Lord's while Trott one day was seeking to conquer fresh empires in aerial space. " Aye," said Ted, " Ah were standin' deep long-on, near t' nursery, and Albert gets reight under one of Bobby Peel; and Ah saw ball goin' oop and oop, an' Ah loses 'er agenst pavilion; then Ah sees 'er reight over me, 'igh as Blackpool Tower, an' Ah gets into position an Ah says to misel', ' Tha's got 'er, Ted, aye, tha's under 'er,' and Ah coops mi 'ands "—pause—" an' then Ah thinks, ' Oh, to hell with 'er,' an' Ah let's 'er go."

The ball fell down in front of him. " Ah never touched it," added Ted. " By goom, you should 'ave 'eard 'Is Lordship; 'e coom stridin' over grass an' 'e *did* carry on, 'e did an' all. . . ."

Frank Mann, though never clearing the pavilion's roof at Lord's, was probably an even more powerful and longitudinal hitter or driver for Middlesex than Trott; he certainly was a sounder batsman. He could be as obstinate as forcible, with a defence almost mulish in its inexpressive sullen stability. Jim Smith, another and burly hitter of Middlesex, seldom propelled a ball as far as he sent it upwards. He stood firm of foot, rooted to the earth; and his power was generated by swing of shoulders and arms alone. He was once given out " stumped," and he regarded the decision not only as a miscarriage of justice but as a verdict which overrated him technically as a batsman. He never

93

left the crease in his life. I often wondered if Smith used a bat of his own, or included a bat as part of his essential outfit. I imagined that when about to go in last, or thereabouts, he picked up any piece of wood lying about in the dressing-room ; an old table leg maybe . . .

Fifty years ago it was still possible to see our cricketers against the clear sky of the early morning of the game's history. The air was unstaled ; achievement remained touched by wonder. We were still in the presence of our first, oldest and greatest of Masters—W. G. Grace. To score a century for England against Australia was not all in a cricketer's day's or season's work ; to " do the hat-trick " verged on the marvellous. Albert Trott did the " hat-trick," and afterwards took four wickets in four balls, two distinct and separate miracles, in one and the same innings, for Middlesex against Somersetshire. Moreover, he chose his benefit match as the occasion for performing them, and so bowled himself into the bankruptcy court. The match inevitably collapsed to a sudden finish, at holiday time too. No sane county cricketer of our period is likely to encourage visions and ecstasies as flamboyant and so contrary to self-interest as those which sometimes held Trott in thrall. He blew out his brains in the end.

Until I had arrived at my twenties I saw no first-class cricket away from Old Trafford. When Middlesex came to Lancashire the imagination of a provincial boy was inflamed ; I somehow associated Lord's with the House of Lords. There were the London flavours too ; the reporters of the Manchester papers invariably referred to Middlesex as the " Metropolitan Brigade." The names of the players in themselves pervaded Old Trafford with a cosmopolitanism almost esoteric in any North-Country atmosphere and scene—Pelham Warner, in a Harlequin cap, R. N. and J. Douglas, B. J. T. Bosanquet, L. J. Moon and C. M. Wells. A. E. Stoddart, F. G. J. Ford and Sir T. C. O'Brien were just before my time, alas. Two or three professionals and seldom more emerged from the players' " quarters," one of them the incomparable J. T. Hearne, of whom J. T. Tyldesley said : " If I'd waited for a loose ball from *him*, I'd have needed to wait from May to September." The aristocratic face of B. J. T. Bosanquet!—and his " googly " spin that reversed the common order and axis in a far from aristocratic way. Then, later, there was the Hon. C. N. Bruce—Lord Aberdare—whose batsmanship was blue-veined, disdainful in poise but never over-stepping the finest breeding and most polite condescension, as cover boundary after cover boundary from his bat sped over the field. Middlesex cricket, as I think I have written elsewhere in this book, has frequently lacked the common touch. A price has to be paid for everything; and Middlesex cannot live in the atmosphere of Lord's and not feel at times enveloped in a very portentous robe of purple.

But nature's law of compensation gets to work in such cases. From "Tubby" Rawlin, a Yorkshireman, to Jim Sims the balance has been maintained between Pavilion and Tavern at Lord's, West End and East End. The contrast and equipoise was to be enjoyed best whenever J. W. Hearne and Hendren batted together for hours at Lord's—and it seems but yesterday when both of them were inseparably there together, out in the sunshine of a June day, seemingly beyond the wear and tear of Father Time himself: Hearne upright and just a little super-cilious in deportment, Hendren familiar and large of smile, twinkling with his Irish-Cockney wit which ran down from his tongue into his feet, but always, even at his most masterful, the urchin who could never really believe his luck—playing for Middlesex and playing exactly as everybody watching him from near or in the Tavern or on the high "free" stands near the nursery would wish themselves to play, with gusto and vigour, and all the time astonished rather that it's all being done by and happening to oneself.

Hearne dignified, Hendren with the touch of nature. All the energy of Hearne was, and had to be, carefully conserved, for he was not rude of health. Hendren played as naturally as a breeze blows, except at times when he would appear to be remembering that, after all, he was only "Patsy" and perhaps not as good at bottom as they pretended, bless their hearts, to think he was;

95

at such moments we could catch a glimpse of his very likeable fallibility as though through a chink in the great armour of his defensive and offensive technique.

Hearne's deportment suffered violent and allied disturbance one fine morning in the 1920's. On Saturday at close of play he had scored an immaculate 50 not out against Lancashire, and when the match was resumed on Monday morning he at once hooked Macdonald's fastest rising ball first bounce into the grand stand, near "Father Time." To this day I am wondering if he doesn't think of this stroke as a blot on an otherwise untarnished escutcheon. He was one of the most gifted of cricketers, and though he learned the game in the full noon of the "Golden Age," and though his batsmanship was classic in style and prolific of runs, his bowling was inconsistent in performance and ultra-modern in method; for he exploited leg-spin and "googly" under the very nose and beard of "W. G." himself. On his day indeed he was one of the cleverest of all bowlers of his type; I have seen batsmen caught at first-slip off him from balls dropping almost in the block-hole. Between the two wars Middlesex cricket was probably as fascinating to watch, for skill and personal touch, as at any time in the county's history —not excepting even the Stoddart-McGregor-Ford-O'Brien ascendancy, which was rendered the more resplendent by the brief and tragic promise of N. F. Druce—tragic because he slipped after finding a foothold on the upper slopes of greatness. If a man fails outright, suffers total eclipse—well, philosophy will reconcile him to the loss of what was never really put in his way. But in nine innings for England against Australia, during Stoddart's second tour there, Druce scored 20, 44, 15, 24, 27, 24, 16, 64 and 18. Each innings he stayed at the wicket long enough to claim some security of tenure; and nine times he was thwarted with a prize very close to hand.

Since B. J. T. Bosanquet, the persistence of leg-spin and "googly" has seldom been interrupted in the Middlesex XI; his breed is not yet ended—Hearne (J. W.), Stevens, Peebles, Robins, and not the least of these, Jim Sims (q.v.), G. T. S.

Albert Trott at Lords in 1911

Hendren batting at the Oval in the final Test Match against
the South Africans in 1924

Stevens, Peebles and Robins were, as boys, remarkable and fascinating prodigies, and each played for England. Stevens was a batsman as well as a bowler, apparently without a " back-lift "; he was one of the first of the moderns to demonstrate that they know a secret not dreamt of by the Old Masters—how to stay in for hours and score a century unaided by a single discernible stroke.

Peebles might easily have developed into " the bowler of a century," so cleverly and artfully did he spin leg-breaks and the " Bosie " (to use the term by which the Australians have immortalised Bosanquet's master trick). But I am not certain that Robins, season by season, was not the best of the three, the most dangerous spinner. He was certainly the best all-rounder ; indeed, he had few equals as a match-winning batsman-bowler for years ; and none was his superior as a cricketer who was an exemplar of the game, a living repository of the will and the spirit. He is amongst the few players of our time of whom we can confidently say that he has bored nobody for a minute. His every movement on the field told of vision, purpose, adventure and the antagonistic temper. He revelled in his play ; at the crease his footwork was restless and inexhaustible. He went out to meet the ball with a bat raised higher behind him than any in England. His drives to the off-side had both swiftness and a poise and were perfectly timed. He would cut late through the slips, bending down abruptly, perhaps after scuttling back from a too precipitate trip forward ; and he imparted to the pretty stroke a most engaging impertinence. The score-board could never make a faithful valuation of an innings by Robins : figures cannot account for relish, for a lover's happy and active absorption in what he loves. From the point of view of cricket as one of summer's sources of open-air delight, designed to keep us young and alive, Robins must be remembered amongst the very rarest of the game's exponents.

Tempus fugit, as Patsy Hendren could say. For some of us it might have been only last summer that we sat at Lord's—and not always did we remain seated—watching Middlesex win the championship against Surrey, a match that simply had to be won, at the end of the season, to wrest the laurels from Lancashire, who, we heard at lunch on the third day, was for the time being at the top of the table, having defeated Worcestershire at Old Trafford. At the beginning of this third and final morning, Middlesex, batting a second time, were 46 behind, ten wickets in hand. That is to say they needed to wipe out a deficiency before they could go " all out " for the necessary victory. So, as the old music-hall song put it, they'd a terrible lot to do to-day; and only six hours available. Imagine : the county championship of 1920 would come the way of Middlesex and " Plum " Warner in his last season for the county only if Middlesex were able to get a big score quickly and also bowl out a Surrey team which included Hobbs, Sandham, Ducat, M. Howell, Shepherd, Peach, Fender and Hitch; everything to be accomplished between half-past eleven and half-past six of a day as mellow as the eve of " Plum's " career.

A grand send-off was given by Harry Lee and C. H. L. Skeet, who, each in first, scored centuries ; Lee, doubled down on his bat, but a pugilist at the hook. Worse than Lee have played for England against Australia and he was never asked. Skeet, who batted No. 9 for his university and was thought of mainly as the finest cover-point since Hobbs or Spooner, played the innings of his life. Warner was able to make a declaration, leaving Surrey 244 in just under three hours. Harry Lee caught Hobbs in the slips of Nigel Haig, who leapt in the air high and excitedly. After that only Sandham could stay the course of G. T. S. Stevens and J. W. Hearne, who found spots in the dry earth. Still, there were doubting Thomases at Old Trafford who remarked, on hearing that Shepherd had been caught near the nursery sight-screen and that Sandham whacked a full-toss back to Hearne—when they heard of these things the long-faced and long-mouthed ones, a little green of visage, pointed out that a time comes in a match when if you can't win, it's all hands on deck to try to save it.

But the fates rightly connived that Pelham Warner should on

August 31st 1920, be granted an occasion when, out of a swelling
and thankful heart, he could chant his *Nunc dimittis*. These days
and such days, so warm and palpitating at the time—yet they
pass. We can't hold but only remember them. That's the irony
of it.

When I was a boy " Plum " was as authoritative of Middlesex,
" stood for " and symbolised Middlesex, as much as Lord Hawke
Yorkshire, and Maclaren Lancashire. The Harlequin cap !—and
it sat well upon him, for at any rate he was always young and
not a man who easily settled grimly in one place, except at the
wicket. (It is one of cricket's best jokes that D. R. Jardine tried
to disguise himself in the cap of a Harlequin.) When I first saw
" Plum " on the field of Old Trafford he came out with Frank
Tarrant to open the Middlesex innings. Tarrant was perhaps
the best cricketer never to play in a Test match between England
and Australia ; a superb defensive bat with strokes, and one of
the nastiest left-handed bowlers of a period rich in them. He,
too, was an Australian. People in the North of England were
unusually sarcastic when they talked about Middlesex cricket,
which was seldom. " League o' Na-tions," they scoffed, adding
something (strictly in parenthesis and *sotto voce*) about if a certain
ritual was performed in Charing Cross railway station, anybody
became automatically qualified to play for Middlesex on the
spot. As we have seen, Middlesex has to pay a certain price in
county identity to enjoy the privilege of Lord's as habitation
and home ; it is only natural that the team should wear the
coloured dress of the great hub of the game, the London Pool
of cricket, where men drop in any summer day from all parts of
the Empire ; Gunesekara and Paravicini to " Plum " himself,
the cricketer of many climes. East End and West End indeed ;
dockyards to Debrett ; Mignon and Enthoven ; Joe Hulme and
G. O. Allen, Board School, Secondary School, London Poly-
technic and Eton.

G. O. Allen, captain of England, one of the most gallant,
was never, I think, officially a regular captain of his county ;
but he did most things for Middlesex a cricketer very well can

do—he even took all the ten wickets in a Lancashire innings in a season when much hard work was required to get a single Lancashire batsman out unless by a petition addressed personally to the umpire. Before Allen's day another amateur, G. W. Beldam, was one of the best swerve bowlers at a time when many of his colleagues made a point of rubbing a new ball in the dust so as to help the spinner's grip. There was, later, Nigel Haig, at times nearly as dangerous with the seam as J. W. H. T. Douglas himself. And how he would move away, while batting, from the line of the ball, until he was contiguous to the square-leg umpire, and crack a fast " bumper " between mid-off and point or third-man, his bat in geometrical accord to the horizon. Under Haig's captaincy Durston bowled quick if not fast for Middlesex, and what is more, he won an England cap, but Murrell didn't, though he could keep an alert wicket and was no fool with the bat. Another Middlesex captain of too brief a reign was George Mann, son of his father and as handsome a picture of a young cricketer as was ever seen in the gilded frame of Lord's cricket ground.

The apparently 999 years' lease of the Hearne-Hendren partnership was renewed by Compton and Edrich, who in different ways sustained contrast of style and personal flavours— Compton the schoolboy's hero, genius without maturity, skill and experience unable to age or stale him ; and Edrich the man of the world, his keen quiet air of knowing the value of things, a fighter by choice, not from provocation, for he seems always self-possessed ; a grand driver, but nobody gets his nose so closely in contact with a difficult ball as Edrich ; he " smells " it, as they say. It was a joy to see him bowl fast in his salad years : the head-down violence of his run to the wicket, the vehemence of the swing-over of the arm, threatened extensive muscular disruption. The follow-through had an impetus that sent him sprawling yards. I sometimes thought he was being drawn down the pitch by the draught. It was not impossible any evening after close of play that odd bits of Edrich's dress and equipment might have been found by the groundsman in the region of the wicket, trousers' buttons or broken boot-laces. A tenacious little man with a mind of his own. When a ball eludes the slips he runs after it chin forward with hell-for-leather determination, and in spite of his lack of tallness he is one of the best of slip-catchers.

Robertson, in first with cheerful ruddy-cheeked Brown, sometimes resembles J.W.Hearne in the stance and the impersonal air he has, and the slight kick backward of his lower legs as he runs a single. He has been known to score a double-century without a smile or a word. There is Jack Young, too, who can pitch a length with any man in England, and he is one of the best and most charming of talkers among cricketers. But I am getting categorical.

Many years ago in an invincible season for Yorkshire, Middlesex trapped them at Lord's. They couldn't hope even to connive a draw. In the crowd adjacent to the Tavern a Yorkshireman watched for long in a silence more eloquent than words, tears, or a beating of the breast. At last he couldn't contain himself. " Fancy," he said, " fancy. Yorkshire being beaten by Middlesex." Then, after a pause, he delivered (as he thought) this Parthian shot : " And wheer *is* Middlesex ? Is it in London ? "

But that was just the point ; Middlesex is in London, and part and parcel of London pride.

Chapter Eight

JIM SIMS

HE IS the most lovable cricketer of these times, and he has gone grey in the service of Middlesex and of the " old googly," as he calls it. Most bowlers of spin, with the " wrong 'un " a delusion and a snare, are secretive fellows, stealthy and enigmatical ; they remain at a certain remove from the understanding and affections of the man in the crowd, like expert forgers or " spivs ;" for the " googly," after all, is definitely a " spiv " ball. But Jim Sims, one of the cleverest and artfulest leg-spinners of his period, is as open-hearted as the day. He exploits his box of tricks as though present at a Christmas party, conjuring rabbits out of a hat, as much astonished himself as anybody else when they appear, and not a little anxious whether a rabbit is there at all, or if and when once produced, it will be found again. He is made of those incongruities which, born in all of us, are the source of fellow-feeling. We laugh at him when he tries to drive and the ball goes for four to fine-leg with a noise like a deck-chair collapsing on a hard floor. We laugh just the same when the drive is perfect in timing, and the poise noble if not majestic. We laugh when he bowls as though from an artificial limb a ball that ambles through the air down the wicket, apparently not closely connected with and scarcely in the dimension occupied by Jim Sims. We laugh when he pitches an unerring length on the leg and middle and over tumbles the off-stump, a ball spinning with a venom not fairly to be associated with anything in the nature of Jim Sims.

After bowling such a ball he walks down the pitch, leaning forward, eager to get to the scene of all the fun and the scattered bails ; and he talks about it. Indeed, he has probably talked about it already, while in the act of bowling, talked about it to the umpire, even while wheeling round his arm, talked about it to mid-off, or to himself. With the " old googly " he entirely flabbergasted Fingleton at Sydney in the second Test match of G. O. Allen's 1936–1937 campaign. Fingleton and Bradman, on a true wicket, seemed planted for hours ; not a trace of mortal fallibility could be seen in their play. Then, with another lick of his right finger and an outward sweep of the wrist, and after a few impatient steps and a pretty shuffle of feet at the crease, Jim circled his arm, loose and casual, and the ball curved lazily but with such a spitting of spin off the earth that Fingleton was entirely late, though he brought his bat down like somebody killing a snake. It was enough to make the pavilion cat laugh its whiskers off, especially the disarming smile that beamed from Sims' face, and the beneficence that shone from his dark handsome eyes—a gipsy's !—on Fingleton. Yes : here is another engaging incongruity. He is supposed to be and to look a man of humour, with a Cockney grimace at the mouth and his list to starboard in attack, and also because of his verbal contributions to one and all. But this is only the half of him. Observe his movements in the field, whether near the wicket or at deep third-man. He is never still, he walks in yards as the bowler runs, swivelling round back to his first position for the next ball, fingers restless. He is a mass of sensitive nerves. He is constantly " in the game," greatly expectant. Anything might happen to him. It is not vain ambition that pricks him on but an anxiety never to give less than his best. This is the essence of him ; here is the secret of our love of him. For all his gifts and experience he remains unsophisticated. Veteran professional though he may be, senior on the staff at Lord's, he has never been hardened by routine and efficiency. He is prone to error. Like all great spirits of comedy, there are hints in him of a price to be paid, of reactions to moods not untouched with gravity.

He can take things very much to heart. In his benefit match in 1950, against Yorkshire, Middlesex were more or less beaten after tea on the third day when Sims went in to bat a second time and as a " last hope." He put his nose over the ball, restrained instincts towards the rhetorical. For half an hour he defended warily. Then he was abruptly bowled by a slow ball that swung with Wardle's left arm and hit the leg-stump. Sorrowful of mien, his shoulders drooping, Sims returned to the pavilion and after a winning half-smile at the sympathetic members in the Long Room, he climbed the stairs to the dressing-room, sat down and, dejectedly taking off his pads, said to Compton : " You know, Denis, I pl'yd forward all right, but I didn't know I'd left the blinkin' gate open."

He is a vintage man and not of the present age, which has witnessed the stabilisation of cricket as a career, with players turning themselves into limited companies. His grizzled hair, his yellowing flannels, his demeanour as a whole, make him the perfect veteran professional of an old school that has won respect because it has always shown respect. Sims is the faithful servant, envying no man and not puffed-up. In July 1949, Middlesex on a third afternoon at Leicester were a team surely past praying for, when in their second innings the eighth wicket fell and they were leading by no more than 73. It was now the turn of Sims to go in. Thoroughly padded, he gripped his bat, and was sallying forth when he turned to his captain, who was sitting on the pavilion balcony, and said out of the corner of his mouth : " What tactics, skipper ? "

He fell upon the Leicestershire bowling with a multitude of strokes ; imposing drives neo-Palladian in style and period, leg-cuts sounding like the xylophone, hits from the middle of the bat, from the edges, from the splice, from the oil-hole. He scored 61 before Walsh bowled him. Then he skittled Leicestershire for 91, taking seven wickets for 38, thus not only saving a match well lost but transforming it to glorious victory, all done in a couple of hours or so.

I first saw Jim Sims at Old Trafford, his first appearance

there, and he bowled leg-spin on a good wicket against Lanca-shire and took eight for 100 in one innings. Later he was entrusted with sharing the onerous burden of opening the innings for Middlesex week by week. For years he was willing and ubiquitous throughout the longest day; but we didn't all at once find out that he really was Jim Sims and none other. Time is the artist who gradually reveals to us a man's centre and quiddity, gets him in the focus of our imagination and sense of humour, so that we not only come to know but begin to look for the unself-conscious traits and oddities of movement by which we identify him at a glance. And Time naturally needs a long " exposure." As recently as 1935, so I find from a book of press-cuttings, I watched the Gentlemen v. Players match at Lord's, and apparently Sims didn't get beyond the suburbs of my affection or attention. I dismissed him in a sentence : " Sims bowled judiciously." But it was a sentence unwittingly prophetic of humour to come.

Middlesex, as I have said, has often been short of that nature which makes us kin with other cricket counties. " Wheer is Middlesex anyway ? "—the county boundaries are obliterated by the vast bulk of London. The M.C.C. casts the dominant shadow over Lord's, so that Middlesex cricket is in a constant vassalage, and is not king in its own castle. But one touch of nature makes the whole world—the M.C.C. not excepted—kin. Exclusiveness thaws in the warmth of a smile from a Hendren; and where'er Jim Sims may walk there can be no frost. For his bounty hath no winter in't; an autumn 't is that grows the more by reaping.

Chapter Nine

CONVERSATION WITH RHODES, 1950

In their old age the mild wide blue eyes of Wilfred Rhodes have lost the keenness that missed nothing on a thousand fields of play; they have become dim, after much peering down the wicket in search of l.b.w.s. Though he visits Test matches still he sees only a " shadowy coast," but he is not blind, as Philip Mead is; yet Mead also attends an occasional Hampshire match. Not long ago, after some young man had played an innings for his county, and as soon as he got out, Mead requested that he should be brought before him. Mead then asked for the young man's bat, and he held it for a while, running the fingers of his right hand over the blade. " You're not ' middling ' 'em yet," was his only comment. Cricket by Braille.

Rhodes can distinguish white flannels from green grass and find his way about happily enough. He came into the pavilion at Trent Bridge on that awful Thursday morning in June 1948 when England collapsed against Australia. At the moment I met him Toshack and W. Johnston were bowling.

" Ah can't see properly now, yo' know," he said, " but they keep on tellin' me that there's two left-handers on, both bowlin' over t' wicket." I assured him that it was indeed the truth.

" So they keep tellin' me," said Wilfred, " but Ah can't see for meself properly, but they keep *on* tellin' me that there's two left-handed bowlers ' on,' both bowlin' over t' wicket, but Ah can't see properly, but they keep on tellin' me. . . ."

106

To those of my readers who cannot get the humour of these remarks without a technical clue, I can only say that for me to provide it would spoil the richness of one of the most amusing and most lovably characteristic remarks I have heard in a lifetime spent in cricket pavilions. Now that Rhodes cannot see much of what is going on he compensates himself by talk—he, once the taciturn Wilfred, cannot be stopped in his flow of chatter, and what is more, nobody would wish to stop him, for history comes from his mouth in rivers. He stopped me at Trent Bridge behind the pavilion while Worrell in front of it was playing a dazzling innings against England in 1950; he button-holed me, and much as I longed to look upon Worrell, I was held as by the eye of the Ancient Mariner; and contemporary greatness happening round the corner was dissolved for me and fused into the immortal past, with Rhodes speaking of it to me in the flesh.

Half a century ago, almost, I had seen him when I was a schoolboy of ten, seen him at Old Trafford standing at the wicket's other end while poor Fred Tate was bowled and England lost a rubber by three runs. Many times had I watched him, with George Hirst, in action against my county of Lancashire; and I had hated the sight of both of them, and had feared them.

And here he was, and here was I, behind the Trent Bridge pavilion in July 1950, the roars of the crowd in the air around us; and Wilfred's talk turned the clock back, yet at the same time somehow merged departed glory with all that was alive and happening here and now, on a lovely summer morning.

I deliberately " drew " him. " What was ' Ranji ' like ? "

" Aye, ' Ranji,' " said Wilfred, " aye, he were a good bat. But Ah used to like bowlin' at him. . . ." (Imagine the high throaty voice of Rhodes, the staccato dialect.) ". . . Aye, Ah, liked bowlin' at ' Ranji.' That leg-glance of his. Ah could get 'im out, y'know. Ah used to send him a top-spinner and he'd miss it. . . . But he were a good bat; aye, he were a good bat."

" And Victor Trumper ? "

" Aye, Victor Trumper. Aye. He were a good bat were

Victor. Ah liked bowlin' at him, though. He was always givin' you a chance. But aye ; he were a good bat."

" And Maclaren ? "

" Aye, Mr. Maclaren ; aye, he were a good bat. But that Harrow drive of his ; yo' know if he'd waited a bit he could have hit ball squarer and safer. Aye, Mr. Maclaren, he were a good bat."

He lavished on no man higher praise than that he was a " good bat " ; none of your extravagances of " great " or " marvellous." " Aye," he nattered on, " M. A. Noble. But Ah never liked bowlin' at him. He never let you see his wicket all day . . . but he were a good bat. Aye, M. A. Noble."

" Aye, Johnny Tyldesley, now he were a good bat—on a ' sticky ' wicket best I ever bowled agenst. But Ah could get him out, yo' know ; he used to drive my spinnin' half-volley and get caught off-side. Aye—sometimes a spinnin' half-volley's best ball of any on ' sticky ' pitch, if batter's quick and a bit rash on his feet, like Johnny. But he were a good bat."

His eyes twinkled ; if they couldn't see clearly across the street to-day, they could see far back and for ever. His cheeks were as fresh-coloured as in his youth when he rose quickly to fame as a slow left-arm bowler worthy to put on the mantle of Peel.

He first played for England at Nottingham in 1899, against Australia : this was " W.G.'s " last match for England and C. B. Fry's and Johnny Tyldesley's first. In 1902 Rhodes was in at the death, as a batsman, in two of the most excruciating Test match " finishes " on record ; at Manchester when England lost the rubber by three runs, and in the subsequent match at the Oval when England won by one wicket, thanks to an incredible innings of 104 by Jessop, cut and driven in one hour and a quarter to the accompaniment of falling slates from the roofs in the Kennington Road and environs.

" Aye," said Wilfred, his eyes seeing his visions still more clearly, " Ah remember—it were a Saturday afternoon at Old Trafford—we used to finish third day then on Saturdays—

sometimes Wednesdays—and Dick Lilley were in wi' me, only Fred Tate to come, and we had to get about twelve to win ; and Hughie Trumble bowls me a half-volley. Ah can see it now —he bowled from far end—Ah think they call it Stretford end— and as soon as Ah sees ball comin' Ah says to miself, ' Ah can 'it this,' and so Ah let go. And Ah drives it clear over yon rails. . . ." Then he paused and another glow of revelation came to his eyes. " Aye, and what's more," he added, staccato as a wood-pecker, " what's more, it only counted four for a hit over rails into crowd in those days. Yo' had to hit out of ground for a six. So reightly speakin' we only lost match by one run, and Ah should have been not out 6 instead of 4."

" Aye," he meditated, " it were a good match. When Dick Lilley and me were in, there were eight on us out and only Fred Tate left. And when we only wanted eight, Dick Lilley hits Trumble, deep square-leg, as good a hit as ever you see, and Clem Hill ran length of a cricket pitch and caught it. Aye, it were a good match. England only wanted 124 to win, and we were 36 for none at lunch. But pitch was doin' a lot and Hughie Trumble bowled off-spinners. He were a good bowler were Hughie. . . ."

On this afternoon of 26th July 1902—at which I was present, a small agonised boy—Maclaren was caught, the first of England's wickets to fall, in the deep field by Duff, off Trumble. Sullen clouds were looming up the sky, and Maclaren feared rain would steal victory from England, and all our chances in the rubber. So he risked it and drove hard, high, majestically, fatally. When he came back to the amateurs' dressing-room he flung his bat on a locker and said to old William Howard, the dressing-room attendant, " William—I've lost the match and the—rubber." But F. S. Jackson died in the belief that it was a mistake on his part that threw the match away. In the first innings he had made 128 ; in his second innings Saunders sent him a full-toss. Jackson vowed to his life's end that he could safely have pushed it to the on or off or anywhere, for a two ; but the goal was so near, so alluring, that he hit too hard and made a present of a catch to Sydney Gregory at cover. In this same intolerable innings Jackson, Abel, Braund, K. S. Ranjitsinhji, Lilley and Lockwood, all perished, after Maclaren's downfall, for less than 90.[1] "Ranji" was l.b.w. Trumble for 2. He was dropped from the England XI forthwith and never played in a Test match again.

Less than three weeks after this Test match at Old Trafford, Rhodes not out 4 (" should 'a counted 6 ") in at the death—he went in last for England at Kennington Oval, where Trumble, Saunders, Noble and Armstrong awaited him, with seven other Australians. George Hirst waited for him too ; fifteen runs were needed for a victory to wash down the dish of irony thrust under our noses at Manchester. It is generally understood that Hirst greeted Rhodes with these words : " Wilfred, we'll get them in singles." It is not more fanciful to say that he added to his instruction : " Aye, and if tha gets out, Wilfred, Ah'll warm thee." The runs were obtained, in singles. But Hugh Trumble, one of the finest men I have known, one of nature's gentlest, swore to me when he was a septuagenarian in Melbourne, that Hirst was " dead " leg before wicket to him when England's score was 259 for nine. If the decision had been answered in Trumble's favour two consecutive Test matches between England and Australia would have been won and lost by three runs.

Last man in for England, sharing the honours in the most stupendous of all victories by England against Australia ; then, a few months more than ten years afterwards, Rhodes went in for England at Melbourne with Jack Hobbs, and played his part in the most prosperous partnership of all for a first-wicket in a Test match—" c. Carter, b. Minett, 179." " Aye," he told me, " Ah remember. Just before we won toss Ah split me fav'rite bat at nets and George Gunn asked me to borrow his, but Ah said, ' It's too heavy for me, George '—two pound ten it were. George always played with a two-pound-tenner—but he said, ' That's what you want, Wilfred, on these fast wickets

---

[1] In this same season of 1902 Lockwood, greatest fast bowler of his day, scored a century for Players v. Gentlemen at Lord's.

—it's on " sticky " wickets you want light bat so's it'll coom up quickly."

" Well," continued Rhodes, eyes again lost to the dark present in the full glowing sight of the past, " Ah borrowed George's bat and, d'yo' know, when Ah starts playin' forward, just defensive, ball goes for four, ay, just defensive push and it goes for four, aye, it goes for four, just a defensive push. . . ." His countenance became suffused with joy—nearly half a century after the event. Something for nothing. Yorkshire. " Aye," he went on, " there was no need to lift George's bat oop ; ball went like a gun off middle of wood, defensive pushes, aye, and they went for fours. . . ."

The Hobbs-Rhodes achievement happened in 1912, eight years after Rhodes, on the same ground, had taken fifteen wickets for 124. He had given up bowling in 1912 ; during the Test matches of this, his great season as Hobbs' colleague at the outset of an England innings, he bowled only eighteen overs for 57 runs and no wickets. After the war of 1914–1918, Yorkshire direly wanted slow bowling, so Rhodes picked up a discarded art exactly where, decades since, he laid it down ; and, recalled to the England XI in a lean period, he bowled against Australia yet again and was not the least important factor in a victory which brought the " Ashes " to us after we had spent fourteen years in the wilderness. He foxed out for 79, Woodfull, A. J. Richardson (twice), Bardsley, Ponsford and Collins. When, to " draw " him, I suggested he wasn't spinning them at that time of his life, he laughed his bland soundless laugh and replied : " If batter thinks Ah'm spinnin' 'em, well, Ah'm spinnin' 'em." At the end of his career it was his modest boast that " Ah were never hooked an' Ah were never cut." It was his sly humour that prompted him to his famous remark about Verity. He travelled from Harrow, where he was coaching, to " look at " his successor at Lord's. After a close inspection, from near the Green Bank, he said : " Aye, he'll do ; he's a good bowler. Aye. He can bounce 'em." Then, following a pause : " Aye, an' he can bowl a ball as I never *could* have."

We all sat up in astonished curiosity. A tribute from the Master !
" What is it, Wilfred ? " " Why, the ball they can tickle down
leg-side for a single." But there was none prouder than Rhodes
at Verity's prowess, though Verity was not really in the Peel-
Rhodes tradition ; he was too quick through the air and not
seductively curved enough in flight for that. " Best ball a slow
left-hander can bowl," he often told me, " is spinnin' half-volley
—on a ' sticky ' pitch." His second thoughts or reservations
are delicious. Of Bradman he said : " Best bat I've ever seen,
aye, best bat I've ever seen—off ba-ack foot." Of square-cuts,
when I deplored to him that nowadays we seldom see cutting
the like of J. T. Tyldesley's : " Aye, a good bat, Johnny. But
cut never were a business stroke." He played " hard." It is
alleged that one day he walked down the wicket while batting
to admonish a newcomer to the team, a greenhorn who began
his innings by hitting two fours, one a cover-drive, in the first
over bowled to him. " Hey," is the remark attributed to Wilfred
on this occasion, " hey, young feller, what y' doin'—we doan't
play cricket in Yorkshire for foon." But he took his portion of
fun all the same. It lent salt to the joke that he was a man of
some caution. When the M.C.C. elected as life-members a
number of distinguished old professional players (regrettably
omitting one of the most venerable and, in his day, celebrated—
W. G. Quaife), the Yorkshire newspapers next morning rang up
those cricketers of the county included among the chosen few.
Each said the right and expected thing. " I'm proud not only
for myself but for Pudsey and Yorkshire." " It's a great pleasure
in my old age and I hope I deserves it." But Wilfred, when
asked for *his* opinion on the honour received, said : " Well—
Ah don't rightly know what it means yet—but Ah'm very pleased
all same."

In an attempt some years ago to write a sketch of Rhodes
I called him " legendary," but that was in my green and salad
and rather yellow days. He is and will remain a Yorkshireman
of any period, typical and indigenous. His spirit lives on, his
technique persists. " The third line of defence for any batsman

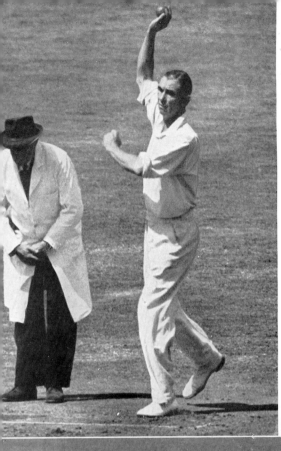

Sims bowling

Sims batting

Hirst and Rhodes in 1950

Rhodes batting

of sense, lad; bat, left pad close to it, then—quick wi' thi'—right pad over, too—never mind what fancy writin' fellows say about 'two-eyed stance' and swashbuckle through covers. We doan't play cricket for foon in Yorkshire." ("Hear, hear," from Emmott Robinson.)

The career of Rhodes spanned two epochs different in conception of the game or the way the minds of players approach it. He began under the amateur influence, when cricket was regarded as one form of outdoor sport amongst others in which an opponent's challenge should be accepted and answered in reason; when indeed cricket was actually played for fun. He lived to see a change of heart; he himself became one of the first and most influential of the realists who reacted against the romantics, one of the hard dour school. " Mak' 'em fetch 'em," was the Rhodesian first principle or attitude. "Give nothing away." The defensive field on batsmen's wickets; the length that made a long-armed drive difficult even to attempt. Yet if we look up scores in *Wisden* of the great period in Yorkshire cricket dominated by Lord Hawke in the early nineteen hundreds, we will find, match after match, a recurring phrase, " c. Denton, b. Rhodes," as familiar during a season of fine weather as the other recurrent phrase of the same illustrious period in wet seasons, " c. Tunncliffe, b. Rhodes." Denton usually fielded at deep long-off where I have, with my own eyes, seen him hold not a few catches from big drives off Rhodes; somebody swallowed the bait and we thought none the less of him for it.

David Denton was one of the best outfields in the land; and as a batsman he himself rendered the lives of all outfielders busy and apprehensive. The Lancashire and Yorkshire match, once on a time, was one of the most brilliant and chivalrous that was played, as indeed it could scarcely help being, with Lord Hawke and Maclaren or Hornby captains, the other combatants including such as F. S. Jackson, Spooner, Frank Mitchell, T. L. Taylor; for the professionals were encouraged, not to say commanded, to trust to their strokes, with the exception of the one or two batsmen whose job it was to hold one end of the wicket steadily. Every team possessed one stout "stonewaller"; Albert Ward went in first with Maclaren for Lancashire in the years of which I am now writing; Tunnicliffe went in first for Yorkshire with J. T. Brown. (But Ward and Tunnicliffe were usually making the recognisable motions of batsmanship, observing the rhythm of it even while they left the boundaries to the activity of others.) It was in a Lancashire and Yorkshire match that George Ulyett tried to drive Johnny Briggs over the boundary for the winning hit, with only one wicket to fall. Ward caught him on the rails and Yorkshire lost by five runs.

About a quarter of a century afterwards two runs were needed for a victory in a Lancashire and Yorkshire match, one wicket to fall, in the last over of the day. Parkin the bowler pitched rather wide to the off, so Rhodes, the batsman, cannily "let them alone" and the match was drawn.

I am pointing no moral story; I merely emphasise again a difference in tactics and mental approach. Both schools of thought have produced cricketers equally great, Rhodes adorned each school. And if the Lancashire and Yorkshire match of Lord Hawke's day was brilliant, the Lancashire and Yorkshire match of the Rhodes-Robinson governance was not less great; for humour and North-Country shrewdness took the place of the cosmopolitan gesture and accent of the amateur presence. During the 1920's, matches at Old Trafford between Lancashire and Yorkshire were seldom finished. On flawless wickets the watchword was: "No fours before lunch on principle, and gradely few afterwards." Visitors from the South of England, not knowing the clue, complained wearily: "What sort of a cricket match is this? Look at the score. Fifty in two hours." But if they had known the secret they would have understood that in a Lancashire and Yorkshire match of those years the score-board meant little or nothing, that the players had other things to do besides worrying about runs. There were all sorts of private and personal grievances to attend to. To enjoy the "foon" you needed to know your Makepeace, your Macaulay, your Emmott Robinson, your Kilner, your Waddington, your Wilfred Rhodes.

No cricketer has more than Rhodes shaped a county's policy, instructed the technical expression of it, linked past skill with present, informed everything with a native wit and wisdom which expressed the man himself and the soil and air which bred him and still breeds all the sons of Yorkshire. If he says he can't see much nowadays, what of it ? He always " smelled-out " as much as he saw. That was the " foon " of it.

PART TWO
★

represented this country at cricket against Australia. It was described as such before it set sail last September from Tilbury, so criticism in this instance is not being wise after the event—though I have never been able to understand why wisdom should not come from the experience of the event. Grave if not grievous risks were taken by the Selection Committee at Lord's when only three seasoned Test match batsmen were chosen, one of them not certain to survive the physical strain of an arduous tour. A breakdown of Compton's doubtful knee would undoubtedly put an unsupportable responsibility on Hutton and Washbrook. As events turned out, Hutton was obliged to shoulder the burden more or less alone. It is always pleasant to encourage young talent, and it is sensible to see to it that young talent doesn't run to waste for want of opportunity. But with no reserves of experienced batsmen in hand, the Selection Committee exceeded the natural shortsightedness of their kind when they entrusted to Dewes, Sheppard, Close and Parkhouse the work of salvage bound to be called for and involved in the event of failure of Hutton, Washbrook and Compton, singly or collectively, at the outset of an innings. Seldom has an untried English cricketer, one not acquainted with the atmosphere of an Australian Test match, played consistently sound innings during a first tour in Australia. To this day Australian students of the game are at a loss to account for a preference of Dewes to Ikin, of Sheppard to Lowson or Robertson. And the passing-over of Edrich is regarded by them simply as yet another instance of " old school tie " officiousness and stupidity. It is a true and remarkable fact that though Washbrook and Compton were barren of runs in the Test matches, and though the " young blood " proved more or less anæmic, the rubber was lost by a hair's breadth. As far as we are free to assume anything about cricket, we may argue that if Edrich had played at Brisbane and in the Melbourne match, lost by only twenty-eight runs—had he been present at these places, with Ikin or Watson of Yorkshire, England would have entered the third Test " two up." Another and more remarkable fact is that England's bowling, obviously inadequate on paper at its fullest possible strength, was, though sometimes crippled by injuries to Wright and Bailey, equal to dismissing Australia in Australia for dangerously low totals ; in fact, Jardine's terrific artillery led by Larwood was scarcely more destructive. In 1946–1947 Bedser, under Hammond, bowled 246 overs in the rubber, for 876 runs and sixteen wickets, average 54 each. Bradman then described Bedser the best of his kind since Tate. Four years later in Bedser's life and career, he bowled 195 overs in an Australian rubber for thirty wickets at 16.06 runs each. Why did Bedser so far surpass the performances achieved when he was a younger man ? There are interesting and perhaps convincing answers.

During the 1950–1951 rubber Bedser was fortunate to bowl on Test match wickets responsive to his skill at swinging by the seam after pitching, wickets peculiarly un-Australian. Moreover, both at Brisbane and Melbourne on the opening days, the density of the atmosphere, almost English, was another unexpected collaborative factor. Last but not least, Bradman was not an obstruction in his path, and—there was no Barnes to counter Bedser's arts with the new ball—a severe deprivation for Australia, especially as Morris long was out of form. Bedser was thus encouraged by a quick wicket before the new ball lost polish and a pliable seam. F. R. Brown in this rubber took eighteen wickets at 21 runs each, not with leg-breaks, mind you, but with swerves or changes of pace mainly medium. He very astutely adapted himself to this, for him, unfamiliar technique ; but without belittling his splendid persistence and steadiness, would any of us expect him to trouble overmuch the defences of a Woodfull, a Barnes, a Ponsford, let alone a Bradman ? The truth is that Australian batting has still to recover from the loss of Bradman and Barnes. Harvey has not yet organised his defences, and Keith Miller is as uncertain and refreshing as an April day. For the first time during many years we have seen the end of an Australian innings visibly approaching after the fall of the fifth wicket—Lindwall, Ian Johnson, Tallon, W.

Johnston and Iverson comprised a " tail " capable of wagging the dog into the pavilion.

In spite of these admissions of Australia's present weaknesses, and allowing that there was the most tantalising slip 'twist cup and lip at Brisbane and Melbourne, I am bound to insist that a substantially different result in the rubber would not have told the truth. Australia in a transition period, with terrific gaps to fill, can none the less put into the field to-day an all-round combination capable of defeating our best most times, unless frustrated by a " sticky " wicket. We have nothing at the moment comparable to Australia's varied and accurate bowling. When an England innings begins Hutton and Washbrook need first of all to face the new ball hurled at them by the two fastest of contemporary bowlers. The possibility or imminence of a " bumper " must constantly be a thought at the back, or the front, of the mind. Then after Lindwall and Miller have been parried, W. Johnston comes on, either spinning slow-medium or directing fast-medium swingers to the leg-stump, seldom loose. At the other end Ian Johnson exploits a puzzling flight and off-spin to a defensive field. If the wicket is at all dusty or even suggesting some surface wear, Iverson spins his " googlies " or whatever they call them.

By sweat of brow the spin-bowlers are kept at bay. But the hard-worked Hutton and Washbrook, if both be still in possession, find time to look at the score-board—a paltry eighty or so (but they didn't during the rubber once go that far together), and Lindwall and Miller are to be tackled again in a few overs. Hutton told me that it is doubtful if Australia has for years had an attack as resourceful and varied as this. A batsman was compelled to play without relaxation at both ends of the wicket, all the time. Obviously no England attack of to-day can in Australia put a similar strain on skill and patience : there is really only Bedser who, ball by ball, makes demands on tireless vigilance. Wright at his very best throws runs away ; and Bailey, much as he added to his stature during this rubber by taking thought, was usually bowling three wide balls an over which a batsman could restfully let go by; and sometimes it was with the new ball. There is no urgent need in English county cricket for a bowler to exercise unfailing accuracy; he can rely on help from the pitch. To watch Warr in Australia, or Hollies or Berry, was to realise how much they owe to English turf or English fresh air: none of them ever looked like getting a wicket in Australia, not in any one of the various ways a wicket may legally be taken. Warr will be glad again to bowl at Fenners. Hollies scarcely made the most of his gifts for want of imaginative control of flight. Had he been an Australian he might from experience in a heart-breaking school have learned something of strategy. This scarcity of accurate bowling in England has produced a race or breed of batsmen who fail in concentration when they are pitted against an attack that regards accuracy as the first of virtues. I make this point as a general principle; for the truth is that in the rubber now being discussed England scored not obviously slower than Australia.

Perhaps the main technical difference between two mediocre teams was a matter of intelligence and toughness of mind. Frankly, much of England's batting was either weak in the head or the heart—" guts " if you like. The loss of three of our wickets in quick succession during a critical moment at Brisbane was the consequence of nothing less than stupidity and failure of nerve. The second Test match, as I hope to show in my description of it in detail, was thrown away for want of resolution. Not until the rubber was settled did the Australians seem to relax a little, and only then for an hour in the fifth game, when Tattersall was permitted to hold the tenth wicket, with Simpson, while England was at the turn of the tide.

I would have regarded the rubber well lost, indeed, if some of our fresh talent had developed and emerged from the ordeal, hardened to some fibre of greatness. Australia can point to Archer, Burke and Hole as young men who seized their chances and revealed themselves as assets for the future. Archer at a crucial beginning of Australia's second innings in the second Test match, as we shall see later in this book, stayed in more than two hours ; had he failed England certainly would have won. Burke scored a hundred in his very first Test match. Hole, also in his first Test match, grappled with odds, not only staunchly but brilliantly. Now you wouldn't claim that any one of these young players is palpably better grounded in technique than Sheppard, Parkhouse or Close, each of whom has enjoyed successes in first-class cricket, over the long duration of an English season, far beyond anything yet achieved by Archer, Hole and Burke. But young Australia gets his nose down to the grindstone and is not afraid. Is this a sign of a national outlook and vitality that are not yet staled and a little debilitated ? The young cricketers of Australia seem keener than ours to study, practise and to talk cricket. I cannot imagine a Burke, a Hole, an Archer on tour in England missing a Test match, and absenting himself from one simply because he happens not to have been chosen to play in it.

I do not find, as a rule, that young Australians speak belittlingly of the great players of the past, though there has been an exception : a certain member of the Australian XI of 1950–1951 stated in conversation that Victor Trumper would not have been thought good enough to be included in Bradman's conquering side of 1948. Cricket wasn't as drastically interrupted in Australia by the two world wars, so that traditions and standards continued to exercise envy and influence, and inspire emulation. Too many English players of the present generation affect to look upon the great masters of the past with scant respect ; inevitably there is a weakening of idealism.

There is, in fact, a widespread deterioration in the mental outlook on the game amongst players, public and the press alike ; and it is affecting Australian cricket, even if in a different way from elsewhere. For if the Australian is not becoming " soft " or slack in conscience, he is inclining towards a point of view which sets the prize above the game in a manner not known to Trumper, Noble, Darling, Duff, Hill, Macartney, Taylor, Gregory, Andrews, McCabe and Kippax, to name a few. We tend to forget that the unique genius of the game came to unfettered expression in a period when the gate-money didn't dictate procedure, but was a by-product, so to say. In other words, crowds once flocked to watch cricketers exhibiting all their arts freely; the cricketers didn't conform to the treasury's need of a good " gate "—and a crowd on several days. Your Maclaren or " Ranji " or Tyldesley or Woolley didn't play one kind of cricket in a county match and another and duller and more acquisitive kind in a Test match. It is often forgotten nowadays that in the greatest days of cricket Test matches in England were confined to three days' play; and—what is more ! —they sometimes began on a Thursday, so that on a Saturday afternoon the turnstiles could be idle, the ground empty, a Test match having come to an end early on Saturday morning. English first-class cricket rose to heights of style and generous sport under a dispensation in which the gate-money was a secondary consideration. All over England—let us repeat it —the county grounds might stand vacant in the sun on Saturday after a decision in two days, owing to a Thursday morning start. The amateur influence and the patronage of wealthy county families, now impoverished, enabled cricket to develop not only as a game but as an art in which there was scope and encouragement for a player to act according to his natural bent. Is it to be thought that men such as Maclaren and Ranjitsinhji would have frittered away their pleasure-loving and civilised lives in the company of dullards who turned cricket into routined labour ? " Ranji " had something better to do than waste his time, mind and sensibilities at such an occupation. He would have gone fishing instead.

I have cause to believe that players of contemporary Test cricket—and of English county cricket too—really do not like it and are relieved when close of play sounds an imaginary " knock-off " in their ears. I see many of our well-paid first-class cricketers nowadays setting forth at week-ends for a day's golf with an avidity they seldom express when embarking on a day in the field at their own game. We are here, surely, at the main source of cricket's frequent failure at the present time as a sport and as an art. It is not played for its own sake often enough. In the past, under the eye of captains such as Maclaren, Warner, Lord Hawke, A. O. Jones and the Fosters—under this aristocratic sway, and a spacious and sometimes even reckless economy, the professional player had before him a constant example of independence of style. Hence the incomparable succession of professionals, brilliant and individual, such as Tyldesley, Denton, Hirst, J. T. Brown, Hayward, Braund, George Gunn, Woolley, to the greatest of them all, Jack Hobbs. All the current talk in England about schools to improve our cricket, with concrete pitches a panacea—this is to talk away from the heart of the matter. The greatness of the game, its immortals and its history, all the inspiration which impelled us to go to the trouble of building and preserving Lord's, all the game's literature and the endless talk amongst friends, years after the event and to a life's end, all these things came to be because one day a number of men and boys and probably a barking dog went into a field with a bat and a ball, intent on fun and no material profit.

II

Nobody can argue that England's players in this rubber didn't have before them an example of the amateur spirit referred to in the foregoing section of this chapter. F. R. Brown was the embodiment, not to say the *embonpointment* of gallant and challenging sportsmanship. Why this example was not bravely followed by one and all is a question not to be answered unless by an invidious exploration of a certain density of imagination on the part of some of his colleagues. Brown was not at all sure himself, as the team voyaged to Australia, that he would be equal to keeping his place in the side; he was prepared to delegate captaincy in the field if he could not contribute his share of technical efficiency. He was not prepared just to give a lead to ten men; in other words, he had no intention of burdening them with a " passenger." At the age of forty there was reason to share his doubts. He conquered by determination. Not only did he bowl hard and well; he twice demonstrated beyond argument that the Australian attack could be driven in front of the wicket and made to look very hot and bothered. As a fieldsman he was one of the most agile of all on view; his nimbleness and accuracy, bending to the ball and picking it up and returning it bang into the gloves of Evans, were a perpetual delight to the eye. His leadership in action left little to be desired; he considered his bowlers, saw to it that the batsmen's strokes were covered. He was " always in the game," helpful and bracing throughout the longest day of " Ethiopic scorchings." His judgment off the field in his arrangement of the order of batting was, it must be confessed, seriously at fault on two occasions—when he decided to depose Hutton from the position of the first man in. This was an error which had dire consequences; but I deal with it in its proper place in my accounts of the Test matches, so I will not harp on it unnecessarily here.

The repeated failures of Compton must remain unaccountable. It is not as though he were out of form during the tour as a whole. Apart from the Test matches, he played well enough and scored 882 runs with an average of 55.12. (And back in England he quickly found confidence and touch again.) He discovered himself caught in a morass of self-doubt whenever the issue was momentous, and he couldn't do anything about it. He succumbed to strokes not recognisably Comptonian and perished almost without fight, rooted to the crease. Nothing like this sequence of futilities has been experienced by a great batsman since Ranjitsinhji's tragic metamorphosis against Australia in 1902. Almost as mysterious were the poor contributions from Washbrook, for he several times began an innings in the Test matches as if in assured and masterful vein. He was possibly embarrassed by conditions and circumstances that caused him to distrust his two most profitable strokes—the cut and the hook. Still, no matter how we probe into the case of Compton and Washbrook in these Test matches, we cannot make sense of it—between them they made 226 runs in seventeen completed innings.

Simpson came into his own exasperatingly late. Many times he suggested that if only he would place some faith in his strokes and move his feet to the ball, he would prevail. When at last, in the fifth match, he had no alternative but to attack—for Tattersall was now his only remaining support—he played beautifully and according to his pleasure. But here again we anticipate—or rather review in advance—a close examination later on in these pages of Simpson's form. In the field he was nearly comparable to Harvey, and that is saying much, but not too much. Bedser surpassed himself, and his performances will be best admired in the context of events which are soon to be described. Bailey compensated for many of the disappointments we suffered from the efforts of the other newcomers to Australian cricket. He pulled himself together after a dubious preliminary canter, so much so that nobody in the team tried or worked harder match by match, whether bowling, fielding or batting. He is not of the authentic Test match class, but this is a common deficiency just now. It is enough that a cricketer should exert himself, body and nerve, to the utmost of his potentialities. Bailey might make much more of his pace if he would give constant thought to his direction and take as much note of the position of the stumps as he takes note of the position of the new ball's seam in his grip. With his unlovely unbalanced action as he releases the ball he invites physical strain, and it is not surprising that at last it betrayed him. When we say that a cricketer is unfortunate to suffer injuries or dislocations of limb and sinew, we should ask ourselves if his style or method doesn't invite such troubles. I cannot remember that Macdonald or Richardson or Brearley often, if ever, " pulled " muscles or left the field for any other reason than to visit the lavatory or to find out the winner of the 3.30. Did W. G. Grace " retire hurt " once in all his career ? It was difficult enough to persuade him to leave the crease at any time.

Wright as usual was a puzzle, capable of winning or of losing a match in a few overs. His best ball is the most dangerous of all. His worst is a batsman's delight—short, ill-directed, with the spin a positive help or motive-force for a stroke. A pretty problem would be presented to any captain of cricket if the other side, seven wickets down, wanted forty to win with no bowler except Wright likely to get anybody out. It would be risky to put him on, risky to leave him off. He can never be taken on trust, one way or the other. Wright is really the sort of bowler who is an asset and a godsend on a perfect wicket if your side has already batted and made round about 500. At Brisbane he was the first in the England attack to ruffle the Australians' complacency; he was excellent at Adelaide; and in the fifth Test at Melbourne he overwhelmed Hassett by a glorious leg-break and settled the day in England's favour. His absurdly long cumbersome, toilsome run, heavily striding as though severe effort were required to propel him along, and his leap and cart-wheel of arms—this is an action that almost defies rhythmical control. Nothing can be done about it at this time in Wright's career; we must put up with it and all his vagaries —I fancy the Australians would, any day. He is a thoughtful bowler, who is never negatively marking time but always attacking, and he is unsparing in determination to do his utmost until he drops flat on his face from exhaustion.

Parkhouse couldn't come to confidence in himself after a touch of illness at the outset of the tour. But in his one or two Test match innings he at least made strokes of class; he was in fact the only one of the recruits whose style pleased C. G. Macartney. I think he was precipitately discarded from the important games. He suffers from a temperament which is easily depressed; it is doubtful if he was sufficiently encouraged. Close didn't give his mind to an effort to overcome the setback of an injury. (The team at one time threatened to become a travelling casualty station.) In the crisis of the second Test match he got out, in an over bowled with the lunch interval imminent, from a stroke that deserved whipping. But he deserves our sympathy, all the same: conscription nipped him in the

bud after a most promising season with Yorkshire. Though
county cricket is of poor quality nowadays, a youth cannot score
a thousand runs and take a hundred wickets in a summer if he is
not gifted.

Sheppard intermittently revealed a latent skill as a batsman,
especially in his adjustment of the forward-push to a back-footed
defensive stroke made from where he could see the ball. His
failure was, I fancy, caused by something missing of hardness
in his temper ; here was a very plain case of talents not sufficiently
sharpened and stiffened against continuously accurate and
antagonistic bowling. A year or two of Australian cricket would
make a first-rate player of Sheppard. Dewes did his best, but
he is simply not flexible enough in stroke-play or footwork ;
he, too, needs experience of the very best, for he has the will
that might find him the way.

Tattersall, called on belatedly, gave all that was expected of
him in usefulness ; he at least was organised technically. It is
hoped that a short sojourn in the land where food is as plentiful
as in England before the war of 1914–1918 will have built up
the health and strength of Statham, so that Lancashire, my native
county, will get the benefit of it all. But why Statham was flown
to Australia as a possible fast bowler is another insoluble problem
put before us by the Selection Committee, who indeed might
acquire unprecedented popularity in the future if they plastered
the London hoardings and the " Tubes " with advertisements,
brilliant of colour of sun and sky and sea, asking " Why winter
in England ? Join an M.C.C. Pleasure Cruise." Hutton, Evans
and Bedser, as well as the captain, emerged from the general
wreckage with reputations fresh polished ; and Berry, though a
misfit as a left-hand slow bowler, at any rate did much by his
happy nature to improve the frequently darkening hour in the
England camp.

Chapter Eleven

BRISBANE

It CAN be argued, by those who are devoted to argument, that the first Test match was decided by the toss for innings. After England's attack—so far held to be of little account by Australians —had put Australia out for 228, thunderstorms over the week-end prevented play from Friday evening until one o'clock on Monday; then twenty batsmen of various sorts and pedigree failed helplessly for the sum-total of 130 runs, in rather less than four hours. The wicket, though causing good balls to spin as well as bad ones to rise breast high or without fair notice to keep low, was by no means as vicious as the Brisbane wicket upon which Hammond's team in December 1946 scored 141 and 172.

Even in the light subsequently and searchingly to be cast into the depths of England's batting strength, it is hard to believe that if England had gone in first on the opening day's nicely-prepared turf they would have scored much less than Australia's 228; and nobody in Australia, or anywhere else, can show the skill of Hutton against the ball that turns, rears and generally gyrates. Indeed, Australia's efforts to cope with a bowlers' wicket in this match were pathetically naïve. But England was not altogether out of fortune's books when Australia batted first; for there was still some moisture left within from the groundsman's nursing; it was, as they say in the North of England, a little " green ' and willing to conspire with Bedser and the new ball—a stroke of luck which again blessed Bedser, a week or two later, at Melbourne.

There are usually storms at Brisbane for Test matches. When Hammond's team played Australia here four years ago, the rain, thunder and lightning were awe-inspiring. Strong men, with scars of battle fresh from the war just over, quailed as the sky became pitch black and the forked heavens exploded, and hail-stones big as cricket balls descended, and the field was engulfed, and furious winds removed the roofs of wooden houses. Yet next morning the flood had subsided. The earth sprouted green again in the burning heat. Primary colours everywhere. Blue sky and palm trees. Jehovah in the storm, then the dove and the vanishing waters. It was a Test match played as though in the Old Testament.

Whether the Brisbane wicket on Monday 4th December 1950 was, at its worst, as spiteful as that of December 1946, is really an academic consideration, very much like inquiring if a tiger is less harmful with two fangs missing from a full set. A " sticky " pitch in Australia is vastly different from one in England, as we shall soon see ; the difference, roughly, is that of the aforesaid ravening tiger from the subtle rattlesnake. English turf after rain and sunshine does not render scientific batsmanship alto-gether inapplicable, abortive and null and void. In Australia the behaviour of a cricket ball, after it has fallen on the glutinous resilient earth, suggests that it is entering, or has entered, a dimension not suspected by Einstein. A good length may rise straight up at an acute angle, removing a batsman's cap. Another ball, same length and flight to an inch, will " shoot " like a stone thrown across ice.

FIRST DAY

AUSTRALIA—First Innings

J. Moroney, c. Hutton, b. Bailey	..	..	..	0
A. R. Morris, l.b.w., b. Bedser ..	..	..	..	25
R. N. Harvey, c. Evans, b. Bedser	..	..	..	74
K. R. Miller, c. McIntyre, b. Wright	..	..	..	15

A. L. Hassett, b. Bedser 8
S. Loxton, c. Evans, b. Brown 24
R. R. Lindwall, c. Bedser, b. Bailey 41
D. Tallon, c. Simpson, b. Brown 5
I. W. Johnson, c. Simpson, b. Bailey 23
W. A. Johnston, c. Hutton, b. Bedser 1
J. Iverson, not out 1
    Extras (b. 5, l.b. 3, n.b. 3) 11

    Total 228

FALL OF WICKETS—First Innings.—1—0, 2—69, 3—116, 4—118, 5—129, 6—156, 7—172, 8—219, 9—226.

BOWLING—First Innings.—Bailey, 12—4—28—3; Bedser, 16.5—4—45—4; Wright, 16—0—81—1; Brown, 11—0—63—2.

ENGLAND.—F. R. Brown, Washbrook, R. T. Simpson, J. G. Dewes, Compton, Hutton, McIntyre, T. E. Bailey, Evans, Bedser, Wright.

The meagre total of 228 caused some consternation in the Australian councils. Until now nobody had clearly foreseen how wide would be the gap caused by the passing or abdication of Bradman; also there had been a universal belittlement of England's resources all round. One or two articles in the profuse, not to say scattered, press of Australia were quite rhetorical in denunciation. So Brown and his men, in the manner of a naughty old lion that defends itself when attacked, went into action with an energy quite beyond the physical resources of many of those of us present on a cool morning. From the fourth ball of the match, bowled by Bailey, Moroney made a glance without looking, which Hutton caught comfortably at fine short-leg. Moroney departed downcast; but he couldn't have known then that he was born; he was doomed for another 0 next innings and to summary expulsion from the Australian XI for the year. This time twelve months since, or thereabouts, he had scored a hundred in each innings of a Test match, against South Africa. He was the first to savour the acid of a " rubber " of increasing irony.

Morris and Harvey played so confidently that none of us put much significance on Moroney's startling act of self-slaughter.

At lunch Australia were 67 for one, and though England had bowled and fielded every ball with a strenuousness exhausting as well as entertaining to see, I imagine that F. R. Brown spent the interval fortifying himself with, amongst other and more material substances, some philosophic resignation and human concern, in advance of the labour to come, for Wright, Bedser and Bailey, himself and one and all.

Immediately after lunch Morris was leg-before-wicket to Bedser in a manner which grew on him rather ruinously as the rubber proceeded. He swung his bat across the ball's line, missed and the umpire deemed him l.b.w. Morris cannot, as he gets on in life, afford to traffic with strokes across the line, his feet moving over and in front of the stumps at the same time.

The fall of Morris, second out at 69, was the cue for the launching of a truly formidable onslaught by Harvey and Miller, Australia's surviving great stroke-players from the Bradman dynasty. Harvey tightened his aggression, adding control over his pulls to leg; and Miller's bat came down on short stuff from Wright with the speed and edge of the executioner's axe on the block. It was Wright who saved England from an apparently inevitable scourging. In his first over, containing three outrageous long-hops, two of which Harvey heaved round to square-leg for fours, he delighted the connoisseur by two entrancing " googlies "; one of them temporarily turned Harvey to stone, blind and immovable. Though aggravated by having to cope for long with a left-hander at one end of the pitch, and in spite of actual punishment and brandished threats of punishment, Wright declined to quail. In every over he posed at least one problem, so that the minds of the batsmen were more than frequently unsettled. It is pretty certain that it was Wright's vagaries of spin and flight that wrinkled the face of the Australian innings; a ball from him positively hovered in front of Miller's bat, hypnotising him to a change of mind, from onslaught to withdrawal. It was a " googly " that didn't rise as high from the pitch as Miller expected, consequently he sent the sweetest little catch to McIntyre, at mid-on, close in. Harvey, as threatening as could be, his bat trenchant and pliant, his feet hunting out the length suitable for his drives and pulls, was scotched by remarkable agility on the part of Evans. Harvey swept at a ball a little short from Bedser; the bat was hungry at the sight of a gift from an unexpected quarter; it was almost a greedy stroke, saliva at the mouth. But it missed its aim save for a hair's-breadth. Evans snapped at the ball, seized it and in one indivisible and almost invisible movement, scattered the bails, appealed for a catch and stumped, and was allowed the former, strictly by virtue of precedence.

Harvey scored 74 in two hours and a quarter, with ten boundaries, one of the few innings played in all five games appealing to that sense and relish of cricket which are oblivious to competitive values and pressure. He was fourth out at 118; and Hassett defended so protectively for half an hour that his movements were scarcely perceptible; we saw him as if he were still in his lair, peering out at the approach of the hunters. But he was quickly bowled, for all his pains, by Bedser. He played forward as correctly as a drawing in a text-book, bat straight, body beautifully forward and over a ball which swung late and just enough to hit the off-stump. From this bald account of Hassett's way of dismissal the student will realise to the full the excellence of Bedser's art.

The accuracy of Bedser and the rococo, not to say eccentric, allurements of Wright made a fascinating contrast. And the fielding was eager and swift; fieldsmen's caps fell off behind them, disturbed in the draught caused by speed in chase. Another catch by Evans, ridding us of Loxton, was as quick in eyesight and calm calculation of pounce as a cat—on a chance only a few inches above the ground in front of the stumps. For the first time we could here nurture the thought that in this Australian XI the end of an innings could be seen in the middle, as though through a chink or cleft. There were no nearly insuperable imponderables to get over at any time : no Woodfull, Ponsford, Barnes, no Bradman. Lindwall and Johnston were allowed to hold the eighth wicket while they lustily clouted the score from 172 to 219. None of us in the English ranks begrudged this brief merry sport. We imagined we had reached a position of advantage and could afford a certain condescension.

The Australians were all out for 228. We all returned to Lennon's Hotel—one of the few places in the public life of Australia where they don't take your wine from the dinner table at 8 p.m.—pleased enough, with good reason. I journeyed to the ground, by the way, with Larwood at the morning's beginning; and when we got there we were refused admission at three entrance gates, in spite of our tickets, marked " Working Journalist." I can well understand that a few years ago the most drastic and far-reaching measures might with justification have been taken to keep Larwood out of all Australian grounds, from Brisbane to Adelaide. To-day he is surely harmless enough.

THIRD DAY (SECOND DAY'S PLAY)

AUSTRALIA

First Innings		Second Innings	
J. Moroney, c. Hutton, b. Bailey ..	0	l.b.w., b. Bailey	0
A. R. Morris, l.b.w., b. Bedser ..	25	c. Bailey, b. Bedser	0
R. N. Harvey, c. Evans, b. Bedser	74	c. Simpson, b. Bedser	12
K. R. Miller, c. McIntyre, b. Wright	15	c. Simpson, b. Bailey	8
A. L. Hassett, b. Bedser	8	l.b.w., b. Bailey	3
S. J. E. Loxton, c. Evans, b. Brown	24	c. Bailey, b. Bedser	0
R. R. Lindwall, c. Bedser, b. Bailey	41	not out	0
D. Tallon, c. Simpson, b. Brown..	5		
I. W. Johnsan, c. Simpson, b. Bailey	23	l.b.w., b. Bailey	8
W. A. Johnston, c. Hutton, b. Bedser	1		
J. Iverson, not out	1		
Extras (b. 5, l.b. 3, n.b. 3) ..	11	Extras (n.b. 1)	1
Total	228	Total (7 wkts. dec.)	32

FALL OF WICKETS—First Innings.—1—0, 2—69, 3—116, 4—118, 5—129, 6—156, 7—172, 8—219, 9—226, 10—228.

Second Innings.—1—0, 2—0, 3—0, 4—12, 5—19, 6—30, 7—32.

BOWLING—First Innings.—Bailey, 12—4—28—3 ; Bedser, 16.5—4—45—4 ; Wright, 16—0—81—1 ; Brown, 11—0—63—2.

Second Innings.—Bailey, 7—2—22—4 ; Bedser, 6.5—2—9—3.

ENGLAND

FIRST INNINGS		SECOND INNINGS			
R. T. Simpson, b. Johnston	12	b. Lindwall			0
Washbrook, c. Hassett, b. Johnston	19	c. Loxton, b. Lindwall			6
Evans, c. Iverson, b. Johnston	16	not out			0
Compton, c. Lindwall, b. Johnston	3				
J. G. Dewes, c. Loxton, b. Miller	1	b. Miller			9
Hutton, not out	8				
McIntyre, b. Johnston	1	run out			7
F. R. Brown, c. Tallon, b. Miller	4				
T. E. Bailey, not out	1	c. Johnston, b. Iverson			7
Bedser	—	c. Harvey, b. Iverson			0
Wright	—				
Extras (b. 2, n.b. 1)	3	Extras (n.b. 1)			1
Total (7 wkts. dec.)	68	Total (6 wkts.)			30

FALL OF WICKETS—FIRST INNINGS.—1—28, 2—49, 3—52, 4—52, 5—56 6—57, 7—67.

SECOND INNINGS.—1—0, 2—16, 3—22, 4—23, 5—23, 6—30.

BOWLING—FIRST INNINGS.—Lindwall, 1—0—1—0; Johnston, 11.2—1—35—5; Miller, 10—1—29—2.

SECOND INNINGS (to date).—Lindwall, 5—3—11—2; Johnston, 3—0—9—0; Miller, 4—3—1—1; Iverson, 3—1—8—2.

The " sticky " wicket.

The sun shone amply if not at all tropically when for half an hour before lunch Washbrook and Simpson launched the England innings bravely and well, after the wet week-end. Washbrook's innings raised hopes sadly to be dashed by his subsequent form. He hit eleven runs from an over by W. Johnston and he looked as much at home as at Old Trafford.

Immediately after lunch Washbrook, over-eager while the wicket was not yet in a bad temper, drove Johnston's second delivery to Hassett at point, so straight and accurately into his hands that Washbrook expressed as much surprise as disgust. The sort of mistake at cricket that shouldn't really count. Now the Australian bowling and fielding, which had been strangely loose, pulled up its socks, at the behest of Hassett, small as Lord Roberts and almost as quietly imperious. Johnston in his seventh over bowled Simpson—vigilant if apprehensive for nearly an hour for 12; three balls afterwards, in the same over,

Evans spasmodically hit in the air to the off-side, where Iverson created a stir by holding a catch on the run. The general assumption amongst his friends to this moment had been that he could neither catch nor run. The batsmen crossed, so Compton faced Johnston's next ball, to which he pranced out of his crease before the bowler's arm had come full circle; he mishit a spinning-away half-volley to Lindwall at second-slip. The ball seemed to brush his elbow in transit. In his innings of five minutes' duration, Compton had more than once pranced out of his ground, and half-turned his back on the ball and thus taken his eye from it, an error never committed by, say, Jack Hobbs against slow-medium spin. The afternoon's fury and fever accelerated; batsmen in the pavilion could not get pads on quickly enough; buckles eluded agitated hands all fingers and thumbs.

Miller in his eighth over sent an incipient flyer at Dewes, who by reflex action steered it to second-slip, where Loxton scooped it up gleefully—forgetting that soon, inevitably, he must himself go forth to be trapped in the same ambuscade and swamp of insecurity. Johnston quickly bowled McIntyre, and McIntyre knew of his fate only, so to say, after the event. Brown's bat clove the air in bulk, but just managed to send a catch at the wicket off Miller. He then declared England's innings closed; and the time of day was 3.20. Hutton for thirty-four minutes had avoided fatal error, had even avoided bad grammar in his defences, while he scored 8, not out. He demonstrated the use of the " dead-bat " for all to see and emulate but none could see, and therefore, could not emulate. " Top o' handle loose " —it is a sort of wise-saw for bowler's pitches in Yorkshire. Rhodes was the philosopher who first thought of it.

Australia's second innings began at twenty minutes to four, and in an hour seven wickets fell for 32. The first three—of Morris, Moroney and Loxton—were taken with the score-board a blank 0 of incredulity. Moroney stuck his pads in front of Bailey's seventh ball for want of a more creative idea, and departed l.b.w. very crestfallen. Bailey caught Morris cleverly at first-slip from the second ball of Bedser's second over; and from Bedser's next ball Bailey caught Loxton first ball, but this was an easy one.

The scorers no doubt experienced some difficulty in accounting for every detail of Australia's palpably inexpert and empirical way of facing the music of the pitch's antics. Nobody hinted of the rudiments of the requisite method. The bat was thrust out fearfully or speculatively or with a "God help me" flourish. Fieldsmen surrounded Hassett so that we couldn't see him. Australia's first run in this very incompetent innings was scored after no fewer than twenty minutes of myopic gropings of the bat. Hassett was l.b.w. to Bailey. Johnston was l.b.w., also to Bailey. Keith Miller at least showed us a great stroke or two; a brilliant back-cut by him from Bailey, and an openly happy cover-drive also off Bailey let us infer how Johnny Tyldesley, at Melbourne in 1904, scored 62 out of 103 for England against Trumble, Saunders, Howell and Hopkins on the vilest pitch in the world. Miller was well caught by Simpson deep in the covers; a hero's end, better than l.b.w. anyway. Harvey also hit two fours, including a blinding cut from Bedser, and he, too, was caught with judgment, by Simpson at cover.

And now Hassett declared—Australia 32 for seven, leaving England 193 to make for victory. The two declarations in an afternoon were, of course, sensible in the circumstances; but in each case they were governed more or less by the logic which persuades a man in a burning building to jump out of a window on an eighth floor, after the fire brigade has gone home by mistake.

Though the wicket was losing something of devil when England went in just before five o'clock, Simpson was entrusted to open the innings with Washbrook, even though Hutton had been "seeing the ball" well enough at the worst of the conditions. Simpson was bowled first ball, and the state of the pitch had nothing to do with this disaster; Simpson completely missed a "yorker" from Lindwall—a "yorker" indeed, almost a sinful ball on a bowler's pitch. The downfall of Simpson provoked the crowd to fearful yells; and Dewes, in next, reached the crease in an atmosphere suggestive of lions and Christian martyrs. He set his jaw and stayed in for forty-four minutes, scoring 9. Washbrook, caught off Lindwall, was second to go at 22; Dewes the third at 23. And at this point words fail me, or nearly fail me.

Play was ended for the day at three minutes to six because of bad light; it should have ceased sooner, for the grey evening changed to a haze akin to darkness. Dewes was out at twenty minutes to six. Bedser joined Bailey, whose watchful resolute straight defence, back and forward, looked safe as a house. Only a few more overs and the dire day would be behind us, with promise of a fair to-morrow, a more or less easy and repentant wicket—and Hutton " in pickle." Bedser for eight minutes was as circumspect and solid of blade as Bailey; at ten minutes to six he drove rashly at a ball, from Iverson, pitching beyond his reach. Harvey caught a high curling catch at cover. Worse and more unutterable, with the score the same and less than ten minutes from close of play, Bailey allowed some imp to jerk him out of the strong shell of protection with which he had covered himself for half an hour. He lashed round and across and upwards at a ball from Iverson, as it was turning harmlessly away on the leg-side; W. Johnston caught him at—of all places at such a moment—long-leg. Poor Bailey walked to the pavilion head down in dejection; probably he was wishing himself dead. And there were friends present who momentarily wouldn't have stood in his way.

Two valuable wickets lost through foolhardiness on the doorstep of the haven of six o'clock. . . . Sickening enough for the strongest English stomach. But the bitter part of the irony —it was a rubber of irony—was still to come, so bitter that " the bitter apple is sweet and the oleander savoury in comparison." McIntyre joined Evans at five minutes to six (remember close of play in Australia is six).

He at once cracked Iverson to the on-boundary, and at once pulled the same bowler to the edge of the field. He and

Evans ran three for this, safely and well. Johnston, who fielded, threw in rather wide, so McIntyre and Evans went for another run as though the devil were after them. Tallon darted after the ball, picked it up and hit the wicket towards which McIntyre hurled himself full stretch in vain. Waste, wicked waste. Eclipse and gathering gloom oppressed us and we wended wearily back from Woolloomgabba to the city lights.

LAST DAY

AUSTRALIA

First Innings		Second Innings		
J. Moroney, c. Hutton, b. Bailey ..	0	l.b.w., b. Bailey		0
A. R. Morris, l.b.w., b. Bedser ..	25	c. Bailey, b. Bedser		0
R. N. Harvey, c. Evans, b. Bedser	74	c. Simpson, b. Bedser		12
K. R. Miller, c. McIntyre, b. Wright	15	c. Simpson, b. Bailey		8
A. L. Hassett, b. Bedser	8	l.b.w., b. Bailey		3
S. J. E. Loxton, c. Evans, b. Brown	24	c. Bailey, b. Bedser		0
R. R. Lindwall, c. Bedser, b. Bailey	41	not out		0
D. Tallon, c. Simpson, b. Brown..	5			
I. W. Johnson, c. Simpson, b. Bailey	23	l.b.w., b. Bailey		8
W. A. Johnston, c. Hutton, b. Bedser	1			
J. Iverson, not out	1			
Extras (b. 5, l.b. 3, n.b. 3) ..	11	Extras (n.b. 1)		1
	—			—
Total	228	Total (7 wkts. dec.)		32

FALL OF WICKETS—First Innings.—1—0, 2—69, 3—116, 4—118, 5—129, 6—156, 7—172, 8—219, 9—226, 10—228.
Second Innings.—1—0, 2—0, 3—0, 4—12, 5—19, 6—30, 7—32.

BOWLING—First Innings.—Bailey, 12—4—28—3; Bedser, 16.5—4—45—4; Wright, 16—0—81—1; Brown, 11—0—63—2.
Second Innings.—Bailey, 7—2—22—4; Bedser, 6.5—2—9—3.

ENGLAND

First Innings		Second Innings		
R. T. Simpson, b. Johnston ..	12	b. Lindwall		0
Washbrook, c. Hassett, b. Johnston	19	c. Loxton, b. Lindwall		6
Evans, c. Iverson, b. Johnston ..	16	c. Loxton, b. Johnston		5
Compton, c. Lindwall, b. Johnston	3	c. Loxton, b. Johnston		0
J. G. Dewes, c. Loxton, b. Miller..	1	b. Miller		9
Hutton, not out	8	not out		62
McIntyre, b. Johnston	1	run out		7
F. R. Brown, c. Tallon, b. Miller..	4	c. Loxton, b. Iverson		17
T. E. Bailey, not out	1	c. Johnston, b. Iverson		7

Bedser	..	..	..	..	—	c. Harvey, b. Iverson	..	..	0
Wright	..	..	..	..	—	c. Lindwall, b. Iverson	..	..	2
Extras (b. 2, n.b. 1)		..	..	3		Extras (b. 6, n.b. 1)	..	..	7

Total (7 wkts. dec.) 68   Total 122

FALL OF WICKETS—FIRST INNINGS.—1—28, 2—49, 3—52, 4—52, 5—56, 6—57, 7—67.

SECOND INNINGS.—1—0, 2—16, 3—22, 4—23, 5—23, 6—30, 7—46, 8—46, 9—77, 10—122.

BOWLING—FIRST INNINGS.—Lindwall, 1—0—1—0 ; Johnston, 11.2—1—35—5 ; Miller, 10—1—29—2.

SECOND INNINGS.—Lindwall, 7—3—21—2 ; Johnston, 11—2—30—2 ; Miller, 7—3—21—1 ; Iverson, 13—3—43—4.

England, four wickets to fall, wanted 163. The wicket had enjoyed the night's repose and, better still if less figuratively, it had been rolled, according to law and order, for ten minutes at 8 a.m. and for seven minutes before noon. When the game was continued spin was practicable, but Monday's venom was no longer there. Good batsmanship could now hope to deal with good bowling without fear of unnatural hindrance to scientific usage. It was just the very wicket to bring the best out of Hutton. Evans hit the fifth ball of the morning, from Johnston, to leg for four ; Hutton moved back on his stumps and cut Iverson square for four, a king of cricket's stroke. In Johnston's third over came the culminating and never to be forgotten or forgiven knock-out. Evans pushed forward at a ball which swung in with the left-arm action of Johnston, and the catch sent to Loxton at forward short-leg, though regrettable, was the mistake that a good wicket-keeper might make without feeling obliged to blush. The next ball from Johnston, much the same in flight and length, was Compton's first and last ; Compton dabbed his bat at it late and wanly, and the ball proceeded to Loxton's hands, standing where he had caught Evans, a few yards from Compton's left trousers pocket. England eight for 46 : 146 runs hopelessly in arrears.

Hutton had no alternative after Compton had seared our hearts but to take complete charge. He played an innings of that technical power, precision and versatility which once on a time was the custom and tradition wherever odds had to be faced. Brown was vigorous for half an hour and smote two fours in his innings of 17; but it was when Wright came in last that Hutton ascended from talent to greatness, all his experience endowed with the eyes of imagination, so that ordinarily good bowling was seen as so much stuff to plunder, or as a grindstone on which to sharpen to brilliance every great swordlike stroke in his armoury. Miller and Lindwall were called up to counter-attack Hutton, who drove Miller through the covers easy of swing as though "trying" his bat; in the same over he hit him—a real clout—over mid-on for four. Hutton next hooked a Miller "bumper" for four, a quite peppery gesture—"Get out of my sight!" He was equally indifferent to the strenuous effort of Lindwall to settle the issue. He scored 62 in an hour and a half before Wright, who experienced no obvious trouble in holding up the impatient Australian attack for thirty-eight minutes, endeavoured himself to hit a four off Iverson to square-leg and was caught by Lindwall. The last stand contributed 45 to England's total of 122. It is a fair assumption that England, even after the wicked squandering of the wickets of Bailey, Bedser and McIntyre in a quarter of an hour (or less) the night before, would have won if somebody had been spared at the finish to stay with Hutton another hour. . . . Waste indeed, unprecedented waste in a Test match. We all left the ground feeling that the gods had sported with us, but so cruelly that surely their humour would now be satisfied. We couldn't suspect that the gods hadn't really begun yet.

I shall always contend that a serious blunder was made when Hutton was not sent in to open England's second innings. There is a surface case in favour of withholding a great batsman from the attack on a dangerous pitch if there are reliable batsmen in reserve to keep him company when at last he goes in. What if your rearguard consist of Bedser, Bailey, Brown, McIntyre, Evans, Wright? F. R. Brown played heroically throughout the rubber; none the less I am certain that he seriously crippled England's chances at Brisbane and Melbourne by not asking the greatest contemporary batsman, on any wicket, to open and give the lead to the England innings. If Hutton had been Hobbs? —very well then, isn't Hutton in the line of Hobbs, his successor, the only one fit to wear the crown of the greatest of all in our time?

Brown driving to leg

Miller, caught and bowled Brown, in the 5th Test at Melbourne, 1951. Brown got him out in this way in both innings of this match

Hutton drives Iverson in the 4th Test at Adelaide

The Australian team clap Hutton as he leaves the field 156 not out in the 4th Test at Adelaide in 1951

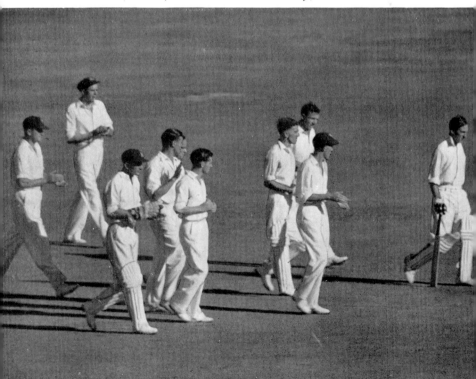

Chapter Twelve

MELBOURNE

THE SECOND Test match was exciting and incalculable throughout, and the end of it was for an Englishman so disappointing
that even now, as I write of it long after the event, I still feel a
certain sickness at heart. Merely a game ?—maybe ; but the
spirit of irony can get at us not only in austere guise in this our
life. On the closing morning the match was England's ; only
151 needed for victory on a pitch that responded to spin but
not at all viciously, eight wickets standing, Hutton unbeaten.
Just before lunch, with but another batsman lost and Hutton
still unbeaten and at his most masterful, 99 would have served.
Dewes got out then, and Parkhouse, who was in next, rose
superior to self-doubt and several horrible glimpses into the pit
beyond the edge of the crease. He actually survived one hundred
and two minutes, a crowning irony ; for Hutton faltered a few
overs after Parkhouse had, unsupported, walked out to face the
music. England's score was 92 for four, 77 wanted, Hutton in
charge 40, when W. Johnston bowled a quick ball a shade short
on or near Hutton's leg-stump. Hutton, as anxious as the rest
of us for the runs that would change agony to rejoicing, shaped
to hit a four to the unprotected on-side boundary. (He had
already driven Johnston in that direction once or twice and
Hassett left the bait of an open field temptingly there while
Johnston was bowling.) At the last split-second, Hutton
apparently checked the swing of his bat across the line of the

ball—and to begin with it was a very commanding swing, a vehement one for Hutton. The mistimed hit soared high and close to the square-leg umpire, and Lindwall ran a few yards but with an assurance and leisure dreadful to see. The suspense was all the more unbearable because we knew he wouldn't drop the catch; Hutton watched him like the rest of us; he was now no more an active and potent factor in the game but suddenly transformed into a helpless spectator. I shall remember this for many a long year; I couldn't believe my eyes. I saw the aggressive sweeping motion of Hutton's bat, an intended pulled-drive, his shoulders finely concentrated. Then I saw the hideous " skier." Naturally I said " No-ball " to myself. Hutton simply doesn't " sky " near the wicket; such a crudity does not come within the normal margin of error of his superb but mortal and therefore not infallible technique. The stroke could not be counted amongst his repertory of possible mistakes; you would have sworn in fact that Hutton could not have committed a stroke so primitive even if he had tried. If ever there was a great cricket match, this was it, of which we could safely say that one stroke and one ball settled the issue irrevocably, yet contrary to all logic and probability. As a last acid-tinctured barb, Bedser at the death was left standing high and dry, batting with the middle of his bat, playing forward as though guaranteed to be there for an hour at least, untroubled but lonely, for want of Hutton —victory only twenty-nine runs distant.

FIRST DAY

AUSTRALIA—First Innings

K. Archer, c. Bedser, b. Bailey ..	..	..	..	26
A. R. Morris, c. Hutton, b. Bedser	..	..	..	2
R. N. Harvey, c. Evans, b. Bedser	..	..	..	42
K. R. Miller, l.b.w., b. Brown ..	..	..	..	18
A. L. Hassett, b. Bailey ..	..	..	..	52
S. J. E. Loxton, c. Evans, b. Close	..	..	..	32
R. R. Lindwall, l.b.w., b. Bailey	..	..	..	8
D. Tallon, not out	..	..	..	7

MELBOURNE

I. W. Johnson, c. Parkhouse, b. Bedser	..	..	0
W. A. Johnston, c. Hutton, b. Bedser ..	..	..	0
J. Iverson, b. Bailey	.. .. ..	..	1
Extras (b. 4, l.b. 2) ..	.. ..	..	6

Total 194

FALL OF WICKETS.—1—6, 2—67, 3—89, 4—93, 5—177, 6—177, 7—192, 8—193, 9—193, 10—194.

BOWLING.—Bailey, 17.1—5—40—4; Bedser, 19—3—37—4; Wright, 8—0—63—0; Brown, 9—0—28—1; Close, 6—1—20—1.

ENGLAND.—F. R. Brown, Hutton, Washbrook, R. T. Simpson, Wright, Close, Evans, T. E. Bailey, Bedser, Parkhouse and J. G. Dewes.

The struggle began three days before Christmas. Shortly before noon on Friday 22nd December, as I walked to the ground through the rich foliage of the Fitzroy Gardens, a slight drizzle of rain sweetened the air but didn't discourage the hurrying throng which swept over the roadways and made for the entrances grim as an invading army. Though F. R. Brown lost the toss I couldn't feel entirely sorry; the atmosphere of the morning and the slight hint of an English " greenness " in the wicket might again stimulate Bedser to uncommon energy and confidence. I ascended to the Long Room of the Pavilion up several flights of steps, past serried ranks of members suitably garbed for all the weathers that Melbourne can show in one and the same day. It really is a " Long Room " at Melbourne, fit to be named with that of Lord's; dignified, polished, quiet, as high and as directly behind the wicket as the topmost gallery at Lord's, over the roof of which an Australian batsman, A. E. Trott, drove a ball from an Australian bowler, M. A. Noble.

From this point of vantage the connoisseur was privileged to enjoy bowling by Bedser of a rare kind. A perfect length, with late swings usually inward for the right-handed batsmen (but with one that abruptly went " the other way "), and outward for Morris and Harvey, the left-handers; vitality from the pitch and almost unerring accuracy of direction. Seldom was it safe to leave a ball alone; this was an attack which challenged the highest skill possessed by contemporary batsmanship ; also it was a joy to watch, and surely a pleasure to play and counter.

The first ball of Bedser's second over veered away from the off-stump, even as Morris found himself lured forward, against his inclinations, I suspect. A catch in the slips was so unavoidable that even a David Hume might well have been persuaded of a causal nexus. Morris himself no doubt appreciated, in the abstract, absolute perfection and rhythm of length and swerve as he went to his doom, much as a man being hanged might (if he were an artist) appreciate the delicate touch and timing of his executioner's technique and apparatus.

Harvey, in next, seemed charmed of life during his first overs from Bedser. A late outswinger left him with no answer except reflex-action ; then Bedser sent him a ball that, instead of " leaving " Harvey's bat, turned rapidly back, missing the leg-stump by an inch. A four over the slips' heads off Bedser was the consequence of the instinct of self-preservation, as if Harvey's bat had become suddenly electrified. Bedser was still " on the spot " ; after an hour of unrelieved effort and after the ball had lost its " newness," he was straining batsmen's nerves and eyesight. He hit Archer's pads with a genuine breakback ; and the collision made a noise like a boxer's glove knocking a man out in the stomach. In a world ruled more by justice than this one, Bedser would have been rewarded by four wickets before lunch, scarcely fewer. But at lunch Australia's score was 67 for one, Archer and Harvey not out. At the end of an hour's play Brown asked Wright to bowl instead of Bailey, whose support for Bedser was always extremely determined, ready to break his back in two, if necessary. Wright unfortunately was at his most unreliable ; he pitched short, and following the severe tightness of the English attack so far, his long-hops must have entered the Australian innings like refreshing air into a lethal chamber. Wright's third over was plundered for fifteen, three fours for Harvey, who in a subsequent over from Wright helped himself to two more boundaries. In Australia's first innings of 194 all out, Wright bowled eight overs for 63 runs and no wickets, in a strap-hanger in a bus turns over a page of a newspaper with his unoccupied hand. Yet again we were gazing upon a rejuvenated England XI fighting hard and cleverly, not at all down-hearted by the loss of Compton, out of the action because of a swollen knee. The Melbourne crowd applauded almost every movement of an English player : Brown was applauded on principle, so to say, whether doing something clever or active or nothing at all. The cool day, now fresh and healthy, was another factor likely to make Englishmen feel at home—that and the fresh green grass of the outfield. Miller, like Harvey, suggested war in the open, out of the trenches, colours flying ; Bedser needed some rest and Wright couldn't be trusted. This surely was a moment for us to fear Miller, for he had played himself in for fifty minutes, scoring only 18. Brown bowled in the responsible place of Bedser, and in his second over deceived Miller, who first shaped to push to the off-side, changed his mind, stood still rather at a loss, while his left heel was struck by the ball. Miller departed l.b.w. This was the beginning of a new lease of life and achievement for Brown which rose to a crescendo without parallel in his career so far ; second-youth came to him, and apparently not only lightened the burden of forty years but, more important, the heavier burden of physical weight and girth. He was not much less quick with a pick-up and a return than anybody else in the English field. Nothing could be done to restore the broken Australian innings after Loxton got out. He defended for eighty-five minutes, while Hassett took charge and pulled four fours from four of Wright's long-hops with a remarkable majesty for a cricketer of his few inches. Loxton endured to compile 32, four runs more than England lost by ! But none of us thought of Loxton or of an English defeat at the close of this enthralling first day at Melbourne ; were not Australia all out for 194, on a wicket good enough for any good batsman ? I doubt if W. G. Grace saw a better in all his life. As I walked through the Fitzroy Gardens, back to Menzies Hotel—and I walked all the way—I was brimming over with the spirit of Christmas, and ready to wish goodwill to everybody.

It was inconceivable that, with the weather set fair, England would not leave Australia's 194 far behind. And yet—some spirit of denial at the back of my mind whispered: " Wait." Remember. The crease. The abyss. Will, this time, the English batsmen see beyond it, and realise it is mainly a figment of their own fearful fancying ? "

SECOND DAY

AUSTRALIA—First Innings

K. Archer, c. Bedser, b. Bailey	26
A. R. Morris, c. Hutton, b. Bedser	2
R. N. Harvey, c. Evans, b. Bedser	42
K. R. Miller, l.b.w., b. Brown	18
A. L. Hassett, b. Bailey	52
S. J. E. Loxton, c. Evans, b. Close	32
R. R. Lindwall, l.b.w., b. Bailey	8
D. Tallon, not out	7
I. W. Johnson, c. Parkhouse, b. Bedser	0
W. A. Johnston, c. Hutton, b. Bedser	0
J. Iverson, b. Bailey	1
Extras (b. 4, l.b. 2)	6
Total	194

FALL OF WICKETS—First Innings.—1—6, 2—67, 3—89, 4—93, 5—177, 6—177, 7—192, 8—193, 9—193, 10—194.

BOWLING—First Innings.—Bailey, 17.1—5—40—4 ; Bedser, 19—3—37—4 ; Wright, 8—0—63—0 ; Brown, 9—0—28—1 ; Close, 6—1—20—1.

ENGLAND—First Innings

R. T. Simpson, c. Johnson, b. Miller	4
Washbrook, l.b.w., b. Lindwall	21
J. G. Dewes, c. Miller, b. Johnston	8
Hutton, c. Tallon, b. Iverson	12
Parkhouse, c. Hassett, b. Miller	9
Close, c. Loxton, b. Iverson	0
F. R. Brown, c. Johnson, b. Iverson	62
T. E. Bailey, b. Lindwall	12
Evans, c. Johnson, b. Iverson	49
Bedser, not out	4

Wright, l.b.w., b. Johnston 2
Extras (b. 8, l.b. 6) 14

Total 197

FALL OF WICKETS—FIRST INNINGS.—1—11, 2—33, 3—37, 4—54, 5—54, 6—61, 7—126, 8—153, 9—194, 10—197.

BOWLING—FIRST INNINGS.—Lindwall, 12—2—46—2 ; Miller, 13—0—39—2 ; Johnston, 9—1—28—2 ; Iverson, 18—3—37—4 ; Johnson, 5—1—19—0 ; Loxton, 4—1—14—0.

On the second day before lunch a reaction set in that was rather more than " equal and opposite." How we English tasted the first of many of the rubber's dishes of humiliation served us ! On an excellent wicket, with little of the " greenness " which had favoured Bedser the day before, England's major batsmen broke down deplorably and six wickets fell for 61. The innings was retrieved by a brave and determined innings by F. R. Brown, who, from this moment onwards, interrupted only by the accident that removed him from the team and the scene five weeks afterwards at Adelaide, played and worked and led his broken forces day after day with an energy so tireless, a spirit so firm, and a wholesale expenditure of nature so infectious, that before long a street hawker in Sydney was shouting from the pavement to the crowd : " 'Ere y'are ; lovely lettuces—all got the 'eart of Freddie Brown." On this second day of the Melbourne Test match, 23rd December, Brown, with a John Bullish and Johnsonian girth, blood and authority, put the advancing Australian attack temporarily in its place. He had so far not scored fifty in an innings during the tour ; to-day he batted with a hope that was a triumph over experience. Six out for 61, he lumbered to the crease, reminding me curiously of Warwick Armstrong in middle age ; and he wasted no time or breath before he lambasted Miller for 3 to leg. In two hours he scored 62 out of 99, with a sixer and four boundaries.

The morning's first over was bowled by Lindwall, and it was as amiable and harmless as a Christmas cracker. Miller was quickly provoked into sending a " bumper," always a sign that he isn't in the mood to bowl or doesn't like the pace of the wicket. But he caused the beginning of England's rot ; as he was destined not once but thrice to do, subsequently, whether with malice prepense on his part or not. Simpson held out a bat almost sightless with speculation and was caught by first-slip. The ball which was his undoing swung to the off, the sort of ball which Sutcliffe scarcely deigned to recognise, let alone play, as he watched it go by, his bat withdrawn, as though the Sutcliffes declined to touch such stuff with their finger-tips.

Dewes, in next, England 11 for one, walked to the wicket slowly. Batsmen go in to bat differently. Bradman took his time, but he was surveying the land, " prospecting " it, so to say, staking his claim. Miller saunters forth to begin an innings, toes straight but the rest of him inclined to wander and look around, as though for familiar faces in the crowd or on the field of play. Dewes went to the crease on the present occasion apparently absorbed in himself, maybe reviewing his technique in the abstract and running over in his mind the different ways a cricketer can get out, from clean-bowled to handled-the-ball. He contrived to avoid a fatal pitfall for half an hour and actually was gathering confidence from the middle of his bat when he slashed at an off-side ball from Johnston, sent it to the slips, where Miller made a catch with his favourite flourish, diving low, swiftly and beautifully. With another fieldsman I could name the stroke would have gone for three runs, if not four. Then Washbrook, not for the first time, frustrated ours and his own hopes ; his innings of promise was cut down in the blossom. Lindwall, obviously about to take a rest, pitched a not at all vivid ball well up to Washbrook, who sought to turn it to leg instead of forcing it, as easily he could have done, to the on. He missed aim and the umpire deemed him l.b.w. For fifty-three minutes he had comfortably, we thought, played himself in. Hutton, in fourth, two wickets down for 33, seemed not as depressed as the rest of us at the downfall of Washbrook.

When Iverson bowled instead of Lindwall, Hutton drove

him through the covers with his left leg forward, his balanced body and the beautiful swing and follow-through of the bat indivisible in rhythm—a stroke of grandeur and noble lineage. He coped almost condescendingly with Iverson's off-spin and three short-leg fieldsmen; and he " took " leisurely singles at will to protect Parkhouse from Iverson. But to the second ball of Iverson's fourth over of the morning Hutton shaped for a sweep square to the on from a well-flighted length, then as though thinking better of it, he raised his bat above and away from the off-break, and the ball struck him near the knee, bouncing upwards. Iverson impulsively called out " Catch it ! " and Tallon swooped forward, made a catch, and he and Iverson appealed. The umpire's finger went up. A mistake of judgment; but nothing could be done about it. The umpire's decision is final on the cricket field, whatever may be the case when he is in his own house.

Good God, we said, whoever heard of Hutton hitting a ball up over his head in a Test match, or anywhere else; he couldn't make such a stroke if he tried. We couldn't guess that next innings Hutton would get out from as " unlikely " a stroke, one not remotely connected with him, yet caught near the umpire, victory within reach. This unjust blow to England should have inspired Close, another Yorkshireman, to most grim obduracy, but it didn't. On the contrary, Close " swiped " horribly across another nicely-flighted ball from Iverson; and it is fervently to be hoped he was suitably chastened to see himself caught not far behind his back on the leg-side. In an Eton v. Harrow match, in a situation as serious for his side as this, any boy who lost his wicket through such weakness, such lack of sense and effort, would not be forgotten or forgiven for it all his life, wherever he might isolate himself in the world, Tanganyika, the Melbourne Club or Montreal. Close was out—five for 54—in the last over before lunch, Parkhouse not out, 7, after much labour.

At a quarter-past two the game proceeded, watched by a great concourse tier on tier, thousands in the shade in the great enclosures, thousands packed side by side in the sun, everybody quiet as a mouse as the bowler began his run. In Miller's second over following the adjournment, Parkhouse received a short rising ball that whistled past his left ear, probably making the sound of a tuning-fork. He struck at the next ball without conviction as it went past the off-stump; Hassett, at short "gully" moved quickly sideways and caught him. Parkhouse for three-quarters of an hour had hinted at a liking for strokes of taste; but his general aspect recalled the old hymn: "Brief life is here our portion."

With Bailey his companion at the wicket, Brown began his onslaught, not at first with as much accuracy as belligerence. A perfect drive to the off from Iverson got his eye in focus; he hit his six, beyond long-on, from Ian Johnson; and he will hear the generous roar of Melbourne's fifty thousand to his life's end. It was a Rubicon stroke. While Bailey stuck to the crease as though by some physical act of clinging to it, Brown put red corpuscles into England's innings; he usually looks as if he knows what red corpuscles are, also phagocytes well stimulated. When he reached 50 with a drive that changed his bat (to the eye of imagination) to a hammer in a smithy, the multitude roared louder, affection in the sound and the tumult. The seventh wicket added 65 in seventy-one minutes. Bailey, who scored 12 of them, was too late against a grand inswinger from Lindwall, goaded to his fastest. As he heard the rattle of the stumps Bailey bowed a sorrowful head; but he had done his side some service.

As we watched Brown and Bailey—not England's two most skilful batsmen—lift the score from 61 for six to 126 for seven, we could realise how many opportunities had gone abegging. Brown, aiming red as a lobster at another six, was caught soon after tea, eight out at 153; then Evans demonstrated what quick feet and impertinence could do with bowlers now desperately keen to get England out for less than Australia's first innings score of 194. The fight for first innings lead, indeed, aroused the crowd to hysteria. Evans batted like a cheeky

Cockney, yet there was skill as well as character in his cricket. A drive through the covers, off a fast ball from Miller, was faultless and timed so well that it raced over the grass and hit the fence with a resounding crack. Sixty thousand Australians were with Evans to a man, even to a small boy—and it is not easy for a small boy to rise above patriotism. The acclamation which announced that England had passed Australia's 194, and the greeting to Evans as he came home, caught at square-leg from another pugnacious stroke, was like the myriad-throated applause to Brown, of the warmth that fills the heart and makes the lover of cricket love the game more than ever. But at the day's end, the eve of Christmas, something of the season's cheerfulness was shaded by the thought of how England had missed a rare chance to leave Australia's 194 so far behind that now we might have been in a position to toast victory in the champagne (Australian) at the parties and celebrations imminent and about to engulf us. We couldn't believe in another breakdown of Australia's batting —and this Melbourne wicket wasn't likely to be an easy one on which to play a long innings if England should be set 300 to win ; and none of us dreamed there would be fewer needed.

THIRD DAY

AUSTRALIA

FIRST INNINGS		SECOND INNINGS	
K. Archer, c. Bedser, b. Bailey ..	26	c. Bailey, b. Bedser	46
A. R. Morris, c. Hutton, b. Bedser	2	l.b.w., b. Wright	18
R. N. Harvey, c. Evans, b. Bedser	42	run out	31
K. R. Miller, l.b.w., b. Brown ..	18	b. Bailey	14
A. L. Hassett, b. Bailey	52	c. Bailey, b. Brown	19
S. J. E. Loxton, c. Evans, b. Close	32	c. Evans, b. Brown	2
R. R. Lindwall, l.b.w., b. Bailey ..	8	c. Evans, b. Brown	7
D. Tallon, not out	7	l.b.w., b. Brown	0
I. W. Johnson, c. Parkhouse, b. Bedser	0	c. Close, b. Bedser	23
W. A. Johnston, c. Hutton, b. Bedser	0	b. Bailey	6
J. Iverson, b. Bailey	1	not out	0
Extras (b. 4, l.b. 2)	6	Extras (b. 10, l.b. 5) ..	15
Total	194	Total	181

MELBOURNE

FALL OF WICKETS—First Innings.—1—6, 2—67, 3—89, 4—93, 5—177, 6—177, 7—192, 8—193, 9—193, 10—194.

Second Innings.—1—43, 2—99, 3—100, 4—126, 5—131, 6—151, 7—151, 8—156, 9—181, 10—181.

BOWLING—First Innings.—Bailey, 17.1—5—40—4 ; Bedser, 19—3—37—4 ; Wright, 8—0—63—0 ; Brown, 9—0—28—1 ; Close, 6—1—20—1.

Second Innings.—Bailey, 15—3—47—2 ; Bedser, 16.3—2—43—2 ; Wright, 9—0—42—1 ; Brown, 12—2—26—4 ; Close, 1—0—8—0.

ENGLAND

First Innings		Second Innings	
R. T. Simpson, c. Johnson, b. Miller	4	not out	10
Washbrook, l.b.w., b. Lindwall	21	b. Iverson	8
J. G. Dewes, c. Miller, b. Johnston	8		
Hutton, c. Tallon, b. Iverson	12	not out	2
Parkhouse, c. Hassett, b. Miller	9		
Close, c. Loxton, b. Iverson	0		
F. R. Brown, c. Johnson, b. Iverson	62		
T. E. Bailey, b. Lindwall	12	b. Johnson	0
Evans, c. Johnson, b. Iverson	49		
Bedser, not out	4		
Wright, l.b.w., b. Johnston	2		
Extras (b. 8, l.b. 6)	14	Extras (b. 8)	8
Total	197	Total (2 wkts.)	28

FALL OF WICKETS—First Innings.—1—11, 2—33, 3—37, 4—54, 5—54, 6—61, 7—126, 8—153, 9—194, 10—197.

Second Innings.—1—21, 2—22.

BOWLING—First Innings.—Lindwall, 12—2—46—2 ; Miller, 13—0—39—2 ; Johnston, 9—1—28—2 ; Iverson, 18—3—37—4 ; Johnson, 5—1—19—0 ; Loxton, 4—1—14—0.

Second Innings (to date).—Lindwall, 3—0—6—0 ; Miller, 2—1—4—0 ; Johnson, 4—1—6—1 ; Iverson, 4—1—4—1.

This was one of the most astonishing and thrilling days in the annals of cricket, and it ended with the balance so precarious that the merest wisp of a straw from luck would sway it decisively, England's or Australia's way. Yet again Australian batsmanship was rendered poverty-stricken ; the second innings was all over at five minutes to five for 181. England counter-attacked grandly from the position to which they were thrown back on Saturday ; the wicket, though not altogether after a contemporary batsman's heart, was on the whole true—in spite of a ball that kept low now and again—and easy for run-making. Keener bowling than Bedser's, Bailey's and Brown's, and keener fielding, couldn't be imagined; and the raging battle was infused by a spirit of sportsmanship that honoured the finest and oldest traditions of cricket, the Melbourne crowd contributing a generous if ear-shattering part.

After a two-days' pause the match began again in hot weather, the sun streaming from a sky of blue satin stretched without a crease in it. From the heights of the members' pavilion, looking straight down and behind the line of the ball's flight, the wicket resembled a light-brown oblong coffin in which, you might have said, reposed the hopes of all bowlers. But it was a deceptive wicket really—good enough for a good batsman, but, as I say, a ball occasionally kept low; and there was always enough hardness in the rolled baked earth to create that illusion in cricket of increase of speed after the ball has pitched. A Test match wicket in Australia, let alone Christmas Day and Boxing Day, could scarcely be expected to remain sober all the time. So once again we were privileged to enjoy a fair fight between bat and ball, fortune never distributing her favours unequally among the opponents. At first I resigned myself to hours of slow attrition while Morris and Archer set themselves to reduce Bedser, Bailey and Wright to limp, moist, ineffectual bodies. Only one wicket fell before lunch, and in ninety minutes not more than 57 runs were scored; and now Australia were 79 ahead, nine batsmen to come. Morris played back to a well-flighted length from Wright, got into position for a glance to leg, changed his mind, and allowed his pads to stop a " googly ", and to his unconcealed surprise was given out l.b.w. Still, nobody foresaw the wrath to come. Archer suggested obduracy if not a technical control that has been taught by experience to work at leisure and by instinct.

The fun began at half-past two when the great ground was packed and inflammable. Archer was caught a few yards from the bat by Bailey, off Bedser in the " gully," and five minutes afterwards Harvey backed-up impulsively as Miller stabbed defensively forward at a surprisingly quick one from Wright. Washbrook, at mid-off, fielded swiftly, threw at one wicket and struck it with Harvey yards out. I was obliged to ask the brilliant fielder's name; he was so thoroughly disguised in a white hat that he might have been wearing the Tarnhelm. Miller also protected himself from the sun by use of a cap; and Miller with his hair invisible is as though W. G. Grace had appeared without his whiskers. Indeed, Miller was not happy; his aggression hinted of some mental unease. Clearly the occasion was not going to be a sort of extra Christmas dinner for Australian batsmen. He made two great strokes off Wright, a voracious sweep to leg, the whole man coming full circle, and a leap of a drive to the off. Then Bailey clean-bowled him with dramatic abruptness. Miller tried to change from offence to defence, but the ball's speed was even quicker than Miller's eyesight; the middle stump was hit before the bat could intervene.

Now Brown came into action again, rolling to the crease like a man-of-war. A rasping ball removed Loxton, caught at the wicket: Australia five for 131, and what with the boiling temperature of the afternoon and the roars and the zoological screams of the women in the crowd, the wonder is that typewriters in the Press Box were not dislocated and infinitives split asunder. The frenzy of it all was intensified by the impersonal tranquillity of the stainless blue sky. Brown next got rid of Lindwall, also caught at the wicket; and in the same over Brown, insatiable and very warm, defeated Tallon, who played back to succumb l.b.w.

After tea Bailey held a catch worth going miles to see, even by transport in Melbourne. Hassett, who was batting belligerently, edged a ball from Brown low to the grass and Bailey grasped it one-handed, flinging the heart and soul of him at the chance. Brown's antagonistic bowling, which had disposed in rapid sequence Loxton, Lindwall and Hassett and changed the day's course, was all done with an old ball and less by the arts of length and variation of pace (which were excellent) than by vehemence of will and power of a good right arm. With every run invaluable and every ball a nail in somebody's coffin for certain—England's or Australia's—a stand by Johnson and

Johnston (only Iverson to come) came as more and more fuel to the flames of a game which burned and singed us as though all of us, crowd, cricketers, bats and balls and surrounding nature, were being caught up in the conflagration of an Australian midsummer. The ninth wicket added 25; Ian Johnson's portion was 23; and England to-morrow, so it was written, but mercifully we couldn't know it, would lose by 28. A day of irony, a day of cricket long to be remembered.

Brown again sent Simpson in first with Washbrook to begin England's task (if it couldn't be called a duty); a mere 179 to win a victory. It was a risky move surely, for if ever an England innings needed a masterful lead it was now. But Washbrook was the first to fall, well beaten by Iverson with a ball that kept low. Hassett lost no time before he brought his spin-bowlers into action, but I fancy he was as hopeful of collaboration from the batsmen's fears or imaginings as from the wicket itself, which if it didn't reject spin, scarcely imparted the pace or " snap " that kills. Bailey, sent in twenty minutes before close of play, was bowled by Ian Johnson for nothing, stretching forward to an off-break. Why was Bailey asked to bat in a position so responsible at the end of an afternoon on which he had not spared himself in the field ? Hutton, who was possibly becoming accustomed to arriving at the crease not with a clean, confident sheet behind him but in the midst of falling wickets, dallied calmly with the last long agonising minutes, as the sun cast the shadows of the great stand over the grass in stark black blocks.

FOURTH DAY

AUSTRALIA

FIRST INNINGS			SECOND INNINGS		
K. Archer, c. Bedser, b. Bailey	..	26	c. Bailey, b. Bedser	.. ..	46
A. R. Morris, c. Hutton, b. Bedser		2	l.b.w., b. Wright ..	.. ..	18
R. N. Harvey, c. Evans, b. Bedser		42	run out	.. ..	31
K. R. Miller, l.b.w., b. Brown	..	18	b. Bailey ..	.. ..	14
A. L. Hassett, b. Bailey	.. ..	52	c. Bailey, b. Brown	.. ..	19
S. J. E. Loxton, c. Evans, b. Close		32	c. Evans, b. Brown	.. ..	2

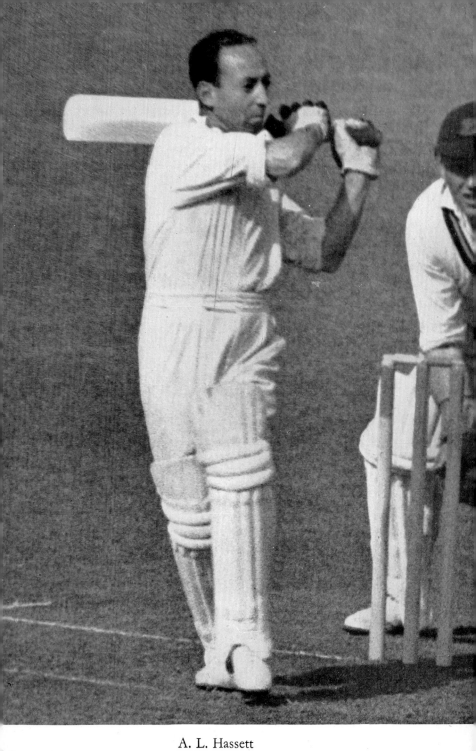

A. L. Hassett

Bedser in action

R. R. Lindwall, l.b.w., b. Bailey ..	8	c. Evans, b. Brown	..	.. 7
D. Tallon, not out ..	7	l.b.w., b. Brown ..	..	.. 0
I. W. Johnson, c. Parkhouse, b. Bedser	0	c. Close, b. Bedser	..	.. 23
W. A. Johnston, c. Hutton, b. Bedser	0	b. Bailey	..	.. 6
J. Iverson, b. Bailey	1	not out	..	.. 0
Extras (b. 4, l.b. 2)	6	Extras (b. 10, l.b. 5) ..	..	.. 15
Total 194		Total	..	.. 181

FALL OF WICKETS—FIRST INNINGS.—1—6, 2—67, 3—89, 4—93, 5—177, 6—177, 7—192, 8—193, 9—193, 10—194.

SECOND INNINGS.—1—43, 2—99, 3—100, 4—126, 5—131, 6—151, 7—151, 8—156, 9—181, 10—181.

BOWLING—FIRST INNINGS.—Bailey, 17.1—5—40—4 ; Bedser, 19—3—37—4 ; Wright, 8—0—63—0 ; Brown, 9—0—28—1 ; Close, 6—1—20—1.

SECOND INNINGS.—Bailey, 15—3—47—2 ; Bedser, 16.3—2—43—2 ; Wright, 9—0—42—1 ; Brown, 12—2—26—4 ; Close, 1—0—8—0.

ENGLAND

FIRST INNINGS		SECOND INNINGS		
R. T. Simpson, c. Johnson, b. Miller	4	b. Lindwall	.. ..	.. 23
Washbrook, l.b.w., b. Lindwall ..	21	b. Iverson ..	..	.. 8
J. G. Dewes, c. Miller, b. Johnston	8	c. Harvey, b. Iverson	..	.. 5
Hutton, c. Tallon, b. Iverson ..	12	c. Lindwall, b. Johnston ..		.. 40
Parkhouse, c. Hassett, b. Miller ..	9	l.b.w., b. Johnston	..	.. 28
Close, c. Loxton, b. Iverson ..	0	l.b.w., b. Johnston	..	.. 1
F. R. Brown, c. Johnson, b. Iverson	62	b. Lindwall	..	.. 8
T. E. Bailey, b. Lindwall	12	b. Johnson	..	.. 0
Evans, c. Johnson, b. Iverson ..	49	b. Lindwall	..	.. 2
Bedser, not out	4	not out ..	..	.. 14
Wright, l.b.w., b. Johnston ..	2	l.b.w., b. Johnston	..	.. 2
Extras (b. 8, l.b. 6)	14	Extras (b. 17, l.b. 2) ..	..	.. 19
Total 197		Total	..	.. 150

FALL OF WICKETS—FIRST INNINGS.—1—11, 2—33, 3—37, 4—54, 5—54, 6—61, 7—126, 8—153, 9—194, 10—197.

SECOND INNINGS.—1—21, 2—22, 3—52, 4—82, 5—92, 6—95, 7—122, 8—124, 9—134, 10—150.

BOWLING—FIRST INNINGS.—Lindwall, 12—2—46—2 ; Miller, 13—0—39—2 ; Johnston, 9—1—28—2 ; Iverson, 18—3—37—4 ; Johnson, 5—1—19—0 ; Loxton, 4—1—14—0.

SECOND INNINGS.—Lindwall, 12—1—29—3 ; Miller, 5—2—16—0 ; Johnson, 13—3—24—1 ; Iverson, 20—4—36—2 ; Johnston, 13.7—1—26—4.

As we have seen, England stumbled on the doorstep of victory. The first ball of the morning, almost a " shooter," from

Ian Johnson, nearly sped under Hutton's bat. Moreover, such a ball, so early in the day, sounded an alarm. Simpson was as a man encased in heavy armour of suspicion and self-distrust; yet he rendered his side staunch service for forty minutes. Hutton soon settled down to a chess-player's scrutiny of every gambit of the bowlers. With time to spare he played any dangerous off-spinner, especially from Iverson, down to the earth with the break, thus frustrating the leg-side fieldsmen clustered round his legs. Iverson bowled with no slips, not a single one, a sign that he wasn't spinning away from the batsman. I cannot agree that he is yet a great, as distinct from a good, bowler if he doesn't command that trick.

At half-past twelve Iverson was "rested" for Lindwall. I breathed relief; this change of bowling was a testimony to the defensive play of Hutton and Simpson in the crucial opening period. England would prevail if a good stand occurred now. But I chafed for signs of strokes calculated to put the bowlers out of conceit with themselves. It was not a fast bowler's commission to win the match on this wicket. Lindwall, though, is not one of those whom George Lohmann counted amongst the "brute force" school of fast bowlers; Lindwall has brains— so many, apparently, that it is a wonder he went in for fast bowling at all. His fourth ball, indeed, which clean-bowled Simpson, was a shade less than fast, with a curved flight; and it swung in. Simpson, before he left the crease for the pavilion, picked up one of the fallen bails and gave it to the wicket-keeper, a sad but courtly action.

Dewes, straight from a sickbed (he had caught a chill on a chilly Christmas Eve following a sweltering day), brought his bat down in the nick of time to a "yorker" which Lindwall sent him as soon as he could get at him. For nearly two hours Dewes stuck to his wicket; it was pure adhesiveness. When at last Dewes scored a single he ran like a sparrow that has quickly and apprehensively picked up a crumb, after long inspection of it from a distance. A cover-drive by Hutton, off Ian Johnson, announced and made plain to everybody present that we were looking at the greatest contemporary batsman, the most thoroughly organised in technique, the most soundly schooled in first and last principles; never an improviser, always an architect of an innings.

When Iverson bowled again in place of Lindwall, an off-spinner bounced abruptly, but Hutton dealt with it one-handed, so that the ball came into contact with a " dead " or passive bat and fell harmlessly to the earth, all venom spent. In the same over Hutton drove to the off for four, a perfectly poised hit, bat swinging on high; so, in a few balls, we were shown models of acts of self-preservation and of confident self-expression.

Five minutes before lunch Dewes pushed his bat too forcibly and fatally at a spinner he couldn't reach because he would or could not " go to the ball "; and twenty minutes after lunch, the disaster and the ironic sport with Hutton occurred. He left the field, leaving behind him a mortal wound; not a lover of cricket in the crowd saw this dethronement without sorrow. . . . The rest should be silence. Close was miserably l.b.w. to Ian Johnson, bereft of ideas, synthetic or analytical. Six for 95, and now Brown joined Parkhouse, whose occasional strokes of bright decision were as flickering fireflies in the night of doubt that mainly covered him.

England's only chance at this point was dependent on assault and battery; but even Brown groped shortsightedly out at Iverson. The Australian attack was too accurate to encourage any belief that eighty runs could be obtained by waiting for them. I still dared to hope that Parkhouse might prevail; for his cricket improved in touch when speed was employed by Hassett instead of spin. But again we were mocked: Lindwall redis-covered in his rusting armoury a magnificent ball, vintage or arsenal of 1948, and he wrecked Brown's stumps entirely; then Miller, on for Johnston, trapped Parkhouse leg-before. Wright prolonged the agony by putting a quite affable blade to an attack which was now as ravening as triumphant; and Bedser was not out at the end, standing like a solitary column left erect, on the bare plain of England's defeat.

Chapter Thirteen

SYDNEY

If the Test match at Melbourne was a sad disappointment for England, the one succeeding it at Sydney came upon us as a hollow anti-climax. It is little use complaining of "bad luck." Fortune runs after competence in this world more often than not. It is much the same with umpires' decisions at cricket. I once said to Bradman, to mollify him during a period when certain English critics were protesting against poor Australian umpires : "Well, Don : as you know, it's usually the losing side that complains about bad umpiring." He replied : "I can't agree." I thought he hadn't correctly understood me. "But, Don," I repeated, "I said it's usually the losing side that complains about bad umpiring." "I heard you," he said. "Well then?" I inquired. "You say it's usually the losing side that complains about bad umpiring," he said; "I disagree. It's *always* the losing side ! "

England would have lost this Sydney match just the same if Bailey and Wright had escaped those dangers to health and limb which seemed to pursue our cricketers throughout Australia from October to March. No team playing in a Test match in Australia can truly hope to get off scot-free if in two innings on a good pitch their chosen batsmen are able to score only 413, with the leading players—in this instance, Hutton, Washbrook, Compton, Simpson and Parkhouse—mustering not more than 235 for ten wickets. Australians themselves were to clinch this argument in the fifth Test, which brought them down from a rather complacent Olympus.

FIRST DAY

ENGLAND—First Innings

Hutton, l.b.w., b. Miller	62
Washbrook, c. Miller, b. Johnson	18
R. T. Simpson, c. Loxton, b. Miller	49
Compton, b. Miller	0
Parkhouse, c. Morris, b. Johnson	25
F. R. Brown, not out	36
T. E. Bailey, not out	9
Extras (l.b. 10, n.b. 2)	12
Total (for 5 wkts.)	211

Evans, Bedser, J. J. Warr, and Wright to go in.

FALL OF WICKETS.—1—34, 2—128, 3—128, 4—137, 5—187.

BOWLING (to date).—Lindwall, 9—0—37—0 ; Miller, 10—3—23—3 ; Johnson, 21—5—63—2 ; Johnston, 18—4—39—0 ; Iverson, 10—1—25—0 ; Loxton, 5—1—12—0.

AUSTRALIA.—A. L. Hassett (captain), A. R. Morris, K. R. Miller, D. Tallon, R. R. Lindwall, I. Johnson, W. Johnston, N. Harvey, S. Loxton, J. Iverson, K. Archer.

On a hot but not as affecting a December morning as Sydney can produce F. R. Brown won the toss. At noon the Australians walked into sunshine streaming down as though filling the world. From the great height of the Press Box—a hot-house of glass—the packed ground could be seen in isolation from the neighbouring places outside, trams and cars going their different ways, houses and gardens and people. There is always piquant contrast when we watch a public event from a position where we can see it as though a thing in itself, with the rest of the world, only just over the wall, oblivious. Sydney is a less solid and imposing stadium than Melbourne ; there is space between stands and enclosures ; there is the open air of a cricket field. The pretty colours of the painted chairs in the Ladies' Pavilion lend an air of social ease and amenity not always to be felt at

Test matches in Australia. The famous " Hill " gathered in strength but not in vocabulary, as Washbrook and Hutton went forth to bat, their shadows like black velvet pools in which they walked or waded. The " Hill," indeed, needs to enlarge its stock of wit and epigram. " 'Ave a gow " is no longer as funny or as withering as it used to be ; nor is " Get a bag." Failing an entirely new idea or invention, perhaps either of these two *bons mots* might acquire fresh sparkle if intoned or pronounced differently. But during one rare period when Australia couldn't get an English batsman out for an hour or so, a voice from the " Hill " shouted, with rare and sudden inspiration : " Put Neville Cardus on."

Lindwall began his physical exercises before bowling, swinging his arms, bending to touch his toes and kicking up his heels. Hassett set his fieldsmen to an inch. The " Hill " of Sydney was as bees swarming : the hum and buzz of expectation announced that Lindwall was ready—then that dead silence in which the first ball is bowled of every Test match between England and Australia. Hutton—in first at last !—drove Lindwall's second ball for three, forcibly to the off, a smack in the face for any fast bowler so early as this in the New Year. The wicket was a batsman's sure ally. Washbrook sliced Lindwall for two, and hit him to square-leg for two from the " meat " of the bat, seven runs off the first over. The batting was supple and even affable, as if the warmth of the morning had already got into the cricket. Miller attacked with his own downward thrust of the head and his sudden turn from his bowling mark, after walking to it tall and straight as a guardsman, no part of his upper body moving, his eyes " straight." Washbrook drove him to the on for three at once, clearly a case of taking a liberty. Miller's bowling was improvisatory : a " bumper," a flying-saucer of a ball, seemed to give him much amusement. In three overs from Australia's fast bowlers, disporting themselves on their native heath, nineteen runs were pillaged. Then Miller showed the ball to the umpires, who looked carefully all round it and held it up to the light like an egg ; another ball was brought into play, but before handing it to Miller one of the umpires bounced it up and down on the hard earth like a man indulging in a little game of his own. One of the spectators, a Central European, found this the most puzzling thing of a wholly mysterious day. He was told that the umpire bounced the ball to get it to the same state of wear and tear as the discarded ball. " But zen I read in the papers zat it is the Herr Miller who makes ze bouncers."

Hassett asked Ian Johnson to bowl instead of Miller at half-past twelve, England 31 ; there is usually a breath of relief in the England dressing-room—and at both ends of the wicket—when Miller " goes off." But a first-wicket stand of Hutton and Washbrook, for which we had waited so long and were destined to wait longer and in vain, came to grief through the sheer negligence or thoughtlessness of Washbrook, apparently at the top of his form. Johnson bowled a short ball going away from outside the off-stump, bouncing bail high : Washbrook cut at it rather as though by an afterthought ; he didn't move across and over the stroke, to play it down. Miller at slip " saw it all happening " in advance ; he went to earth quick as a ferret to a hole and held the catch in an outstretched right hand as he fell and rolled round, every motion suggesting veins suddenly injected with mercury. A cricketer as alive as Miller, the impulse and instinct of him flashing to visible beauty of movement, is worth his weight in gold to the game.

The fall of Washbrook restored to Hutton's shoulders his daily burden of responsibility ; we could see it sitting there again, Old Man of the Sea ; see it from the Press Box's dizzy altitude, a Press Box in the stratosphere. A cricket-writer may as well go up in a balloon.

Simpson opened with a handsome drive to the off for four, from W. Johnston, who was now on for Lindwall. But the England innings lost the flush of health ; a green-sickness came over the complexion. Simpson began to defend as though his bat had little organic connection with his legs, and as though his pads really had no legs in them or, if at all, wooden legs.

Nobody would have suspected that this was the Simpson who a day or two earlier had scored a double century on the same ground against " an Australian XI." Ian Johnson was clever enough to spin an off-break even on a wicket of unflawed surface ; and Simpson's bat ventured into the danger zone with the dubious hesitations of a man trying the heat of a bath with his toes.

All credit to Simpson that he contrived to stay in ; it is easy to deal with cunning bowlers when you are in form. To frustrate them when you have temporarily lost skill and the crease is as a pit of hidden menace—here is proof of good faith, which is esteemed by the angels above cleverness.

After lunch Iverson twice nearly goaded Simpson to desperate remedies by flight as much as by break ; also Simpson was run out but for an inch of his life. Still, he remained on view for the great multitude to see or inspect. Hutton brought into action one or two of his most matured strokes, a cover-drive from Iverson, and a drive forced with strong arms to the on. Iverson gnawed away on the leg-stump ; he is often what is known as a " negative " bowler ; his attack is not persistently direct, but trusts to a batsman's impatience on a good wicket. And to hope to wear away a contemporary batsman's patience on a good wicket is optimism carried to the extreme. Seldom during this rubber did I see a ball from Iverson spin from leg, or spin " the other way " at all ; his use of a first-slip was a decoration rather than an accessory. Ian Johnson beat Hutton in the air, and only Hutton's experience saved him when the ball pitched, the prettiest off-spinner ; his feet moved rapidly across the stumps and, though he was out of his ground, the pads defeated the wicketkeeper's anticipations. Johnson deserved some applause—but didn't get it, for the poor bowler many times does good deeds anonymously—for challenging Hutton with such a ball, unaided by anything except his own arm, fingers and intelligence.

The England total rounded the 100 before half-past three, for only one wicket, with the crowd as quiet on the whole as a painted back-cloth in one of Arthur Collins' Drury Lane sporting dramas of old. Simpson's defence, for long anxious and suggesting a struggle with his own misgivings as well as against the Australians, changed to wilful obstinacy. The Australian attack was here accurate rather than difficult. There wasn't a cloud in the sky to throw a shadow on the England innings now. Hassett, rather at a loss, called on Miller, though a new ball would not be at his service for half an hour and after the tea interval. Miller had strayed from the slips to the outfield on the off, near the Sheridan stand and the colour of the dresses of pretty girls. He swung the wheel of the match in one over, an over which became historical before he had finished it. Hutton, who it seemed was beyond legal ways of getting out, was leg-before to an inswinger; no, not fast. Any ordinary fast bowler might have hurled a " bumper " with an old ball at Hutton in the circumstances. Miller floated a medium-pace, a curving flight which " dipped " so late that Hutton was in the act of pushing it towards cover when the ball got past the inside edge of his bat and struck the pads fatally. The master played his stroke perfectly; the master was mastered, brought down as some interfering force outside nature might bring down the sun at high noon. Hutton's 62 lasted nearly three hours. Compton stopped the fourth and fifth ball of this same catastrophic over. He played back to the sixth, thrusting out from his back foot a bat all aslant to another inswinger which touched the inner edge of the blade and sped thence to the leg-stump with a terrible rattle. England lost the rubber in this over of opportunist imagination. What a cricketer is this Miller! Sometimes he lapses into loose ends, bowls all over the place and bats with the irresponsibility and flail-like strokes of Saturday afternoons elsewhere. When he extends himself, though, in effort and purpose, antagonism runs through all his nerves and body with electrical concentration; then he seems to say that he will move this mountainous obstacle, this hateful impediment to progress—by God he will—he knows not what things he will do, but they shall be the terror of the earth. After tea, Simpson, seeking a single for his 50 in the fashionable manner of the day—that is, by means of a push round to leg—steered Miller (now with the new ball) into Loxton's hands near the square-leg umpire : prey to a booby-trap. Simpson bit his lip, cursed his folly, but what was the use of that ? England 128 for one ; England 137 for four. As Miller wrecked England's innings the noise of the crowd was fearsome, for in the acclamation was a sound of appetite satisfied. Into the arena strode Brown, not to be baited but to bait. Parkhouse suffered agonies for half an hour without a ghost of a scoring stroke, but took courage and pulled Ian Johnson's short off-spinner to the on-boundary. Loxton bowled in place of Miller ; distant thunder after the storm. Brown tempered aggression with discretion. Parkhouse, at last something like himself, drove Johnson beautifully, a cricketer's stroke, and cut him sweet as fruit, with a stylist's poise and relish. Parkhouse was dropped from the England XI after this match : a queer action in a fairly strokeless contingent. He and Brown scored 50 for the fifth wicket ; Parkhouse, hunting another four from Johnson, lofted a catch to the on and Morris, running after a ball that was always leaving him, hugged it with relief as well as judgment. In the deepening shadows over the grass Brown battled to the end, and Bailey, not for the first time and almost certainly not for the last, tackled the ordeal of the closing period like a man.

SECOND DAY

ENGLAND—First Innings

Hutton, l.b.w., b. Miller	..	..	..	..	62
Washbrook, c. Miller, b. Johnson		..	..	..	18
R. T. Simpson, c. Loxton, b. Miller	..	..	..	49
Compton, b. Miller	..	..	..	..	0
Parkhouse, c. Morris, b. Johnson		..	..	..	25
F. R. Brown, b. Lindwall	..		..	..	79
T. E. Bailey, c. Tallon, b. Johnson	..		..	..	15
Evans, not out	..	..	..	..	23
Bedser, b. Lindwall	..	..	..	..	3
J. J. Warr, b. Miller	..	..	..	..	4
Wright, run out	..	..	..	..	0
Extras (l.b. 10, n.b. 2)	..	..	..	..	12
Total	..	..	..	..	290

high over his genuflected body. A forcing stab from Lindwall, off Brown's left hip, which twisted round with astonishing agility in a man of some heaviness and circumference, could be counted amongst the cleverest strokes of the match. Then Brown drove Ian Johnson straight for four, his bat swinging down and upward easily, finishing manfully aloft, a stroke as natural and as much a part of cricket as green grass. Nobody in the rubber equalled Brown's forward drives in strength, aggressive intent and power of execution. When Johnston bowled instead of Johnson, Brown drove him square, left hand of cover, who was rendered apparently immobile by the speed of Brown's hit. Brown, reddening from sun, expense of energy and lust for plunder from Australian bowlers, drove again at Johnston to the off and the ball sped from the edge of his bat through the " gully." Brown, at 79, fiercely cut Lindwall for nothing ; then abandoning science for natural ability, he sliced the last ball of this Lindwall over into the gloves of Tallon, whence it escaped and also eluded Miller's efforts to make a catch at first-slip, though he performed a whole anatomy of muscular adjustments, diving, darting and leaping like a cage of monkeys. Lindwall, next over, bowled Brown while the crowd groaned with sorrow, spreadeagling the stumps as the bat once again heaved aloft, having just missed aim at another straight four, if not a sixer, out of the premises. Brown's reception to the pavilion was so royal that it might well have been a procession with the decorations up and the red carpet down. This gallant retaliation for England's seventh wicket had hauled the total from 187 for five to 258 for six in 106 minutes, making the game " alive " again. Brown batted two hours thirty-eight minutes for his 79. It was here that Bailey was hit on the right thumb by Lindwall, after his two hours of noble if martyred stonewalling for 13. He endeavoured to bat again after receiving surgical aid, but he scored only two more runs when he came back. He was caught at the wicket and looked as pale as a ghost. Evans saw him depart with even more than general regret, for obviously he was setting his mind on a terrific century. The " Game Chicken "

of cricket—but in trying to "keep" the bowling he ran
desperately for a single, and Wright, late to start, failed to get
home, though he risked rupture in the effort and escaped with a
strained groin, which put him, also, out of the game for weeks.
Hassett curiously didn't ask Iverson to bowl throughout the
Brown-Bailey stand. As he is no use in the field, was he, I asked
myself, being played for moral support? The answer was given
a day or two later, in no uncertain voice. On a wicket he wouldn't
himself offer to his worst enemy, Ian Johnson bowled thirty-one
overs for three wickets and 94 runs, delighting the connoisseur
by examples of the off-spinner's art; his curve through the air,
ample but seductive, pleased the eye apart from whether it was
effective or not. It is not only batsmen but bowlers, who
can make a contribution to the beauty of the game, which even
at the present time remains one of the most beautiful of them all.

Against only three bowlers to do the main work, one of
them Warr, Australia went in at five minutes to three, the afternoon a hot-house, the crowd at times a parrot and monkey-
house. Archer turned an inswinger from Bedser for one. Morris
stopped Bedser's third ball, bat in front of the pads. He endeavoured to turn the fourth to leg, but walked across his stumps
too far to the off, leaving all three of them as uncovered and
naked to the world as a new-born baby. He was rightly bowled.
Many times this rubber Morris contributed to his failures by
moving over the wicket with his bat held out before peripatetic
pads. It is a fault likely to betray any batsman not endowed with
the comprehensive eyesight of Argus. The crowd seemed to
deafen the remote blue of heaven as Morris fell. Time was when
an advance by England at the outset of an Australian innings
was an event scarcely credible in nature, whether the dispossessed
batsman were Woodfull, Ponsford, Brown, Fingleton or Barnes.
Even then, some gigantic explosive from Larwood's arsenal was
needed to bring it about.

Warr supported Bedser with the new ball and flung all his
lean young life into his attack; twice in one over he caused a
draught near the off-stump, as Archer lunged forward and missed.

But already, in spite of the spur to energy given England by Morris's quick departure, we could see heavy labour ahead of Bedser, Brown and Warr; and we recollected in time that there is a precedent in the annals of Test matches for employing your wicketkeeper as bowler—what is more, a remarkably successful one, underhands too; lobs and probably " grubs," with Alfred Lyttleton bowling them in his pads and, doubtless, a smoking-cap.

Bedser in his sixth over didn't spare himself in an attempt to get Hassett out before Australia's soundest batsman settled down. Hassett, with no choice, was obliged to use the extreme edge of his blade, near the splice, to save himself from a late outswinger; any relation of Miller in the slips might have caught him, and he was only 13 and prevailed until, on Monday, he reached 92. Hassett and Archer proceeded to play to fight again on Monday; they defied not only Bedser at his best but they defied the foul fiend, or rather the raucous voices on the " Hill," who couldn't see the point of the slow scoring. With the air sultry enough to hint at storms not far away, the Australian policy might best have been served by some show of enterprise and of stroke-play while the wicket remained trustworthy. Hassett responded to the " Hill's " irony by patting a full-toss back to Bedser, who probably bowled it ironically. At close of play—I decline to use the Australian term " stumps "—Australia were 110 for one, Archer not out 44, after 174 minutes; Hassett not out, 62, in 170 minutes. As the players came from the field, the multitude was dispersing as agitatedly as they had assembled at noon; and they were still saying " Rhubarb, rhubarb."

THIRD DAY

ENGLAND—First Innings

Hutton, l.b.w., b. Miller ..	..	..	..	..	62
Washbrook, c. Miller, b. Johnson		..	..	..	18
R. T. Simpson, c. Loxton, b. Miller		..	..	..	49
Compton, b. Miller	..	..	..	..	0

174

SYDNEY

Parkhouse, c. Morris, b. Johnson	25
F. R. Brown, b. Lindwall	79
T. E. Bailey, c. Tallon, b. Johnson	15
Evans, not out	23
Bedser, b. Lindwall	3
J. J. Warr, b. Miller	4
Wright, run out	0
Extras (l.b. 10, n.b. 2)	12
Total	290

FALL OF WICKETS.—1—34, 2—128, 3—128, 4—137, 5—187, 6—258, 7—267, 8—281, 9—286, 10—290.

BOWLING.—Lindwall, 16—0—60—2 ; Miller, 15.7—4—37—4 ; Johnston, 21—5—50—0 ; Johnson, 31—8—94—3 ; Iverson, 10—1—25—0 ; Loxton, 5—0—12—0.

AUSTRALIA—First Innings

K. Archer, c. Evans, b. Bedser	48
A. R. Morris, b. Bedser	0
A. L. Hassett, c. Bedser, b. Brown	70
R. N. Harvey, b. Bedser	39
K. R. Miller, not out	96
S. J. E. Loxton, c. Bedser, b. Brown	17
D. Tallon, l.b.w., b. Bedser	18
I. W. Johnson, not out	64
Extras (b. 3, l.b. 7)	10
Total (for 6 wkts.)	362

R. R. Lindwall, W. A. Johnston, and J. Iverson to go in.

FALL OF WICKETS.—1—1, 2—122, 3—122, 4—190, 5—223, 6—252.

BOWLING (to date).—Bedser, 36—3—95—4 ; Warr, 30—4—110—0 ; Brown, 40—4—133—2 ; Compton, 6—1—14—0.

A dour business ; compared with it a Lancashire and Yorkshire match of the Rhodes-Robinson-Makepeace oligarchy might have seemed skittish. Hassett's plan of campaign was merciless. The wicket would get dustier every hour; so Australia's first innings must be prolonged until a total large enough had been scored to ensure that a fourth innings, if any, would be merely formal. Over by over the conditions more and more if almost imperceptibly favoured spin, and the Australians grinded into the gathering dust the crippled English bowlers. Hour after hour, exposed to burning sun, we saw Bedser and Brown or Brown and Warr wheeling their arms, Bedser and Brown lumbering uphill, " bits in their mouths " like cart-horses, while Warr threatened to dislocate himself as he goaded tired young limbs to unnatural spurts of temper and vitality. The hours crawled by and Brown's movements, as he rumbled to the bowling crease with his rotating arm, began to create the illusion of perpetual motion rendered fixed, static and unplastic.

In ninety minutes before lunch 68 runs were observed by the scorers and written down in their account books. Between lunch and tea, 105 minutes, 74 were added ; and from tea to six o'clock close of play, 110 in 105 minutes—in five hours 252, of which 110 were flogged from thoroughly exhausted bowlers in an hour and a quarter. Ian Johnson was at liberty to drive right and left as he chose for 64, with seven boundaries. From the competitive view, from the contemporary attitude to Test matches, and an attitude economic and as unlovely as the age we live in, not a word of criticism could be levelled at the Australian policy. Miller, who with Worrell is by nature and technique the free-est and most dashing stroke-player to-day, schooled himself to the hair-shirt of self-denial and in four hours and a half made only 96, with three fours. But O my Trumper and my Darling long ago ! When the long-drawn afternoon had ended I met MCabe and asked him if he had ever stayed in nearly five hours for less than a hundred. " No," he replied, " I was never clever enough."

Again a big crowd was present at noon, Monday morning or not. Apparently there is no unemployment in Sydney except on principle. Warr bowled one over, then Brown swung into action with Bedser ; and during a few overs two wickets were taken with no help from the pitch. In Bedser's third over Archer snicked to the leg-side to be caught by Evans leaping sideways. The next over bowled by Brown wakened panic (but she was soon able to sleep again). From the third ball of this over, a leg-break, Hassett was beaten, and Brown unavailingly appealed for a catch at the wicket. The next ball was nearly a long-hop, and Hassett, risking a forcing hit to the on, erred in timing and didn't try to hide his mortification when Bedser at forward square-leg caught him negligently. Hassett's innings scorned delights for 192 laborious minutes. Australia 122 for three, and Miller was in now with Harvey, who when only 2 slashed hastily, and indifferent to science, at an outswinger from Brown. The ball skimmed above Compton's head. Compton's arms, rather than his hands, went up protectively rather than acquisitively, so the ugly stroke escaped just punishment. Harvey faltered in his timing ; he missed more balls in an innings than Woolley missed in a season. Brown kept at it for three-quarters of an hour ; after lunch he bowled from 2.45 to 4 ; and after tea for nearly another hour. Also he was alert in the field ; he picked up a fierce drive from Miller at mid-off, saving a four and bending down and swivelling round amazingly. Miller spoke plainly of his intention, though for long I couldn't believe it, so quickly he picked up his bat. On other days this aspiring attack would have put before him irresistible temptations. At lunch Miller was 16 after sixty-six minutes of his partnership with Harvey, who was 34 ; Harvey cannot easily not hit a loose ball. He hasn't quite graduated yet. He was bowled by Bedser immediately after lunch, driving inaccurately to the off-side ; if the bat found some contact with the ball it was less by design than by the operation of that mysterious law of gravitation which momentarily brings foreign bodies together.

The cricket here taxed the patience even of the partisan ; for my part, I thought it was unchivalrous. Three bowlers on a hot day, Warr a spent force if plucky ; an afternoon on which it was exhausting even to walk a few yards to a refreshment bar. The point is that not only was the batting mainly inert : it was not even good and canny stonewalling after the great Lancashire and Yorkshire tradition of humorous shrewdness. Much of it was inexpert, and I sighed for a Larwood or an O'Reilly to expose it. Miller, at least, played his part skilfully, he who in his heart was surely chafing. But was he ?—one never knows the secret inclinations of our cricketers nowadays. Still, I could understand at a glance that cricket was Miller's vocation, his way of life. Of the others I was nearly persuaded to suppose that maybe they did other things for a living : possibly we were looking at a good plumber, a capable furniture remover ; maybe even an accomplished trombonist.

Loxton when 13 mowed at an off-side ball from Bedser, transforming his bat into some sort of antique agricultural weapon ; but he wasn't clever enough to send the catch which Evans, like a good logical cricketer, rightly expected. Scarcely a stylish stroke was to be seen for an hour after lunch. Miller remained quiescent, if grammatical and principled. Warr, almost breaking his back with willingness, came close to ridding us of Loxton leg-before by means of a ball whose only menace was that it travelled the shortest distance between two points. Fast bowling was vanity on a wicket which was preparing itself gradually, if slowly, for an alliance with the Australian spinners.

Silence reigned supreme during this tediousness. What, I asked myself again, had happened to the " Hill " ? In fact, the " Hill " has scarcely opened its mouth since the Australian Barnes retired ; probably he exhausted them. But when Barnes batted hours without runs he stonewalled skilfully, with character and intent to annoy thousands. Loxton, unable to get out from good bowling for want of certainty of timing, asserted his essential mortality by pulling a long-hop from Brown to the region of square-leg, and Bedser caught him judiciously, on the run. Tallon cut Brown to the boundary before Bedser claimed him l.b.w. ; but if half a dozen good strokes, stimulating to the æsthetic senses, occurred between lunch and tea they escaped my vigilance, which, I confess, was not eternal.

After tea, as I have recorded, Ian Johnson flogged the limp, footsore but not broken-spirited attack. Brown was reduced to automatism ; he went on and on in benumbed rotation. Johnson, without shame, snicked him for two, and thumped him to the on-boundary. He and Miller added 110 together in 105 minutes, and Miller permitted Johnson to score the faster, 64 of them. Miller revealed no hint of jealousy as Johnson helped himself like a soldier at pillage ; I even suspected that he was not willing to join in a massacre of England's pathetic remnants worn down to no more than their shadows on the grass. He had done all that had been asked of him, held one end of the Australian innings for four and a half hours at heaven knows what cost to his impulses and inclinations. Next day he broke free of the leash, hit Warr with a magnificent six, and in eighty minutes his score travelled from 96 to 145, and he was not out at the end ; but his innings in all lasted six hours.

Though we had to deplore a conception of Test match cricket which puts the strokes of a Miller in chains, and renders his attitude to the game as obsolete as chivalry, we none the less couldn't withhold admiration of the intelligent control he exercised over his temperament, which was indeed proof of his quality as a cricketer. Not many of us who are naturally spend-thrift and glamorous can embrace austerity and endow it with style.

FOURTH DAY

ENGLAND

First Innings		Second Innings		
Hutton, l.b.w., b. Miller	62	c. Tallon, b. Iverson ..	..	9
Washbrook, c. Miller, b. Johnson	18	b. Iverson	..	34
R. T. Simpson, c. Loxton, b. Miller	49	c. Tallon, b. Iverson ..	..	0
Compton, b. Miller	0	c. Johnson, b. Johnston ..	..	23
Parkhouse, c. Morris, b. Johnson..	25	run out	..	15
F. R. Brown, b. Lindwall	79	b. Iverson	..	18
T. E. Bailey, c. Tallon, b. Johnson	15	not out	..	0
Evans, not out	23	b. Johnson..	..	14
Bedser, b. Lindwall	3	b. Iverson	..	4
J. J. Warr, b. Miller	4	b. Iverson	..	0
Wright, run out	0	absent hurt	..	0
Extras (l.b. 10, n.b. 2)	12	Extras (b. 1, l.b. 5) ..	..	6
Total	290	Total	..	123

FALL OF WICKETS—First Innings.—1—34, 2—128, 3—128, 4—137, 5—187, 6—258, 7—267, 8—281, 9—286, 10—290.

Second Innings.—1—32, 2—40, 3—45, 4—74, 5—91, 6—119, 7—119, 8—123, 9—123.

BOWLING—First Innings.—Lindwall, 16—0—60—2 ; Miller, 15.7—4—37—4 ; Johnston, 21—5—50—0 ; Johnson, 31—8—94—3 ; Iverson, 10—1—25—0. Loxton, 5—0—12—0.

SECOND INNINGS.—Lindwall, 4—1—12—0 ; Miller, 6—2—15—0 ; Johnston, 13—6—31—1 ; Iverson, 19.4—8—27—6 ; Johnson, 10—2—32—1.

AUSTRALIA—FIRST INNINGS

K. Archer, c. Evans, b. Bedser	48
A. R. Morris, b. Bedser	0
A. L. Hassett, c. Bedser, b. Brown	70
R. N. Harvey, b. Bedser	39
K. R. Miller, not out	145
S. J. E. Loxton, c. Bedser, b. Brown	17
D. Tallon, l.b.w., b. Bedser	18
I. W. Johnson, b. Brown	77
R. R. Lindwall, l.b.w., b. Brown	1
W. A. Johnston, run out	0
J. Iverson, run out	1
Extras (b. 3, l.b. 7)	10
Total	426

FALL OF WICKETS.—1—1, 2—122, 3—122, 4—190, 5—223, 6—252, 7—402, 8—406, 9—418, 10—426.

BOWLING.—Bedser, 43—4—107—4 ; Brown, 44—4—153—4 ; Warr, 36—4—142—0 ; Compton, 6—1—14—0.

Australia's first innings came to an end for 426, just before lunch ; and at a quarter-past two Hutton and Washbrook began England's uphill fight, 136 behind. But only for a while was there fight at all. This defeat, and the one to follow at Adelaide, left for some of us a taste in the mouth that couldn't be washed away by the victory in the fifth match.

The wicket no doubt began to collaborate with Australia's spin-bowlers. Hutton and Washbrook again set about the fast bowling confidently and well ; in half an hour the score was 28, Washbrook quite brilliant and contumacious. This time it was Hutton who was the first to get out and then the whole world of England's innings, with no Atlas to hold it up, or elephant on elephant, fell into the abyss. Iverson came on and drew Hutton out full stretch many times, then bowled him one of the few balls which Iverson turned slightly from leg. It " went away " a little, also it bounced at an unpleasant angle, very quick, to the bat's shoulder. Hutton's defensive " dab " for once in a way, was too positive, not " dead " enough. The ball was probably played on to Hutton's knee ; anyhow it rotated to Tallon's gloves, squirmed from them, bounced towards the earth where Ian Johnson at first-slip could only scoop it upwards, but Tallon dived as it fell again and the catch at last was completed. It was all very hard to follow—as agile as a tree of monkeys. And a really unpleasant ball.

Simpson's brief innings was that of a cricketer whose strokes seemed to have been entirely and painfully extracted; we breathed relief and compassion when he held out his bat nebulously to another lively ball from Iverson and Tallon caught him. Then Iverson clean bowled Washbrook, a quick off-spinner and a good one; Washbrook played forward and his bat, I suppose, did all that a defensive bat can do—as Doctor Johnson on his death-bed said of a pillow. Washbrook had stayed in an hour and a quarter, but at the first sight of spin he abandoned the determined offensive methods which had put Lindwall and Miller out of action. But it wasn't a fast bowler's wicket. For that matter, Iverson for all his cleverness would not, I think, have worked havoc so easily against players who trusted to quick feet. Nobody, Compton least of all, challenged him by aggressive drives or pulls to the on " with the spin "; and, as I must insist, Iverson seldom bowls a dangerous leg-break. No doubt some risks would have had to be taken in an attempt to " knock " Iverson off, because his length was so steady; but was it safer to stretch out from a rooted back foot which stole all forcibility from resistance? Batsmen came in, bowed down, and died the death. Nobody changed method or attitude; Iverson was free to do as he liked. At tea his analysis was ten overs of eight balls each, five maidens, eleven runs, three wickets.

Iverson's first rank bad ball was swept to leg for four by Compton after tea; and Parkhouse " lay back " and cut Iverson for three, a refreshing sight indeed. Moreover, Parkhouse began to move boldly forward to Iverson, who at once looked less insoluble. Parkhouse, taking heart, drove Iverson straight for three; it could be done, you see, and has been done, often too, against spin as good as, if not better than, Iverson's. Alas, Parkhouse lost his wicket after he had made a clean square-cut forward of point. Loxton fielded, both batsmen dithered before running ; then Compton sent Parkhouse back ; and Parkhouse was run out. Most run-outs of this kind are the consequence of hesitant " calling." As J. M. Barrie advised, sagely and soundly : " When you make a stroke don't stop to cheer ; run at once."

Brown came next, cheered affectionately by thousands. It was high time for a sortie to break the cordon. Nobody, I repeat, was solving the problem. Compton, though he was playing watchfully enough now, allowed Iverson to dictate the terms. England was heading surely for disaster—with not a gesture even of bad-tempered desperation. A clean swinging drive by Compton mocked us with temporary hope and delight. Brown actually lofted Iverson to the on for two, and Iverson rested after bowling eighteen overs. W. A. Johnston, the next bowler, sent a swinging half-volley to Compton, who in 1947 would have annihilated it ; on 9th January 1951 in a Test match, he thrust his bat at this half-volley, driving from where he could not reach it masterfully, and he was caught in the slips. The rest should be silence. Evans suggested tantrums until he hit hideously across a ball tossed well up to him by Ian Johnson ; and after Bailey had been warmly welcomed for venturing out from the casualty ward, Iverson returned to the attack, bowled Brown first ball, bowled Bedser next over, and next ball bowled Warr, whose only means of retaliation was a grotesque " swipe."

It was all very sad for an Englishman who remembered the dignity of Maclaren, the composure of Hayward, the D'Artagnan temper of Tyldesley, the majesty of Hobbs, the calm lovely power of Woolley, the dictatorial obstinacy of Sutcliffe—but I am becoming irrelevant. Australia's excellent attack—Iverson's in particular—merited more mettlesome opponents. Another rubber lost by England from behind the batting crease. Nothing venture, nothing win. Iverson bowled nineteen overs four balls, eight maidens, twenty-seven runs, six wickets. Whaur's your Hughie Trumble noo ?

Chapter Fourteen

ADELAIDE

THIS WAS a boring match on the whole, containing little more than a statistical interest. No connoisseur would have watched it for more than a few hours each day if the score-board had been removed from the premises. Worse than that cannot be said of any cricket match. There are times when the score-board is a thermometer which takes the temperature, the blood-pressure, of a game—as at Brisbane. At Adelaide the score-board was as dull as a railway guide, telling us only of arrivals and departures, the comings and goings of batsmen.

So I shall in this report refer as little as maybe to the figures and general accountancy, so capably attended to by Mr. Ferguson. None but contemporary players could have resisted the invitation of a beautiful turf and a beautiful setting to engage in enjoyable stroke-play. But cricket, like most things in life, is an organism in an environment. The present age is parsimonious, starved imaginatively, lacking eccentricity of character. Why should cricketers be expected to rise superior to it?

FIRST DAY

AUSTRALIA—First Innings

K. Archer, c. Compton, b. Bedser	..	..	..	0
A. R. Morris, not out ..	..	..	..	140
A. L. Hassett, c. Evans, b. Wright	..	..	..	43
R. N. Harvey, b. Bedser	..	..	..	43

K. R. Miller, not out 24
Extras (b. 2, n.b. 1, w. 1) 4

Total (for 3 wkts.) 254

J. Burke, D. Tallon, I. W. Johnson, R. R. Lindwall,
W. A. Johnston and J. Iverson to go in.

FALL OF WICKETS.—1—0, 2—95, 3—205.

BOWLING (to date).—Bedser, 19—3—48—2; Warr,
13—1—55—0; Wright, 14—0—66—1; Tattersall, 14—1
—46—0; Brown, 3—0—24—0; Compton, 1—0—11—0.

ENGLAND.—Hutton, Washbrook, R. T. Simpson,
Compton, D. S. Sheppard, F. R. Brown, Evans, Bedser,
Wright, J. J. Warr and Tattersall.

It was a day of blazing Australian summer on one of the
most handsome of the large grounds of the world. In the distance
the hills, the field itself graced by the presence of the cathedral.
Sympathetic hearts went out to the bowlers, white figures
moving in Nebuchadnezzar's furnace. In short, it was very hot.
After an hour and a half Australia, in first, scored 52 for the loss
of Archer, caught at short-leg from Bedser's inswinger, third ball
of the match. There was no evidence deducible from Australia's
batting that Australia had won three Tests and were in the position
of a team with everything to gain from some show of adventure,
and little to lose.

As I looked at this undistinguished and limp cricket, and
saw and heard the grim activity of the journalists at their typewriters, I thought to myself—it is the solemn duty of the gentlemen of the Press (and this includes everybody) to beguile the
public that this rubber is still alive and to be taken as seriously
to the bitter end as by the players themselves. I was reminded
of a hen which, after its head has been chopped off, continues to
run on and on, under the sad but entirely mistaken impression
that it is still alive, saying to itself: " My goodness, that was a
narrow shave, but I'm still here and clucking—good lord, no,
I'm not; I'm dead ! "

Morris, his reputation in the balance, avoided the Bedser
embarrassment by keeping away for a time from the wicket to

which Bedser bowled, thus exercising the discretion that is the better part of valour. While the ball remained shiny, he was content to watch Hassett deal with Bedser, which Hassett, the most soundly organised of Australia's batsmen to-day, did ably enough, though when he was only six a lovely outswinger from Bedser shook him. Warr again bowled hard, with an optimism quite heroic. If he could have lost weight at all he would have lost pounds. At the end of each over he sadly contemplated existence as it was being presented to him in the shape and terms of the Adelaide cushion of a wicket; he drooped but revived, and set about it, himself again, straining young nerve and sinew to the full. Yet the batsmen could play him with time to spare. One boundary, looked at from the wicket, probably was located on the horizon. Hassett and Morris did not appear to be concerned with any entertainment, either for their own or for the crowd's satisfaction. The match yawned. A brief little whirlwind on the far end of the field was the only proof afforded by the scene that nature, visible and adjacent, was not wholly inanimate. It was cricket that might well have been as per-manent, unchanging, and as devoid of human purpose as the eternal Lofty hills miles away. A full-toss by Tattersall, struck for four by Morris, was a noisy disturbance of the peace; and when Hassett positively pounced out of his crease to drive a no-ball from Wright for six I imagined I detected a momentary expression of disapproval falling as a shadow on one of the cathedral's two spires. A bird, a Willy Wagtail, ventured to the heart of the match, near the bowler, and remained there or there-abouts for quite a while; but probably needing some warmth of human or animal or vegetable contact he skimmed away to the crowded if not congested stand named after the immortal son of Adelaide, George Giffen, whom (we wished on a day like this) God had preserved.

Morris reached 50 in two hours and twenty minutes: he was combating not only England's efforts to get him out but his own recently exposed proneness to error. On the docile pitch he was free to move his legs anywhere, defying the foul fiend of science.

At last and at long last, Hassett, always a cricketer of tenacity whenever he comes to the wicket in a dubious hour, sunshine or cloud, fell to a catch at the wicket; moreover, he tried a cut. His innings of 43 consumed two hours twenty minutes. Morris here added some slight freedom of play to his persistent defence; he sent a ball from Bedser speeding for four—another cut!—and momentarily brought back to memory—momentarily, mind you—an almost legendary left-handed Australian batsman named Clem Hill.

The England attack stuck to the broiling task like galley slaves. Tattersall, in his first Test, though unable to spin on the cruel wicket, was steady and in technical control. His analysis for this Australian innings was three for 95 in twenty-six overs, a very good piece of work. Brown surprisingly contributed only three overs: and before the match had entered its fourth day he would join the team's hospital, victim of a motor-car accident, which is a fate that can easily befall anybody in Australia.

In some hundred minutes before tea, on this first day, the crowd sat in placid silence while the score crawled from 52 for one to 148 for two, and I wondered if any except peoples of the English race could witness so much pompous competence and not laugh or shrug it out of existence. The Frenchman who said we took our pleasures sadly never saw a contemporary Test match; think of it.

After tea, Morris, more resembling himself and not a near relation, glanced Wright prettily for four. Another stroke by Morris, a late cut off Wright—a short leg-break—was worthy of the summer afternoon passing before us like a dream. They can do it when they like. Morris came to the hundred he was pretty certain to make before the rubber was at an end; he took 215 minutes over it; but in the second half he recaptured nearly his nicest touch and even created the illusion towards six o'clock that we had been present at one of our national and manly field sports. But we hadn't.

Harvey began sketchily, again missing aim repeatedly. Then his innings assumed some certainty of shape and glow, much as a candle after much sputtering in the wax, comes to a flame, steady if susceptible to draughts. Bedser bowled him at 5.15 precisely —quarter-past seven on a foggy and bitter morning in England. Australia 205 for three : Miller came forth, no part of his body moving except his legs, with toes pointing straight ahead. He was cheered lustily by schoolboys naturally rather tired of looking at middle-aged sobriety. He drove Warr at once, a low swift swoop of a forward drive, and ran four like the wind, cheating the ball which stopped short of the boundary. His every movement told of a cricketer who, if he had his way, would change even a Test match of these times into occasions of challenge, hazard and chivalry.

SECOND DAY

AUSTRALIA—First Innings

K. Archer, c. Compton, b. Bedser	..	..	..	0
A. R. Morris, b. Tattersall	..	..	..	206
A. L. Hassett, c. Evans, b. Wright	..	..	..	43
R. N. Harvey, b. Bedser ..	..	..	..	43
K. R. Miller, c. Brown, b. Wright	..	..	..	44
J. Burke, b. Tattersall	..	..	..	12
I. W. Johnson, c. Evans, b. Bedser	..	..	..	16
R. R. Lindwall, l.b.w., b. Wright	..	..	..	1
D. Tallon, b. Tattersall ..	..	..	..	1
W. A. Johnston, c. Hutton, b. Wright ..	..	..	..	0
J. Iverson, not out	..	..	..	0
Extras (b. 2, l.b. 1, n.b. 1, w. 1)	..	..	..	5
Total	..	..	..	371

FALL OF WICKETS.—1—0, 2—95, 3—205, 4—281, 5—310, 6—357, 7—363, 8—366, 9—367, 10—371.

BOWLING.—Bedser, 26—4—74—3 ; Warr, 16—2—63—0 ; Wright, 25—1—99—4 ; Tattersall, 25.5—5—95—3 ; Brown, 3—0—24—0 ; Compton, 1—0—11—0.

ENGLAND—First Innings

Hutton, not out ..	..	..	..	..	56
Washbrook, c. Iverson, b. Lindwall	..	..	..	2
R. T. Simpson, b. Johnston	..	..	..	29
Compton, not out	..	..	..	5
Extras (l.b. 3, n.b. 1) ..	..	..	..	4
Total (for 2 wkts.) ..	..	..	..	96

D. S. Sheppard, F. R. Brown, Evans, Bedser, J. J. Warr,
Wright and Tattersall to go in.

FALL OF WICKETS.—1—7, 2—80.

BOWLING (to date).—Lindwall, 5—0—23—1 ; Miller,
7—2—18—0 ; Johnson, 8—0—26—0 ; Iverson, 9—2—
20—0 ; Johnston, 5—2—5—1.

Again a morning of hot sunshine which, one could have
imagined, consumed the world. Australia 254 for three wickets :
Morris, with a hundred already behind him, and Miller to tackle
on an inhumanly sedative pitch—once more our hearts bled for
the bowlers, for now for sure the long-promised or long-
threatened (according to the point of view) massacre by Miller
of Bedser, Brown, Wright and one and all was upon us. Miller,
whom even a contemporary Test match has not yet altogether
chastened, though his wings may be losing feathers from beating
many days against the iron bars of precaution and efficiency, hit
boundaries from the first three balls of the day, each bowled by
Bedser, one of them the longest long-hop ever bowled by Bedser.
Miller from his back foot struck it to the off, and the speed of
the stroke deceived us about its power. The fieldsman at cover
could merely turn round and look at the ball as it went by ;
apparently he was turned to stone.

But Wright in two clever overs furrowed Miller's narrow
brow, and Miller's eyes were knit together as he tightened his
grip, bent a little closer to his bat, and peered down the pitch
at Wright, but with time to fling his mane of hair back over his
head with a sweep of the left hand. Miller doesn't really like a
ball that now and again tends to spin away or possesses the
flight and curve in the air which asks questions. His technique
is not complex, and it thrives best on speed and a direct line of
attack. Wright thumped Miller's pads with his second ball. His
fifth whipped past perilously close to a bat which was drawn
suddenly away from the line of a leg-break as though stung.

A few moments later Wright hit Miller's pads again, also his
body. The brilliance abruptly fused, so to say. Morris took
charge of the bowling for a while, not drastically, for it was

very good. An interruption while another ball was found to take the place of a damaged one was an additional check or hiatus. When the cork is drawn and the " fizz " splutters, the champagne should not be allowed to remain still and go flat. Miller's rhythm was indeed broken ; he tried to return to his original key and tempo by means of a sweep to leg from Wright. The hit carried no farther than Brown at forward fine-leg, and the catch was held on the second attempt. Wright deserved this wicket ; but another eclipse of Miller was a sad loss to a match sorely in need of light and felicity. After his departure even the shadow cast by the magnitude of Morris's innings could not hide much mediocrity in Australia's batting. Morris reached 200, out of a total of 365, in seven hours twenty-five minutes ; he was educated and perfect of taste all the time and not more interesting than is suggested by these terms. But only a very good player is able at the pinch to reassert himself, confound his critics, clear his own mind of unease, and discover at the right moment the best in him. England's bowlers, yet again, utterly staggered the expectations and fondest wishes of their closest friends. Australia lost seven wickets for 117 after the day's effervescent beginning at 254 for three. Wright, four for 99 in twenty-five overs, seldom bowled an over which didn't at least once tax not only footwork but brainwork. Tattersall, accurate and intelligent for the most part, bowled Tallon with a rasping top-spinner. No batsman, except Miller, suggested he was prepared to risk something to find the boundary. At one period, in fact, the Australian innings was becoming porcine ; the bulk was provided by Morris, the others were the litter. After the counter-attack of England, which changed a menacing score of the first day to one which put a true value on a preponderant mediocrity, Washbrook failed once more, caught for two on the leg-side off Lindwall from a stroke which has often been his undoing ; and what is more, caught by Iverson nimbly and dexterously. So, as usual, an England innings was born in travail, the wet-nursing in the hands of Hutton. Simpson might have been soon caught and bowled by Iverson if Iverson had

equalled his best efforts as a fieldsman. More peculiar still was
the behaviour of Hutton, who mingled superb strokes with a
nerve-taxing dubiousness against Ian Johnson. This bowler
bothered Hutton throughout the rubber. Hutton played him on
this occasion from behind the crease, poking and pushing. When
he did go out to Johnson he missed the spin completely and
Tallon should have stumped him by yards. Hutton was then
34; had he gone England would have been 55 for two. And
half an hour from six o'clock a cunningly flighted ball from
W. Johnston deceived and bowled Simpson. Johnston is no
slave to seam and new balls. We wended our way home hoping
Compton on Monday would conquer himself and be inspired by
the example of Morris.

THIRD DAY

AUSTRALIA

First Innings		Second Innings				
K. Archer, c. Compton, b. Bedser..	0	not out	..	..	..	.. 12
A. R. Morris, b. Tattersall	.. 206	run out	..	..	..	.. 16
A. L. Hassett, c. Evans, b. Wright	43	not out	..	..	..	.. 5
R. N. Harvey, b. Bedser ..	.. 43					
K. R. Miller, c. Brown, b. Wright	44					
J. Burke, b. Tattersall ..	.. 12					
I. W. Johnson, c. Evans, b. Bedser	16					
R. R. Lindwall, l.b.w., b. Wright..	1					
D. Tallon, b. Tattersall ..	.. 1					
W. A. Johnston, c. Hutton, b.						
Wright	.. 0					
J. Iverson, not out	.. 0					
Extras (b. 2, l.b. 1, n.b. 1, w. 1)	5	Extras (b. 1)	..	..	..	1
	—					—
Total	.. 371	Total (1 wkt.)		..	..	34

FALL OF WICKETS—First Innings.—1—0, 2—95, 3—205, 4—281, 5—310,
6—357, 7—363, 8—366, 9—367, 10—371.

Second Innings.—1—26.

BOWLING—First Innings.—Bedser, 26—4—74—3; Warr, 16—2—63—0;
Wright, 25—1—99—4; Tattersall, 25.5—5—95—3; Brown, 3—0—24—0;
Compton, 1—0—11—0.

Second Innings (to date).—Bedser, 5—3—6—0; Warr, 2—0—10—0; Wright,
3—0—16—0; Tattersall, 1—0—1—0.

ADELAIDE

ENGLAND—First Innings

Hutton, not out	156
Washbrook, c. Iverson, b. Lindwall	2
R. T. Simpson, b. Johnston	29
Compton, c. Tallon, b. Lindwall	5
D. S. Sheppard, b. Iverson	9
F. R. Brown, b. Miller	16
Evans, c. Burke, b. Johnston	13
Bedser, l.b.w., b. Iverson	7
Tattersall, c. Harvey, b. Iverson	0
J. J. Warr, b. Johnston	0
Wright, l.b.w., b. Lindwall	14
Extras (b. 15, l.b. 5, n.b. 1)	21
Total	272

FALL OF WICKETS.—1—7, 2—80, 3—96, 4—132, 5—161, 6—195, 7—206, 8—214, 9—219, 10—272.

BOWLING.—Lindwall, 13.3—0—51—3; Miller, 13—2 —36—1; Johnson, 15—2—38—0; Iverson, 26—4—68—3; Johnston, 25—4—58—3.

It was, as usual, left to Hutton to render an England inning vertebrate: the rest lacked backbone and applied technique, on a turf so good that "W.G." wouldn't have expected or wished the like of it in the next world, let alone this. Wright helped Hutton to hold the last wicket while the score was stiffened by 53 and gave us very plainly to understand how the moderate bowling might have fared if tackled with aggression. But aggression seems fashionable everywhere nowadays except in Test matches between England and Australia.

Hutton was not out 156, after six hours ten minutes, and is now one of the only two England cricketers ever to carry a bat through a Test match innings against Australia. The other was Bobby Abel, and his bat was supposed to be crooked.

The fourth ball of the morning, bowled by Lindwall, produced a feeling of tragic misfortune suffered not only in person, but generally. Compton was caught at the wicket, anxiously glancing to leg. Fortune so far from being blind sometimes seems to hunt out a chosen victim and pursue him pitilessly. Only the cynic is likely to say that in such cases the fault, dear Brutus, is not in our stars. Poor Compton came back to the pavilion on a heavenly day—came back disconsolate on the field where, four years before, he had scored two centuries for England. Not for nothing do I call this the Ironic Rubber. Compton might have found some ameliorating philosophy in the knowledge that Victor Trumper was once dismissed in three consecutive Test match innings for noughts, including a " pair of spectacles " administered by S. F. Barnes and J. N. Crawford. And Fuller Pilch was once discovered during a period of failure stretched on the grass under a tree crying : " O I shall never score a run again ! "

As soon as Sheppard faced the situation he nearly ran Hutton out, but he kept his nerve and for nearly an hour he used a straight bat, surviving mainly by resisting all allurements until Iverson tempted him with a half-volley which he missed fatally by driving across the line, head moving up rather than down. Hutton was as austere as skilful : there was a long vacant space on the on-side between leg and mid-on. I couldn't imagine any batsman, as strongly fortified in spirit as in technique, allowing his dignity to be impeached as openly as this. Brown, according to his custom, showed belligerence in a straight drive off Miller ; and so Miller bowled him off his pads. Just before lunch another old ball was called for even though a new one was legally permissible ; and after lunch and after the new ball had been in play about half an hour, this was exchanged for yet another ball of equivalent condition and aspect. I have in my time known the need in cricket matches of several fresh bats, but never before of so many balls in so short a time. It is said that Augustine Birrell, last of the nineteenth-century essayists and a statesman and scholar, once broke a borrowed bat while playing for J. M. Barrie ; moreover, he had never handled a bat before, and when he had broken this one, he brandished the splintered blade at the pavilion, calling out : " Bring me some more bats."

Evans pranced up and down and gave his wicket away, not for the first time. He seems occasionally a little light-headed. When Hutton saw that the other end of the wicket was in the care of those of his colleagues who were in the team for reasons not closely connected with batsmanship, he enlivened his style just a little, though it was clear that he was set on an undefeated innings if they had to trample the life out of him. We are bound, while we praise him, to deplore that this thoroughbred cricketer was not playing during the period when he would have been constantly in the company of those who were not only masters of all the strokes, but considered it a point of honour constantly to make them, fair weather or foul. Hutton is not inferior in artistry to any or most of them. But the best of us are influenced, no matter how little, by environment and by precept and example.

FOURTH DAY

AUSTRALIA

FIRST INNINGS		SECOND INNINGS	
K. Archer, c. Compton, b. Bedser	0	c. Bedser, b. Tattersall	32
A. R. Morris, b. Tattersall	206	run out	16
A. L. Hassett, c. Evans, b. Wright	43	l.b.w., b. Wright	31
R. N. Harvey, b. Bedser	43	b. Brown	68
K. R. Miller, c. Brown, b. Wright	44	hit wkt., b. Wright	99
J. Burke, b. Tattersall	12	not out	37
I. W. Johnson, c. Evans, b. Bedser	16	not out	1
R. R. Lindwall, l.b.w., b. Wright	1		
D. Tallon, b. Tattersall	1		
W. A. Johnston, c. Hutton, b. Wright	0		
J. Iverson, not out	0		
Extras (b. 2, l.b. 1, n.b. 1, w. 1)	5	Extras (b. 1)	1
Total	371	Total (5 wkts.)	285

FALL OF WICKETS—FIRST INNINGS.—1—0, 2—95, 3—205, 4—281, 5—310, 6—357, 7—363, 8—366, 9—367, 10—371.
SECOND INNINGS.—1—26, 2—79, 3—95, 4—194, 5—281.

BOWLING—FIRST INNINGS.—Bedser, 26—4—74—3 ; Warr, 16—2—63—0 ; Wright, 25—1—99—4 ; Tattersall, 25.5—5—95—3 ; Brown, 3—0—24—0 ; Compton, 1—0—11—0.
SECOND INNINGS (to date).—Bedser, 19—4—62—0 ; Warr, 15—0—55—0 ; Wright, 19—2—85—2 ; Tattersall, 18—1—78—1 ; Brown, 3—1—41—1.

ENGLAND—First Innings

Hutton, not out	..	..	..	156
Washbrook, c. Iverson, b. Lindwall	..	..	..	2
R. T. Simpson, b. Johnston ..	..	..	..	29
Compton, c. Tallon, b. Lindwall	..	..	..	5
D. S. Sheppard, b. Iverson	..	..	..	9
F. R. Brown, b. Miller ..	..	..	..	16
Evans, c. Burke, b. Johnston ..	..	..	..	13
Bedser, l.b.w., b. Iverson	..	..	..	7
Tattersall, c. Harvey, b. Iverson	..	..	..	0
J. J. Warr, b. Johnston ..	..	..	..	0
Wright, l.b.w., b. Lindwall	..	..	..	14
Extras (b. 15, l.b. 5, n.b. 1) ..	..	..	..	21
Total	..	..	..	272

FALL OF WICKETS.—1—7, 2—80, 3—96, 4—132, 5—161, 6—195, 7—206, 8—214, 9—219, 10—272.

BOWLING.—Lindwall, 13.3—0—51—3 ; Miller, 13—2—36—1 ; Johnson, 15—2—38—0 ; Iverson, 26—4—68—3; Johnston, 25—4—58—3.

Australia, leading by 133, took no risks while they made assurances doubly—not to say trebly—sure in their second innings. Apart from Harvey and a comparatively austere yet recognisable Keith Miller, it was again not an easy day to sit through without unashamed yawns and dreams of what might have happened, and what indeed has often happened on this same beautiful field in the past. For ninety minutes the match dragged drearily ; Hassett and Archer did nothing in particular against Bedser and Warr on the drowsy couch of the wicket ; and when Wright was at last asked to bowl they continued to do nothing in particular and they didn't do it very well. In an hour and a half 68 runs were added to Australia's 34 for one—Monday's close of play—with only one boundary hit and only one attempt at a boundary hit.

The match seemed becalmed. Presumably the Australian batting was once more putting into practice " a wearing-out process " calculated to grind the wicket to dust and the England attack with it. The policy these days is not so much to score many runs in Tests as to prevent others from scoring at all, At Adelaide such a " process " was as palpable and as arresting to the naked eye as the gradual but unending dissolution, disintegration and wear and tear going on minute by minute in the adjacent and dreamlike hills—and about as closely related to sport.

Wright heaved himself along the earth with strides that were not so much leaps as ponderous exhausting propellings from the earth ; time after time his arm cart-wheeled and the sweat poured from him. He bowled admirably, turning the ball now and again with, of course, loose stuff as the price to pay for finger and wrist spin on such a turf. He beat Hassett from the moment the ball left his hand : Hassett, quite baffled, sought to hide behind his pads—and he is tiny enough—and though he was l.b.w. it was as good and clinching as a flattened middle-stump. Archer had, sixteen runs earlier than this, been caught on the on-side driving boldly at Tattersall ; possibly he was a victim of some psychological reaction. Even a contemporary batsman is subject to changes of blood-pressure.

At lunch Australia's score was 102 for three. Off seventy-seven balls from Bedser, nineteen runs were scored by a team which, having already won the rubber, might have been expected by those not " in the know " to risk a generous gesture. . . . Such thoughts or fancies may have passed through the minds of Harvey and Miller, for the match actually acquired some lustre and style after lunch. Harvey, who seldom is unwilling to play cricket, given the cue, put bloom on to his strokes—long-armed drives all the more appealing because not absolutely " safe." Harvey is out of his period ; a decade or two ago he would have been encouraged in a Test match, if his side stood in an advantageous position, to bat on the rim of security to his heart's content, and good luck to you ! He reached 50 in an hour and a half, what time Miller chafed much on the leash, while Warr bowled wide. In the nick of time Harvey and Miller reclaimed the Australian innings to the side of the angels of sportsmanship. The game seemed to spring into the gleaming sunshine of the afternoon ; Harvey used his feet, dancing on his toes, and his bat scintillated in the light. Miller, if he contented himself with a checked forward action, a thrust rather than a drive, arrested our attention. He cannot bore us, for at those times when he is scoring slowly we wonder why, and get ready for a sudden explosion of impatience. This Harvey-Miller stand promised a really flamboyant assault every over, plunder and plumage. It ended abruptly when Brown came on and bowled Harvey. Still, Harvey had cleared the air, so that we could see in the proceedings some family resemblance to a game. Miller reached 50 in an hour and fifty minutes ; in comparison with the sluggishness which had preceded him, he created the illusion, almost, of Keith Miller. He, at any rate, occasionally taxed the quickness of our vision to appreciate to the full his downward darting late-cut.

After tea attrition set in once more. Burke naturally could do nothing about it ; in his first Test match he had to deal with two enemies : his own inexperience and anxiety as well as the bowling. We didn't suspect it yet but he was, before long, to astonish us and, doubtless, himself. Miller, one short of his hundred, chopped a ball on to his stump. His innings lasted nearly three hours and a half, a long time for Miller, but champagne after the small beer of What's-his-Name and Never Mind. Miller seemed just for a moment disappointed that he had missed a century so narrowly, then he tossed his head and his hair and came back to the pavilion apparently without a care in the world. Perhaps he remembered that Clem Hill once scored, in three consecutive Test innings, 99, 98 and 97—98 and 97 in one and the same match.

FIFTH DAY

AUSTRALIA

First Innings		Second Innings		
K. Archer, c. Compton, b. Bedser	0	c. Bedser, b. Tattersall	..	32
A. R. Morris, b. Tattersall	.. 206	run out ..	..	16
A. L. Hassett, c. Evans, b. Wright	43	l.b.w., b. Wright ..	..	31
R. N. Harvey, b. Bedser ..	.. 43	b. Brown ..	..	68
K. R. Miller, c. Brown, b. Wright	44	b. Wright ..	..	99

ADELAIDE

J. Burke, b. Tattersall 12	not out 101
I. W. Johnson, c. Evans, b. Bedser 16	c. Evans, b. Warr 3
R. R. Lindwall, l.b.w., b. Wright.. 1	run out 31
D. Tallon, b. Tattersall 1	c. Hutton, b. Compton 5
W. A. Johnston, c. Hutton, b.	
Wright 0	not out 9
J. Iverson, not out 0	
Extras (b. 2, l.b. 1, n.b. 1, w. 1) 5	Extras (b. 7, l.b. 1) 8
Total 371	Total (8 wkts. dec.) 403

FALL OF WICKETS—First Innings.—1—0, 2—95, 3—205, 4—281, 5—310, 6—357, 7—363, 8—366, 9—367, 10—371.

Second Innings.—1—26, 2—79, 3—95, 4—194, 5—281, 6—297, 7—367, 8—378.

BOWLING—First Innings.—Bedser, 26—4—74—3 ; Warr, 16—2—63—0 ; Wright, 25—1—99—4 ; Tattersall, 25.5—5—95—3 ; Brown, 3—0—24—0 ; Compton, 1—0—11—0.

Second Innings.—Bedser, 25—6—62—0 ; Warr, 21—0—76—1 ; Wright, 21—2—109—2 ; Tattersall, 27—2—116—1 ; Brown, 3—1—14—1 ; Compton, 4.6—0—18—1.

ENGLAND

First Innings	Second Innings
Hutton, not out 156	c. sub., b. Johnston 45
Washbrook, c. Iverson, b. Lindwall 2	l.b.w., b. Johnston 31
R. T. Simpson, b. Johnston .. 29	not out 23
Compton, c. Tallon, b. Lindwall .. 5	c. sub., b. Johnston 0
D. S. Sheppard, b. Iverson .. 9	not out 6
F. R. Brown, b. Miller 16	
Evans, c. Burke, b. Johnston .. 13	
Bedser, l.b.w., b. Iverson 7	
Tattersall, c. Harvey, b. Iverson .. 0	
J. J. Warr, b. Johnston 0	
Wright, l.b.w., b. Lindwall .. 14	
Extras (b. 15, l.b. 5, n.b. 1) .. 21	Extras (b. 6, n.b. 3) 9
Total 272	Total (for 3 wkts.) 114

FALL OF WICKETS—First Innings.—1—7, 2—80, 3—96, 4—132, 5—161, 6—195, 7—206, 8—214, 9—219, 10—272.

Second Innings.—1—74, 2—90, 3—90.

BOWLING—First Innings.—Lindwall, 13.3—0—51—3 ; Miller, 13—2—36—1 ; Johnson, 15—2—38—0 ; Iverson, 26—4—68—3 ; Johnston, 25—4—58—3.

Second Innings (to date).—Lindwall, 5—1—19—0 ; Miller, 7—1—17—0 ; Johnston, 13—2—30—3 ; Burke, 3—1—7—0 ; Johnson, 14—4—32—0.

Australia's innings was extended beyond lunch only to give young Burke the chance of scoring a century in his first match; and right well and surely he seized it. But I was reminded of Makepeace, of Lancashire, who in one of his first seasons was 99 not out at lunch against Essex and he had not yet scored a century for his county. None the less, A. C. Maclaren declared the Lancashire innings at an end during the interval, then he went to Makepeace and said : " Sorry, Makepeace, but we've got to win this match and my team must be my first consideration. Well played—besides, don't worry. You'll get your century for Lancashire before long." And added, after a pause : " And if you don't I'll bloody well sack you."

Apart from Burke's innings, sprouting with promise of defence and stroke-play, the only event of the latter part of Australia's second innings was Warr's first wicket in a Test match : he had bowled for it since the New Year, bowled innumerable persevering overs for it, and it cost him more than 250 runs. He got Ian Johnson caught at the wicket ; and the umpire hesitated before announcing a verdict in Warr's favour. Possibly the umpire thought the news had best be broken gently. Maybe something like the following conversation ensued :

" Are you in good health, Mr. Warr ? "

" Yes."

" Heart sound ? "

" Quite."

" Very well, sir, I'll put my finger up."

Just before three o'clock England went in again, to try to bat seven hours to avoid defeat or to score 503 to win. Iverson could not take the field, the latest victim of this increasingly dangerous game known as Test cricket. He damaged an ankle at practice, treading on a ball in an attempt to stop it with one of his boots. Hutton immediately forced Lindwall square to the on for four and drove him straight to the boundary. Some of Hutton's finest hits, if not all of them in this rubber, were from Lindwall's bowling. Washbrook didn't make a run for twenty minutes, whereat he drove W. Johnston over the on-boundary for six, without due and fair warning. Our cricketers, who day by day are our joy and despair, frequently behave according to uncharted or uncodified psychological laws ; they seldom dream of hitting for six when they are comfortably established on a good wicket and their team is as soundly placed as the Great Pyramid. Ian Johnson, as usual, disturbed Hutton's poise and rhythm as soon as he came on, but Hutton, all the same, drove him for four, moving forward on feet that might have been padded like a cat's. My sympathies at this moment were all for the poor moist bowlers, mad dogs of Australians running about in the sun, 90 degrees in the shade. If the wicket was of any use to bowlers, only Iverson from the cool shade of the pavilion could have told us why and where.

As the afternoon mellowed and the shadows of the cricketers became not pools of black velvet on the grass but miniatures or silhouettes of themselves drawn out of scale, it was pleasant to sit back and watch Hutton's strokes. He seemed more than usually ready to attack the loose ball and, somehow, I wasn't surprised when a pull intended to reach the boundary provided means for a splendid catch by Loxton (substitute—as Ko-Ko says), who leaped upwards and held the ball in one hand. Then the damnably iterative anti-climax occurred in the England innings. Washbrook played back and across a good length from W. Johnston and perished l.b.w. Worse still and shocking and sad, Compton steered, spooned, patted—what you will—his second ball straight into the hands of forward short-leg. Compton expressed dismay ; and the hearts of many lovers of the game were sorely with him. But why didn't he " chance it," try to blaze his way back into form, damning the consequences ?

So the bottom fell out of the match with a dreadful sub-sidence. Tallon missed stumping Simpson a yard out of the crease off Ian Johnson, though goodness knows where Simpson thought he was going. Against a ball now gently and not for-midably spinning, creeping paralysis afflicted England's batting. Ramadhin, Valentine, W. Johnston, Ian Johnson—who next ?

SIXTH DAY

AUSTRALIA

First Innings		Second Innings	
K. Archer, c. Compton, b. Bedser	0	c. Bedser, b. Tattersall	32
A. R. Morris, b. Tattersall ..	206	run out	16
A. L. Hassett, c. Evans, b. Wright	43	l.b.w., b. Wright	31
R. N. Harvey, b. Bedser	43	b. Brown	68
K. R. Miller, c. Brown, b. Wright	44	b. Wright	99
J. Burke, b. Tattersall	12	not out	101
I. W. Johnson, c. Evans, b. Bedser	16	c. Evans, b. Warr	3
R. R. Lindwall, l.b.w., b. Wright..	1	run out	31
D. Tallon, b. Tattersall	1	c. Hutton, b. Compton	5
W. A. Johnston, c. Hutton, b. Wright	0	not out	9
J. Iverson, not out	0		
Extras (b. 2, l.b. 1, n.b. 1, w. 1)	5	Extras (b. 7, l.b. 1)	8
Total	371	Total (8 wkts. dec.)	403

FALL OF WICKETS—First Innings.—1—0, 2—95, 3—205, 4—281, 5—310, 6—357, 7—363, 8—366, 9—367, 10—371.

Second Innings.—1—26, 2—79, 3—95, 4—194, 5—281, 6—297, 7—367, 8—378.

BOWLING—First Innings.—Bedser, 26—4—74—3 ; Warr, 16—2—63—0 ; Wright, 25—1—99—4; Tattersall, 25.5—5—95—3; Brown, 3—0—24—0; Compton, 1—0—11—0.

Second Innings.—Bedser, 25—6—62—0 ; Warr, 21—0—76—1 ; Wright, 21—2—109—2 ; Tattersall, 27—2—116—1 ; Brown, 3—1—14—1 ; Compton, 4.6—0—18—1.

ENGLAND

First Innings		Second Innings	
Hutton, not out	156	c. sub., b. Johnston	45
Washbrook, c. Iverson, b. Lindwall	2	l.b.w., b. Johnston	31
R. T. Simpson, b. Johnston ..	29	c. Burke, b. Johnston	61
Compton, c. Tallon, b. Lindwall ..	5	c. sub., b. Johnston	0
D. S. Sheppard, b. Iverson ..	9	l.b.w., b. Miller	41
F. R. Brown, b. Miller	16	absent hurt	0
Evans, c. Burke, b. Johnston ..	13	c. Johnson, b. Miller	21
Bedser, l.b.w., b. Iverson	7	c. Morris, b. Miller	0
Tattersall, c. Harvey, b. Iverson ..	0	c. Morris, b. Johnson	6
J. J. Warr, b. Johnston	0	b. Johnson	0
Wright, l.b.w., b. Lindwall ..	14	not out	0
Extras (b. 15, l.b. 5, n.b. 1) ..	21	Extras (b. 15, l.b. 3, n.b. 3, w. 2)	23
Total	272	Total	228

FALL OF WICKETS—First Innings.—1—7, 2—80, 3—96, 4—132, 5—161, 6—195, 7—206, 8—214, 9—219, 10—272.

Second Innings.—1—74, 2—90, 3—90, 4—181, 5—221, 6—221, 7—228, 8—228, 9—228.

BOWLING—First Innings.—Lindwall, 13.3—0—51—3 ; Miller, 13—2—36—1 ; Johnson, 15—2—38—0 ; Iverson, 26—4—68—3 ; Johnston, 25—4—58—3.

Second Innings.—Lindwall, 10—3—35—0 ; Miller, 13—4—27—3 ; Johnson, 25.6—6—63—2 ; Johnston, 27—4—73—4 ; Burke, 3—1—7—0.

If England had contrived to make a draw in spite of the loss overnight of Hutton and Compton I shouldn't have described the performance as more than meritorious. The match was surrendered after a reassuring stand by Simpson and Sheppard, who seemed so unlikely to get out that the Australian attack began to look as though in need of attention from the Official Receiver. Then on the verge of 1.30, the last over before lunch, if Simpson didn't take leave of his senses and strike most injudiciously at a ball which he could have played defensively, or left entirely alone, with a broomstick. He was caught from a feeble " skier " on the off-side. Simpson had shown us several excellent strokes ; and twice in the over of his ruin he drove Johnston straight for fours. Wine—rare wine for him so far in the rubber —went to the head. Sheppard improved in method as soon as he moved his feet forward and ceased to lunge into the obscure. He began to allow his bat freedom of swing and, ball by ball, he grew in confidence. Had it not been for Simpson's rashness, this fourth wicket stand surely should have—but the history of England's batting this rubber prompted never-ending and painful conjecture.

Evans, in a shapeless white hat, battled for a while and England rounded 200 with only four wickets down. I was wondering now whether Iverson would be called on by Hassett, even if in a bath-chair ; and there is a precedent in cricket for so extraordinary a resort. David Harris, of Hambledon, once bowled in a match at a ripe age, and after each over reposed in a chair near the square-leg umpire, whence he looked on with interest and dignity until it was his turn to bowl again.

Miller, unpredictable by prophecy, stars in their courses, cards, palm of the hand, or tea-leaves in the cup, changed the day—the phrase comes back to my ears, as I write it down, like an echo. So far he and Lindwall had used the new ball with an almost cynical regard for the conservation of energy on a hot day. Miller, with the old ball, took a few paces, turned round, and bowled medium-pace off-breaks as though for fun. He was aided and abetted by one or two batsmen who seemed to suggest, with equal frankness, that hard work, concentrated and tiring, would scarcely prove worth while in the circumstances. Bedser swung his bat quite aimlessly at his first ball and, like Simpson, sent a gift of a catch to the off-side, not far away. D. R. Jardine, had he been present and captain, would have awaited Bedser's return to the pavilion with a countenance stern and Caledonian, if not wild. Evans snicked Miller to first-slip and Miller trapped Sheppard l.b.w. So the inglorious end—not to be cast out of memory by the victory a week or two afterwards at Melbourne. Sheppard was able to hold off the Australian bowlers for three hours; that he was able to do so much, in his first Test match, says little for the fighting temper of certain of his colleagues. Brown was, of course, absent and obviously badly wanted. Seldom have I left a cricket field more disgusted.

Chapter Fifteen

FIFTH TEST

THE VICTORY at Melbourne in the fifth match provoked rejoicings not less in Australia than in England. We deserved it ; for with all their faults, Brown and his men played better cricket than might have been signified by five defeats. From Brisbane to Perth there was a widespread relief that after thirteen years Australia had at last been forced to their knees by their oldest and most respected opponent at cricket. Her players, it was generally thought, had become complacent ; and indeed I could find evidence amongst them, during this very match which revealed their vulnerability, that one or two of them were until the crisis slackening, consciously or subconsciously, the will to win both on and off the field. Not until the writing could unmistakably be seen on the wall did I get a sense of the authentic Australian concentration and ruthlessness. One of the turning points—if not *the* crucial turning point—occurred when in England's first innings Tattersall was able to stay in while 74 runs were scored for the last wicket. The ninth wicket fell at 246 and England's lead, with Australia to bat again, was merely 29. Tattersall put a straight bat to the ball and let us understand that he comes from Lancashire, so cleverly did he smother spin and frustrate a leg-side field. Simpson then took charge, and for the first time in the rubber liberated his fine range of strokes. But is anybody prepared to believe that if England had needed not 74 to win but half that amount, and only Tattersall to hold one end of the crease—is anybody in his senses prepared to believe England would have won, with the rubber undecided ? Without detraction from Simpson's superb innings, I go so far as to doubt if he, let alone Tattersall, could have then wrested victory from the Australian grip. After all, in this Melbourne match the onus was on England to make a supreme effort ; psychological pressure was on their side. I'm not saying that Australia didn't " try " ; but there are different ways and temperatures of effort. Australians know better than cricketers anywhere that needs must when the devil drives.

The victory was hailed in England as a sign of the turning of the tide in our Test match fortunes and recent history, as the rising star of a new and better day. So it may have seemed to those who read the good news on a cold foggy morning at the dimly illuminated breakfast table. But in Australia we could see things differently. While the Sydney and Adelaide defeats still rankled, because of England's open avowal of little stomach for a fight, this triumph at Melbourne appeared to some of us to be not more than, in the revealing glare of an Australian day of summer, the sudden splutter of a burnt-out candle. Even Simpson's 156 not out was, from one point of view, the last and most acid dose of irony : if only at Brisbane and Melbourne ! . . . when he was as starved for strokes as charity. As we cheered his undefeated century and admired the ease and style which went to its making, we could understand that he was asserting himself with mixed feelings and regrets.

FIRST DAY

AUSTRALIA—First Innings

J. Burke, c. Tattersall, b. Bedser	..	..	.. 11
A. R. Morris, l.b.w., b. Brown ..	..	..	.. 50
A. L. Hassett, c. Hutton, b. Brown	..	..	.. 92
R. N. Harvey, c. Evans, b. Brown	..	..	.. 1
K. R. Miller, c. and b. Brown ..	..	..	.. 7
G. Hole, b. Bedser	..	..	.. 18
I. W. Johnson, l.b.w., b. Bedser	..	..	.. 1

R. R. Lindwall, not out 18
D. Tallon, c. Hutton, b. Bedser 1
W. A. Johnston, not out 4
Extras (b. 2, l.b. 1) 3

Total (8 wkts.) 206
J. Iverson to go in.

FALL OF WICKETS.—1—23, 2—111, 3—115, 4—123,
5—156, 6—166, 7—184, 8—187.

BOWLING (to date).—Bailey, 9—1—29—0; Bedser,
20—4—44—4; Brown, 15—4—40—4; Wright, 9—1—
50—0; Tattersall, 11—3—40—0.

ENGLAND.—F. R. Brown, Compton, Hutton, Washbrook, R. T. Simpson, D. S. Sheppard, Evans, T. E. Bailey,
Bedser, Tattersall, Wright. *Twelfth Man*—McIntyre.

Again Australia won the toss and again the batting was
funereal; though the rubber had died the death weeks since,
an unconscionable time was being taken disposing of the body.
The lack of energy and enterprise in the Australian innings was
scarcely a fair recognition of the capital England attack on a
wicket so lifeless that to bowl on it must have conveyed the sort
of sensation obtained from working on one of those noiseless
typewriting machines. Admittedly not a lot of loose stuff was
sent down by Bedser, Bailey, Wright and Brown; but do Test
match batsmen of the present generation need half-volleys and
long-hops to encourage them to some attempt at handsome
entertaining strokes? Do they believe that Bradman, McCabe,
Kippax, Archie Jackson, Woolley, Hammond—to mention
recent names without remembering the fabulous Trumper,
Tyldesley and K. L. Hutchings—do they really believe that these
great players of the day before yesterday could drive, cut and
glance and pull only rubbish? If they do believe as much, then
I must quote the remark of the Great Duke, who when a man
came up to him one night in Willis's Rooms and said, "Dr.
Jones, I believe?" replied, "Sir, if you believe that, you believe
anything."

Burke was caught at ten minutes to one at short forward-leg
off Bedser: I had now become quite sick of the sight of this

fashionable and stupidly dangerous push-stroke, speculative and congested, legs in front of the wicket, bat blind in front of the pads, and moving across the line and actually *steering* the ball to the expectant fieldsman.

Hassett also groped at Bedser's inswinger ; Bedser from time to time caused us to imagine that the pitch contained some resilient foreign body ; but this was proof, yet again and more, of his art. The toil went on and on under the cloudless sky, interrupted only by refreshments, brought out no doubt as sustenance every forty-five minutes. The threat of an approaching storm in mid-afternoon probably galvanised Hassett into a sudden and brief sequence of fine hits. (Every effect has a cause, deep laid though its operations.) These, our contemporary heroes of the cricket field, reverse the doctrine of Falstaff ; they become lions under compulsion. Hassett, who can play all the strokes, would, under different dispensation have been akin to J. T. Tyldesley, giving delight to thousands ; but instead he has distrusted his gifts, and provoked even his friends and admirers to almost unrelieved hours of boredom. In no other game except cricket do the great exponents deliberately, in a great contest and on a great occasion, withhold their best and most commanding ability.

The first hour of the day under notice produced 25 ; at lunch, after an hour and a half, Australia's total rested at 48 for one, Morris 25 not out. In two hours and three-quarters the 100 was attained : on this same ground in 1908, K. L. Hutchings, playing for England against Australia with Cotter, Noble, Armstrong, Saunders and Macartney, scored 126 in two and a quarter hours, with twenty-two fours and a six. But my mind is wandering again. Some plausible and quite scientifically argued excuses were put forward on behalf of all this dismal nonsense. W. J. O'Reilly and others maintained that the unusual slowness of the pitch, and its holding effect on the ball, " made it very difficult to make attacking strokes." Apparently the ball " wouldn't come quickly off the face of the bat." I have myself, in my innocence, imagined that it was the wielder of the willow

—as once on a time he was called, not altogether figuratively—
who put the force into the bat, which force, by the law of
dynamics or something or other, was immediately infused into
the ball. I can understand that the ball will not " come off "
the face of any bat if the said bat is held out only to deflect, or
obtain a ricochet. Clearly if the wicket is slow it will not
provide the motive-power of a speedy deflection, but only enough
to send the ball along the ground to the adjacent fieldsman. It
is essential, to obtain runs with destructive and effectual stroke-
play, to *hit* the ball hard from time to time. And why the contemporary reluctance to hit over the fieldsmen's heads, or into
the unprotected outfield ? Must every stroke be played on the
grass ? Even the scrupulously classic William Gunn loved, when
he was set, to drive over mid-off's head.

England's attack was again reduced when Bailey twisted a
foot while bowling ; he returned to the casualty ward he had
just left and in the match delivered only seventeen overs, nine
in Australia's first innings, eight in the second. So Brown, still
stiff from his accident in Adelaide, came into force once more,
according to precedent, and he split the becalmed Australian
ship as though a thunderbolt, or three thunderbolts, had been
aimed from the sky in a burst of bad temper by one of the watching and yawning gods of the game sitting on the Mount Olympus
of cricket. Brown so far had obviously not enjoyed himself in
the match ; once he tried to field by a sudden bending of the
body, and he shook off a twinge of pain like a pugilist shaking
off a nasty punch. He chased a hit with sweaty effort. Morris
and Hassett at half-past three were rooted to the earth ; they
had taken the score from 23 to 111, when Brown was chosen as
the instrument of justice. With the eighth ball of a maiden over
he seduced Morris into l.b.w. by means of a good length ball
that slightly turned from leg off the ground. Harvey, after a
single from Wright, cut hard at a medium-paced ball and sent
it into Evans' gloves, another maiden and wicket for the gallant
captain. Miller, obviously determined to put an end to all these
negations and abortions, drove Wright fiercely and gloriously

to the off-boundary, then confronting Brown, struck "too soon"—deceived as much by flight as the pace off the pitch—and was caught and bowled with the flourish of a farmer's boy. So Brown took three wickets for none in ten balls. Bravo, but who in Northamptonshire could be expected to believe it unsupported by evidence of the eye? Brown in this Australian summer changed his methods as a bowler, abandoned leg-spin and trusted mainly to length and seam-swing. Hutton, who from first-slip was in the best possible position to judge, expressed his surprise and admiration at the excellence of Brown's attack on the whole. But in the interests of truth and out of respect for standards set up in Test cricket in the past, Brown is not a bowler of the highest order; he himself would be the first to laugh at any excessive praise of his talents in this direction and class. I doubt if the great Sydney Barnes at his best could have removed Bradman, Ponsford and Woodfull in ten balls on a dead pitch. Did he ever, even at Melbourne in 1911, get three first-class players out in so quick a time? History answers in the negative.

Brown's face reddened not only because of the warmth of the afternoon and the elated occasion but because of the sunshine radiantly falling on him from the Indian summer of his career. We have to go back in the history of Test matches as far as F. S. Jackson to find an England captain of cricket who as a "change" or reserve bowler has equalled Brown's performances in this rubber. Hole, from Adelaide, held up his end for three-quarters of an hour in an unpleasant situation—his first Test match—and we hadn't to wait for his brilliant second innings to understand, that here was another Australian youth of much more than promise. Bedser bowled him with a swinging "yorker" and a new ball. Hassett was the next out; when he was 88 he drove Brown for a truly regal four to the off, and in the same over tried another but less drastic hit to the off, edged the stroke, which was clearing the slips when Hutton caught him shoulder high as the ball was speeding away. Had it not been for a few moments of vigour by Lindwall in the day's closing moments, Australia, in five hours, would have acquired even fewer than 206 for eight wickets. Hassett's innings of 92 lasted three hours and a half; its value in the current economy was beyond question, so was the skill and patience which were involved. But as I say, he should have been born heretofore!

THIRD DAY (SECOND DAY'S PLAY)

AUSTRALIA—FIRST INNINGS

J. Burke, c. Tattersall, b. Bedser	11
A. R. Morris, l.b.w., b. Brown	50
A. L. Hassett, c. Hutton, b. Brown	92
R. N. Harvey, c. Evans, b. Brown	1
K. R. Miller, c. and b. Brown	7
G. Hole, b. Bedser	18
I. W. Johnson, l.b.w., b. Bedser	1
R. R. Lindwall, c. Compton, b. Bedser	21
D. Tallon, c. Hutton, b. Bedser	1
W. A. Johnston, not out	12
J. Iverson, c. Washbrook, b. Brown	0
Extras (b. 2, l.b. 1)	3
Total	217

FALL OF WICKETS.—1—23, 2—111, 3—115, 4—123, 5—156, 6—166, 7—184, 8—187, 9—216, 10—217.

BOWLING.—Bedser, 22—5—46—5; Bailey, 9—1—29—0; Brown, 18—4—49—5; Wright, 9—1—50—0; Tattersall, 11—3—40—0.

ENGLAND—FIRST INNINGS

Hutton, b. Hole	79
Washbrook, c. Tallon, b. Miller	27
R. T. Simpson, not out	80
Compton, c. Miller, b. Lindwall	11
D. S. Sheppard, c. Tallon, b. Miller	1
F. R. Brown, b. Lindwall	6
Evans, b. Miller	1
Bedser, not out	3
Extras (b. 1, l.b. 9)	10
Total (for 6 wkts.)	218

T. E. Bailey, Tattersall, and Wright to go in.

FALL OF WICKETS.—1—40, 2—171, 3—204, 4—205,
5—212, 6—213.

BOWLING.—Lindwall, 16—1—65—2 ; Miller, 14—4—
39—3 ; Johnston, 9—1—36—0 ; Iverson, 14—3—29—0 ;
Johnson, 8—1—29—0 ; Hole, 5—0—10—1.

At six o'clock the English camp was profoundly disconsolate.
Victory had been sighted not far away from a position of
advantageous eminence. Australia were all out 217, and at tea
England, with only Washbrook lost and 160 scored, stood in a
position to administer a stunning knock-out. But Hutton
faltered ; 204 for three—and at close of play our lead was a
beggarly single run and only four wickets left. Not a man in the
England XI, save Hutton, deserved to escape whipping, not
excepting Simpson, 80 not out ; for when ruin was enveloping
England's innings he, though well set after two and a half
hours, added but three runs in the last hour. He could not know
that to-morrow Tattersall would astonish the world by unusual
resistance ; he couldn't know anything of the sort. He wasted
the beautiful wicket, too, on an evening as humid as a monsoon.
All's well that ends well, I suppose ; next morning Simpson
cleared his character of every perceptible stain. For the time
being he tried our good opinion of him during a most mournful
night, so mournful as far as I was concerned that I sat in lonely
disillusionment at dinner at Menzies Hotel inconsolable even by
a bottle of Australian hock.

There was no cricket on Saturday, 24th February, owing to
rain. But the wicket was unspoiled, flat as a pancake, for Hutton
and Washbrook when England went in an hour before lunch on
Monday to begin their first innings. From Lindwall's first over
runs rippled the grass ; we couldn't believe it—brilliant strokes
without any preliminary pushing or shuffling ugliness. Strokes
to the on were hit from Lindwall with impunity. Lindwall was
at this stage as tame and harmless as one of those beautifully
preserved lions which we can admiringly look at in glass-cases
in museums. Washbrook also glanced Miller for four off his left
glove, shaking his hand in momentary pain. Six overs pro-

duced 34, seventeen from Miller, seventeen from Lindwall, Washbrook's share 22, Hutton's 12. I thought there were hints of high blood-pressure in Washbrook's cricket : a sort of " red sky at morning " flush. He was precipitately out, caught at the wicket off a wide ball which rose not too high on the off-side from Miller. It was a redundant stroke. Hutton before lunch was a model of technique and poise. A drive through the covers off Johnston was as classic as the Elgin marbles, and much more shapely. A very late leg-glance also off Johnston was executed with the crossed legs and rapidity of " Ranji." I am frequently told that I live in the past when I complain of the commonplace, wooden-footed methods of many batsmen of the present ; but show me true cricket, bred in the bone, and present and past become merged for me in the game's never-ceasing, if occasionally jerked or interrupted, kaleidoscope of flashing and lovely action-pictures.

After lunch Hutton lost something of lustre. Iverson bowled off-spinners at Hutton's left hip, and naturally stroke-play suffered some constipation. Moreover, Hutton's touch faltered —he wasn't feeling too well—for with his score 37 he tried to drive Ian Johnson forward to the off ; indeed, cover-point prepared himself to receive the hit. But the ball floated away, found the edge of Hutton's bat, whence it went to Miller in the slips, and Miller—of all living men—wasn't ready. In the same over Hutton drove again for four and so perfectly timed was the stroke that the velocity of the ball over the slow outfield reduced the fieldsmen to the immobility of tree-trunks. Simpson discovered something of the form known at Trent Bridge. A boundary by him to the off from Ian Johnson was immaculate, a square-drive from Lindwall had power and relish. (But he can be as anonymous as an account-book.) At four o'clock Hutton and Simpson had scored 120 together ; and a tired lot of Australians came to the pavilion for refreshment. Then, the teacups scarcely removed and washed, if young Hole didn't bowl Hutton—clean bowl the master ! Hutton played outside a simple ball which swung away ever so gently. The sight of

Hutton's back no doubt inspired Lindwall and Miller to recharge their batteries; for here ensued the most strenuous and vehement onslaught of fast bowling witnessed in all the rubber. It was magnificent, and it was war. There were short " bumpers " of course. But there was speed as direct and piercing as spears. Certain of England's company of writers for the Press objected to this fusillade; none of them could have seen or remembered Cotter, who at Old Trafford in 1905 challenged Maclaren's hook with the most terrific rising balls I have ever seen. There was nothing not " legitimate ", fair and splendid in Lindwall's and Miller's efforts to snatch the game from England's grip on a wicket senseless as a doormat that has been left out in the porch all night in the rain. We have reached a pretty pass. Here we are in a period of spoon-fed batsmen, spoiled pets of stupid pitches. The breed of fast bowlers is rapidly becoming extinct. Then, when the only two surviving great fast bowlers are exalted by a challenge to do their damnedest and most terrific, the cry is : " Take him off. Take him off." The Soft Age.

Well, then. Compton came forth, still the subject of our prayers. Another failure by him was not to be contemplated. Another failure by him would break the hearts of countless schoolboys in England. Fail he did. Not since Ranjitsinhji in 1902 has a cricketer nationally beloved suffered Compton's scourging from the President of the Immortals, who apparently didn't finish his sport with Tess. Compton played comfortably enough while he was spared; he made his own favourite sweep to leg from Iverson. Lindwall trapped him quite devilishly; he changed from inswingers to his fastest outswinger; Compton essayed a late cut and Miller took the catch off his toes. Sheppard, a run later, was snapped by Tallon off Miller, flicking his bat as empirically as at a mosquito. Lindwall, definitely in full storm, smashed Brown's defences as though they were paper; and Miller not so much as bowled Evans as hurled *himself*, transformed into a cricket ball for one fiery moment, and flattened him out. Simpson's score didn't stir through all this wreckage.

He was as a cricketer petrified. The fast bowlers' hurricane scattered four wickets in less than an hour. Next day, they couldn't in the same time scatter Tattersall's wicket, as all the world knows, still wondering why.

FOURTH DAY (THIRD DAY'S PLAY)

AUSTRALIA

FIRST INNINGS		SECOND INNINGS	
J. Burke, c. Tattersall, b. Bedser ..	11	c. Hutton, b. Bedser	1
A. R. Morris, l.b.w., b. Brown ..	50	l.b.w., b. Bedser	4
A. L. Hassett, c. Hutton, b. Brown	92	not out	44
R. N. Harvey, c. Evans, b. Brown	1	l.b.w., b. Wright	52
K. R. Miller, c. and b. Brown ..	7	c. and b. Brown	0
G. Hole, b. Bedser	18	not out	18
I. W. Johnson, l.b.w., b. Bedser ..	1		
R. R. Lindwall, c. Compton, b. Bedser	21		
D. Tallon, c. Hutton, b. Bedser ..	1		
W. A. Johnston, not out	12		
J. Iverson, c. Washbrook, b. Brown	0		
Extras (b. 2, l.b. 1)	3	Extras (b. 1, l.b. 7, n.b. 1, w. 1)	10
Total	217	Total (4 wkts.)	129

FALL OF WICKETS—FIRST INNINGS.—1—23, 2—111, 3—115, 4—123, 5—156, 6—166, 7—184, 8—187, 9—216, 10—217.

SECOND INNINGS.—1—5, 2—6, 3—88, 4—89.

BOWLING—FIRST INNINGS.—Bedser, 22—5—46—5 ; Bailey, 9—1—29—0 ; Brown, 18—4—49—5 ; Wright, 9—1—50—0 ; Tattersall, 11—3—40—0.

SECOND INNINGS (to date).—Bedser, 12—3—33—2 ; Bailey, 8—0—20—0 ; Brown, 6—1—26—1 ; Wright, 11—1—34—1 ; Tattersall, 5—2—6—0.

ENGLAND—FIRST INNINGS

Hutton, b. Hole	79
Washbrook, c. Tallon, b. Miller	27
R. T. Simpson, not out	156
Compton, c. Miller, b. Lindwall	11
D. S. Sheppard, c. Tallon, b Miller	1
F. R. Brown, b. Lindwall	6
Evans, b. Miller	1
Bedser, b. Lindwall	11
T. E. Bailey, c. Johnson, b. Iverson	5
Wright, l.b.w., b. Iverson	3

Tattersall, b. Miller 10
Extras (b. 9, l.b. 1) 10
_____
Total 320

FALL OF WICKETS.—1—40, 2—171, 3—204, 4—205, 5—212, 6—213, 7—228, 8—236, 9—246, 10—320.

BOWLING.—Lindwall, 21—1—77—3 ; Miller, 21.7—5 —76—4 ; Johnston, 12—1—55—0 ; Iverson, 20—4—52 —2 ; Johnson, 11—1—40—0 ; Hole, 5—0—10—1.

For a while the England innings seemed to be going to a natural end. Lindwall immediately made a mess of Bedser's wickets ; in fact he broke one of them. Bailey, fit again, drove Lindwall to the off for four, unexpected if not unpremeditated violence, a grand hit which no doubt sent shivers of delight from the bat's blade, through the handle, into his nerves and blood-stream. Every cricketer knows this sensation and also the aftermath when, next over, he is caught off a feeble stroke near the wicket, as Bailey on this occasion was caught, a wan push off Iverson to forward short-leg—and how many more times in my reports must I use this same ugly phrase, " caught at forward short-leg " ; I imagine that at least a dozen or so batsmen in this rubber have miserably lost their wickets this way. How much better for them and how much better for my prose style if more players had got out to running catches in the deep field.

Lindwall was surprisingly taken off. He bowled not more than five overs on this third day and was at liberty to watch with a certain disinterest the remarkable stand by Tattersall and Simpson for the last wicket. Simpson, who scored only nine in twenty minutes, was missed in the slips off Miller by Ian Johnson ; he was 89 when he " began again " and, with nobody to rely on for company of any duration and intimacy, proceeded to play the innings of his life, a resurrection and a reformation in one. He went forward to Iverson's spin, danced to it, and in the twinkling of an eye changed not only the aspect of himself but of the match. It was as though a fresh confidence had taken possession of him, or as if for months his own physical shape and vessel had been the bottle imprisoning his genii. Still, even yet, the only question that interested us urgently was whether Wright and Tattersall could survive long enough to enable Simpson to reach a hundred. When Wright was leg-before to Iverson, Simpson needed nine. Tattersall, pale and lanky, a true son of the senior and original and lamented George Formby, took guard and bent himself, so that the upper body nearly described a right angle to the lower part. Fieldsmen swarmed round him. Tattersall, being a left-handed batsman, either from necessity or choice, was presumed to be easy game for Iverson. But Tattersall played forward to the spin-spin, or rather—but the methods of Tattersall cannot be described at the tail of a sentence ; I must begin another.

While the ball was approaching him through the air, Tattersall remained stiff and bent, a sort of human mark of interrogation. Then his left leg advanced as though by volition of its own. The bat went simultaneously with it ; and both as a rule got there rather before the ball pitched. Tattersall was now in a position to look at the ball closely. In fact he adapted to his own purposes and anatomy the great principle of K. S. Ranjit-sinhji : " First find the ball, then go to it." Tattersall merely reversed this doctrine : he preferred, or his left leg and bat pre-ferred, to " go " first to the ball and find it afterwards. Though Tattersall's bat remained thrust forward firmly as it and the leg waited for the ball, it became as if changed suddenly from willow to a woollen lath soaked in chloroform which rendered Iverson's spin at once insensible. Not once was Iverson's spin likely to be propelled by Tattersall to the cluster of fieldsmen ; he smothered it, in a way fit to make Cecil Parkin's cat laugh. Tattersall snicked Miller off the edge of his bat, the same bat, still held forward and quite stationary when struck, and ran a single all legs and neck, so that Simpson could have the bowling ; and Simpson in one over by Miller swept a short length ball to the boundary, dismissing it from his presence (like A. C. Maclaren), cut him for two ; then, leaping out of his ground, hit him past mid-on for three and so arrived at his century. In fifty minutes before lunch Simpson made light of the bowling and scored 40; here was the traditional English gesture of singeing of the beard. He made true cricket and the performance of handsome strokes seem as easy and natural to his nature and style as, in the other matches, he had made crabbed and confined dabs and pushes seem a gross and unfair libel against him.

After lunch Miller and Johnson bowled—not Lindwall. Simpson forced Miller square for four, and drove Johnson high through the covers. This was too much for Miller, who released a really fast one, which immobilised Tattersall's defences entire, leg and bat. Simpson, 156 not out, batted five and a half hours.

Time was when Australia, if 103 behind on the first innings, would have regarded such a disadvantage as unusual but not distracting. Each and every Australian innings is now vulnerable from the first batsmen in; at any rate an Australian innings is no longer—as it was when guarded by Woodfull and Ponsford—like one of those safes which can be opened only by a secret code. At ten minutes to three Bedser bowled a maiden over to Burke. Morris hit a full-toss from Bailey for two. The general impression was that at long last the Australian batsmen would, one and all, come to full form and satisfy their own and their friends' best wishes. Even Hutton prepared for the worst: "They'll get a lot of runs this time," he prophesied. Morris, confident as brass, hit across and with the freeest swing, low and hard at a quick short ball from Bedser: he missed it and was adjudged l.b.w. after some meditation by the umpire. In the same over Bedser caused the new red ball to sting the shoulder of Burke's bat and the young man was caught by Hutton, easily, at second-slip; this was a red-hot ball indeed. So the cat was amongst the Australian pigeons—and there are pigeons in Australia: I have fed them in the lovely gardens at Sydney, looking on the harbour.

Hassett and Harvey each enjoyed narrow escapes. Hassett could not avoid another fizzing ball from Bedser, and Hutton missed him at first-slip. Wright bowled in place of Bailey, and Brown came on for Bedser, whose analysis was 6—2—18—2. Was Maurice Tate asked to " rest " at such a prosperous moment and, if asked, did he listen? At tea Hassett and Harvey had relieved the slight tension in the Australian dressing-room and the score was 65 for two. The counter-attack of England was highly spirited, and deserved to prosper. After tea Harvey hit a short ball from Wright to long-leg, his bat and shoulders heaving prodigiously round. In the same over Harvey risked another stroke, much the same of intention, and it miscarried to mid-wicket, and Compton chased in vain after a catch it was not possible for Compton to make. Harvey appeared ready to gamble in a bold effort to get Australia out of an unsatisfactory, indecisive position. He is naturally a cricketer who loves the generous action; he is unwilling to bow to the current Ten Commandments of cricket, all beginning " Thou shalt not . . ." He was not, I fancy, in consistent health this rubber, and a cricketer of Harvey's dashing stroke-play must trust much to a keen eye and a swift response from nerves and body. He fell to Wright, leg-before; he tried a hit to the off and the ball kept low. His innings of 52 was almost atavistic in its gallantry of poise and its readiness to face the challenge of a determined attack and a vigilant field which scented blood at last.

Only a few minutes after Harvey was out, Miller pushed out his bat to a good length from Brown, who, for the second time in the match, caught and bowled him. Miller had possibly not recovered altogether from an over he had just received from Wright, full of nasty questions of flight and spin. In the day's searching last hour young Hole proved his stuff as he stood there and served attendance on Hassett.

FIFTH DAY (Fourth Day's Play)

AUSTRALIA

First Innings			Second Innings			
J. Burke, c. Tattersall, b. Bedser ..	11		c. Hutton, b. Bedser	..	..	1
A. R. Morris, l.b.w., b. Brown ..	50		l.b.w., b. Bedser ..	..	..	4
A. L. Hassett, c. Hutton, b. Brown	92		b. Wright ..	..	..	48
R. N. Harvey, c. Evans, b. Brown	1		l.b.w., b. Wright ..	..	..	52
K. R. Miller, c. and b. Brown ..	7		c. and b. Brown ..	..	..	0

G. Hole, b. Bedser	18	b. Bailey	63
I. W. Johnson, l.b.w., b. Bedser	1	c. Brown, b. Wright	0
R. R. Lindwall, c. Compton, b. Bedser	21	b. Bedser	14
D. Tallon, c. Hutton, b. Bedser	1	not out	2
W. A. Johnston, not out	12	b. Bedser	1
J. Iverson, c. Washbrook, b. Brown	0	c. Compton, b. Bedser	0
Extras (b. 2, l.b. 1)	3	Extras (b. 2, l.b. 8, w. 1, n.b. 1)	12
Total	217	Total	197

FALL OF WICKETS—FIRST INNINGS.—1—23, 2—111, 3—115, 4—123, 5—156, 6—166, 7—184, 8—187, 9—216, 10—217.

SECOND INNINGS.—1—5, 2—6, 3—88, 4—89, 5—142, 6—142, 7—192, 8—196, 9—197, 10—197.

BOWLING—FIRST INNINGS.—Bedser, 22—5—46—5 ; Bailey, 9—1—29—0 ; Brown, 18—4—49—5 ; Wright, 9—1—50—0 ; Tattersall, 11—3—40—0.

SECOND INNINGS.—Bedser, 20.3—4—59—5 ; Bailey, 15—3—32—1 ; Wright, 15—2—56—3 ; Brown, 9—1—32—1 ; Tattersall, 5—2—6—0.

ENGLAND

FIRST INNINGS		SECOND INNINGS	
Hutton, b. Hole	79	not out	60
Washbrook, c. Tallon, b. Miller	27	c. Lindwall, b. Johnston	7
R. T. Simpson, not out	156	run out	15
Compton, c. Miller, b. Lindwall	11	not out	11
D. S. Sheppard, c. Tallon, b. Miller	1		
F. R. Brown, b. Lindwall	6		
Evans, b. Miller	1		
Bedser, b. Lindwall	11		
T. E. Bailey, c. Johnson, b. Iverson	5		
Wright, l.b.w., b. Iverson	3		
Tattersall, b. Miller	10		
Extras (b. 9, l.b. 1)	10	Extras (l.b. 2)	2
Total	320	Total (2 wkts.)	95

FALL OF WICKETS—FIRST INNINGS.—1—40, 2—171, 3—204, 4—205, 5—212, 6—213, 7—228, 8—236, 9—246, 10—320.

SECOND INNINGS.—1—32, 2—62.

BOWLING—FIRST INNINGS.—Lindwall, 21—1—77—3 ; Miller, 21.7—5—76—4 ; Johnston, 12—1—55—0 ; Iverson, 20—4—52—2 ; Johnson, 11—1—40—0 ; Hole, 5—0—10—1.

SECOND INNINGS.—Lindwall, 2—0—12—0 ; Miller, 2—0—5—0 ; Johnston, 11—3—36—1 ; Iverson, 12—2—32—0 ; Johnson, 1—0—1—0 ; Hole, 1—0—3—0 : Hassett, 0.6—0—4—0.

Australia's main chance depended on Hassett, possibly the one man in the side passionately anxious for an Australian victory. Wright settled the issue and won the match at twenty

minutes past twelve. From his variegated repertory Wright produced a leg-break of perfect length, which curved seductively
through the air, lured Hassett forward, pitched on the stumps,
turned—and yet hit the stumps. There is no scientific answer
to such a ball in all the accumulated technique of batsmanship,
from Fuller Pilch to Hutton.

In this same over of Wright, Ian Johnson smote ambitiously
and high to mid-on, where Brown waited lovingly. Now we saw
a young Australian, in his first scorching baptism, not only
facing but revelling in the ordeal and opportunity. The evening
before, as we know, Hole had shown his mettle and character
in defence during the most searching ordeal he is likely to have
to face in his career. With Hassett gone he straightway began
to attack, in a sequence of resolute, rapid and often beautiful
strokes, the ball travelling as quick as eyesight could follow. No
finer hits were seen in the five Test matches. Lindwall, after
one desperate drive, realised his duty was to discard his
own customary forcibility and to wait on Hole; for over by
over, we all were allowed to know, not by prophecy but spontaneous revelation, that a new star was rising in a rather waning
sky.

Hole twice swung Wright to long-leg with abandon and
power. A fieldsman was placed to frustrate any other liberty
of the same kind in that direction; so Hole cut Wright's next
ball through the almost vacant slips, his bat coming down like
a knife on a spasm of accelerated pace. Hole hit eleven runs from
this over. When Bedser bowled with the new ball, Hole flicked
him impertinently through the slips for four, a yard from
Compton's outstretched arm. But Hole is not at all impertinent
in appearance. He is tallish and quiet-looking, and his preliminary stance at the wicket is rather gawky and straddled;
but the moment the ball is on the way he is erect, with his bat
drawn up higher behind him than is fashionable; and he brings
it down decisively enough.

At one o'clock Australia's lead was 63, four wickets to go.
Hole drove Bailey straight for four and hit him for three by

means of a square-drive partaking of a cut, strong in the wrists. When he was 57 he ventured another naughty flick between Hutton and Compton in the slips. Hole indeed was threatening to put before England the threat of a more than formal second innings until, a minute or two from lunch, Lindwall was well bowled by Bedser. Though at the interval Australia with three wickets in hand led by only 89, nobody in the English camp was counting the chickens. But after lunch anti-climax set in. Hole was splendidly yorked by Bailey, and the last three wickets collapsed for five. Shades of Grimmett, O'Reilly and Fleetwood-Smith. Hole had kindled a torch that didn't deserve such a douche. His innings satisfied me that he has in him the born stuff of a stroke-player who can sternly deal with good balls. I think, too, that he will not only help to win many matches for Australia, but while he is at it, give much delight. That is, if they don't spoil him and he keeps a straight bat and a modest mind. One or two of the modernists praised him reservedly, saying he is " something of a dasher." No doubt they would have passed him with honours if he had stayed in three hours for 50 and got out at last l.b.w., or caught at forward short-leg. Hole will go far— and so will many of the balls bowled to him.

There was a slight concern in the English dressing-room before Hutton and Washbrook went forth to score 95 to win. Another terrific assault from Lindwall and Miller was confidently expected, especially as, earlier in the day, Bailey had hurled a bumper or two at Lindwall, damning the consequences. As a fact, no thunderbolts at all ever threatened Hutton and Washbrook. After a few overs Johnston and Iverson were put on. England didn't exactly run half-way to greet victory; in fact they awaited quite coyly her coming their way again after so long an absence. Washbrook was caught at 32; and Harvey ran Simpson out with a throw like David with the sling. Compton dared scarcely lift his bat, an excusable scepticism considering his long inexplicable succession of failures. It was poetic justice to Hutton that he should pilot his side to the desired end.

TEST MATCH AVERAGES

AUSTRALIA

BATTING

	Matches	Innings	Times not out	Runs	Highest score	Average
K. R. Miller ..	5	9	1	350	145*	43·75
J. Burke	2	4	1	125	101*	41·66
A. L. Hassett ..	5	9	0	366	92	40·66
R. N. Harvey ..	5	9	0	362	74	40·22
A. R. Morris ..	5	9	0	321	206	35·66
K. M. Archer ..	3	5	0	152	48	30·40
I. W. Johnson ..	5	9	0	151	77	16·77
R. R. Lindwall ..	5	9	1	124	41	15·50
S. J. E. Loxton ..	3	5	0	75	32	15·00
D. Tallon	5	8	2	39	18	6·50
W. A. Johnston ..	5	8	2	29	12	4·83
J. Iverson	5	7	3	3	1	0·75

Also batted.—J. A. R. Moroney, 0, 0 ; G. Hole, 18, 63.

BOWLING

	Overs	Maidens	Runs	Wickets	Average
J. Iverson	138·4	29	320	21	15·23
K. R. Miller	106·6	23	301	17	17·70
W. A. Johnston ..	154·1	28	422	22	19·18
R. R. Lindwall	98·3	11	344	15	22·93
I. W. Johnson	138·4	23	311	7	44·42

Also bowled.—S. J. E. Loxton, 9—1—28—0 ; J. Burke, 3—1—7—0 ; G. Hole, 6—0—13—1 ; A. L. Hassett, 0·6—0—4—0.

BATTING

	Matches	Innings	Times not out	Runs	Highest score	Average
L. Hutton	5	10	4	533	156*	88·83
R. T. Simpson ..	5	10	1	349	156*	38·77
F. R. Brown ..	5	8	0	210	79	26·25
W. G. A. Parkhouse	2	4	0	77	28	19·25
T. G. Evans ..	5	9	1	144	49	18·00
C. Washbrook ..	5	10	0	173	34	17·30
D. S. Sheppard ..	2	3	0	51	41	17·00
T. E. Bailey ..	4	7	2	40	15	8·00
D. Compton ..	4	8	1	53	23	7·57
A. V. Bedser ..	5	8	2	43	14	7·16
J. G. Dewes ..	2	4	0	23	9	5·75
R. Tattersall ..	2	3	0	16	10	5·33
D. V. P. Wright ..	5	7	1	23	14	3·83
J. J. Warr	2	4	0	1	1	0·25

Also batted.—D. B. Close, 0, 1; A. J. McIntyre, 1, 7.

BOWLING

	Overs	Maidens	Runs	Wickets	Average
T. E. Bailey	75·4	18	198	14	14·14
A. V. Bedser	195	34	482	30	16·06
F. R. Brown	109	12	389	18	21·61
D. V. P. Wright ..	103	6	500	11	45·45
R. Tattersall	68·5	12	257	4	64·25

Also bowled.—J. J. Warr, 73—6—281—1; D. B. Close, 7—1—28—1; D. Compton, 11·6—1—43—1.

* Not out.